Crickets and Thunder

Following God to the Ends of the Earth

Crickets and Thunder

Following God to the Ends of the Earth

Karen Judd Low

Some names have been changed to protect privacy but the whole account is true to the best of my memory.

Library of Congress
Low, Karen J.
Crickets and Thunder: following God to the ends of the earth
ISBN 978-0-9848430-0-8

Printed in the United States of America

*"God sometimes seems
to speak to us most intimately when
He catches us off our guard."*

C.S. Lewis.

I've known Karen for almost forty years and she is perhaps the most positive, influential, magnetic person I've ever met. She has a warmth and authenticity that opens doors, opens minds and open hearts wherever she goes, in remote villages, major cities and everywhere between. Someone said, "If you're not living on the edge, you're taking up too much room." *Crickets and Thunder* testifies to the fact that Karen has always lived on the edge and always will. Karen's story is amazing because Karen lives amazed. Anyone who deeply desires to live to the fullest will do well to step into the *Crickets and Thunder* story ready for adventure.

--Ken Johnson, Author of Life^2 – The Secret to Limitless Living, Sr. Pastor, Westside Church, Bend, Oregon

"This book gets to the core of what the Christian life is all about: an honest search for God coupled with an unbridled willingness to not only hear His voice, but to respond by putting His calling into action. I wish every Christian would wrestle with the story that Karen so powerfully tells because it speaks directly to the great famine in our Christian culture–namely, the absence of allowing oneself to be humbly and unreservedly available to the God who still speaks."

--Dr.Bruce Hanlon, Former Sr. Pastor, Crossroads Community Church, Framingham, MA, Seminary Professor, Africa Bible College, Malawi

"This is a book I couldn't put down. Having witnessed Karen's life for many years, I can vouch to the way God so mightily works in and through her. Your view of Him will be greatly expanded as a result of reading these pages."

--Dr. Scott Larson, President and Founder, Straight Ahead Ministries, Worcester, MA

"A well told story is one of life's simplest and greatest gifts. Karen Low gives that gift to us in *Crickets and Thunder*. She weaves you through the uncanny marriages of supernatural and simple, hurt and hope, faith and doubt, by painting potent images in your mind. You will want more. Your faith will be stretched as she takes you through the wonder of God doing extraordinary things through ordinary people."

--Chris Mitchell, Co-author of A Place for Skeptics,
Sr. Pastor, New England Chapel, Franklin, MA

"In Crickets and Thunder I experienced two things: first, I was amazed at the way God intervened over and over in the lives of Frank & Karen Low, encouraging and assuring them of his presence, and providing for them in full measure what they most needed at a particular time. It gave me fresh assurance that he is as involved in my life and loves me as much as he does the Lows. The second thing I experienced was a challenge to live as faith-filled and obedient a life as they did."

--Dick Germaine, Pastor, Founder and CEO,
Barnabas Ministries, Boston, MA

"This book is so darn refreshing! It is also so KAREN LOW! If you want hard core, jungle, stunning miracles, and snake stories shared by someone who lived it, here it is! But you will also read of a young couple who heard God's call, and followed that call all the way to tribal redemption."

--Mark Foshager, Global Mobilization Director,
International Teams, Chicago

CONTENTS

Crickets and Thunder
is a collection of true stories about getting
to know the invisible God.

Whether soft as crickets or loud as thunder,
in all his diverse and astounding workings,
He is able, He is with us,
and He wants us
to know Him.

for
Naomi, Jesse, and Isaac,
the delight and joy
of my heart

1. Human Snake

1986

With my trusty Minolta camera strapped around my neck, I swung past the moldy screen door into hot sunlight with a bang. My eyes struggled to focus on a stream of oncoming natives. Roughly two hundred men covered with spotted ferns and smeared with black pig grease wound out of the jungle and snaked across the grassy airstrip into plain view.

Sweat trickled over my lip but that wasn't unusual. In the Sepik Region of Papua New Guinea, temperatures were always high and humidity off the charts, but with my eyes riveted to a giant human snake undulating in my direction, it seemed hotter.

Peering through my lens and narrowing my focus, I saw that they were armed and dressed for war with six foot bows and bamboo arrows jutting out at all angles. Silhouetted against the dark backdrop of jungle foliage, their weapons resembled a hundred spindly legs of a giant centipede, growing bigger by the minute. Rhythmic steps mimicked my drumming heartbeat. My mouth went dry.

I was thirty-one and the mother of three small children. My husband Frank was thirty-three, and the most fluent among us in the tribal language. We'd been living in the tribe for six years. We could speak the language and eat the food; but we still had a long way to go. What was really going on in the minds and hearts of the Iwam[1] people?

I zoomed the lens of my camera as far as it could go, momentarily relieved to see the familiar faces of village friends at the front of the pack. Both Samut, the actor-handsome son of the landowner, and the flamboyant young Tomas in the lead, worked in the office as Frank's translation assistants. Tomas even wore my husband's clothes like his shadow twin. Surely with such good friends and neighbors in the lead, they wouldn't use their weapons against us. Would they?

Two days earlier, Tomas came for coffee and told us they were going to try to settle land disputes. He even asked to use my black markers and paper for placards to welcome government officials. "Oh sure, anything to help settle these talks," I said.

Frank stepped out and stood behind me on the front porch. "They've taken great pains to *bilas* [decorate] for this."

"Yeah, this must be a pretty big deal for them." Fascinated by the colorful décor, I aimed my camera at the head of the pack. Just as I zoomed in for a close-up, they pointed their spears straight at me and the front-runners charged in my direction screaming, *"Ka papa tet! No ken sutim piksa!"* [Stop! Don't shoot!] *But shouldn't that be my line?*

I dropped my camera so it hung by the strap around my sweaty neck. They've seen us with cameras on countless occasions. *What's wrong with this picture?* Then Frank grabbed my elbow and rushed me inside hollering, "Kids! Go to the loft, NOW!"

The click of my camera seemed like the tribal version of the shot heard round the world. The whole mob suddenly broke into a run and circled the house, shooting five-foot bamboo arrows into the roof and whooping loudly in syncopated rhythms, *wooh, wooh, wooh!*

---

[1] Pronounced Ee'-wahm, a tribal people group around May River, estimated population between 5-10,000.

2

The pulsating volume swelled until we could barely hear each other. Spear tips paraded past the windows and their chaotic cries filled the air, but seconds dragged as though the cosmic hands of Father Time were melting in fervent heat.

Inside the house, we looked at each other with eyebrows raised. Unspoken expressions read, "Brace yourself. This could be it." With propane tanks beneath our feet and a dried thatch roof above our heads I thought, one lit match tossed our way and we're goners.

My mind was swirling like the angry parade outside. *Why are they doing this? Why can't we sit down and talk this out?*

Separated only by a few flimsy planks and screens, our options for defense weren't good. Yet, we wouldn't use our hunting gun or lay a hand on any of them. We hadn't come to the jungle to fight these people, but maybe it was time to contemplate our own eternal destiny.

I had to ask myself honestly, am I willing to lay down my life for what I believe today? Dear God, is this how the story's supposed to go?

2. Drifter

"Try this," my brother said after school one day.

"What is it?"

"Speed. Try it. It gives you a buzz and you can stay up all night."

In the summer of 1969, the number of Americans in uniform peaked at 550,000 in Vietnam and in a little town in New York another half million descended on Woodstock to tear off their clothes in rebellion. That same year Neil Armstrong walked on the moon and *Easy Rider* appeared in theaters. It was an age of restlessness and agitation, a time of breaking boundaries. At fifteen, I smoked weed, called myself a freak, and sat in the high school courtyard chanting songs about Uncle Sam sending everyone home in a box. *Oh it's one, two, three, what are we fighting for? Don't ask me, I don't give a damn, next stop is Vietnam!*

By sixteen, my life revolved around a midnight blue sports car, rock music at FULL volume, and a regular pu-pu platter of drugs. On May 4, 1970, four college students were shot by our own National Guard while protesting the war at Kent State. Life is ridiculous. Mindless. *Got a joint?*

In three brief years of high school, very little stands out as vividly as the day the entire student body funneled into the gymnasium to watch a local hero perform. "Muscular senior Frank Low won the state title for all-round gymnast and number one on the rings," the town paper reported. He was the pride of the school—the epitome of everything I was not.

I looked around that packed auditorium with disdain. The "in-crowd," the jocks and cheerleaders with their tight pony tails and phony smiles felt hollow. The meaninglessness of shuffling around those crowded halls for years washed over me with incredible sadness. I didn't fit "the mold" and never would, so I hated all of it.

I watched that gymnast flipping, pointing, and twirling on the rings with expertise. Despite the fanfare of the whole school audience, he seemed so blissfully unaffected. Obviously, he was very good, but more, he was doing something he genuinely loved. What did I love that much? This question helped me make a decision, and at the end of my junior year, I waltzed into the principal's office to talk.

"I'm sorry," the secretary began, "Mr. Earnst is on vacation this week. Let me call the Vice Principal." *Perfect.* I always liked Mr. Hart.

"What can I do for you, Karen?" he came in smiling.

I launched into my little speech. "Mr. Hart, I'm just letting you know that I won't be coming back in the fall, so you can take my name off the roster."

"Why?" he asked sympathetically.

"I'm wasting my life here." It probably required great effort to conceal whole-hearted belly laughs at this point, but Mr. Hart displayed the utmost patience, and took me seriously.

"What do you want to do, Karen?"

"I want to get to work."

"What kind of work?" he raised his white eyebrows.

"The kind where you get a salary with benefits. I don't want another temp job."

"Hmmm. Wait here a minute," he said, and disappeared into the back room. When he returned, he was holding my file. "Karen, I think I have good news for you. You already have enough credits to graduate, and you have real good grades--college prep in a top division. I'd hate to see you drop out." I braced myself, thinking he might try to talk me out of leaving. Instead he said, "Karen, a senior year isn't required by the state, but you can take an evening class to get your required fourth year of English if you want." He smiled.

"Is that all?" I asked incredulously.

"Yes. And when you finish, we can mail your diploma." He was pleased.

I was freed from high school and launched into my wildest years in the age of Aquarius, peace symbols on VW vans, and daisies in our hair. That summer I flew to Puerto Rico for a runner-up to Woodstock and landed in San Juan with thousands of long-hairs from all over the country. Three of us hitched thirty miles in the back of a truck to acres and acres of open fields surrounding the stage of a week-long concert in the mud; a gigantic rock fest complete with outdoor shower spigots and tents. Santana, Grateful Dead and other big names of the era serenaded the melee day and night, filling the air with electronic pulses.

Walking along the beach for an hour or so, I started feeling lightheaded and knew something wasn't right. Some local women waved their hands around excitedly, pointing at the sun and patting their faces. I was over-exposed. Heading for the trees, I walked until I came to the big white tent with a red cross, a recognizable sign in any language. One of the aides handed me a mirror and I was shocked by the moon-face that returned my gaze. My whole face had swollen like a melon!

The unlucky patients under that Red Cross tent were practically enough to scare me sober. Overdoses weren't limited to solar rays, either. Lying on sheets all over the ground were naked men and women on bad trips, some screaming in terror. One fair-skinned northerner was burned bright red and thought demons were clawing at her bloodied body like she had died and gone to hell. Writhing in pain, she cried hysterically while friends tried to "talk her down."

Once rehydrated, a station aide sent me on my way with stern warnings about the dangers of sun poisoning. Turning to leave, I nearly collided with a good-looking Latino near the entry. "Heavy, man, she must have had some pretty bad shit," he shook his head.

"Yeah, it's too bad," I agreed. "She's out of her mind."

"My name's Eduardo," his teeth gleamed against his dark complexion. "You can call me Eddie." Gesturing to my face he said, "Want my hat?" I hesitated, but the writhing woman shrieked once more from her mat behind me.

"Sure, thanks," I said gratefully, the birth of a life-long fetish for head-coverings.

"Can I show you around?" he offered. He took me by the hand and we walked all over the grounds while great name bands played non-stop. Then he led me into one of the heroin tents and offered me some. "You'll love it," he beamed.

I had always drawn the line at needles, yet I was popping pills and smoking weed like a lunatic. No matter how far you spiral down the ladder, a lower rung provides an illusion of sensibility. Thankfully, visions in the Red Cross tent kept me straight that day.

"No thanks," I said, and drifted back into the crowd on my own. My face gradually returned to its usual size—a three-quarter moon instead of a full round orb—and I flew home in one piece.

One hot afternoon that same summer I stormed out of the house in an angry rage and started walking toward the highway. I'd just broken up with my spoiled rich Italian boyfriend and decided to hitch-hike—anywhere would do, just to get out of my room.

Not far from home, a couple of scruffy guys on motorcycles pulled over. "Wanna ride?" they grinned, with engines rumbling. They seemed to be in the same frame of mind, wanting to burn off a little fuel and have some fun.

"Sure," I replied, and hopped on the back of the one I liked best. We blasted around town awhile before stopping at Carvel's Ice Cream and I went to the counter to pour water into a Dixie cup. A real cute guy with long hair and a beard was smiling at me.

"Do you want some water?" I asked, offering the cup.

"Thanks," he smiled and came closer. Our eyes met and we talked briefly. No names or numbers, but something must've sparked like the Karen Carpenter song where angels sprinkle love dust. He said he never felt that way before, drawn to my "kaleidoscope eyes." I didn't realize it, but this bearded hunk was the gymnast who performed in my high school.

His brother took one look at my frayed hip-huggers and traveling companions and dismissed me. "Forget her, Frankie. She's a Sax-ganger," referring to a rough part of town called Saxonville. I wasn't really *with* the Sax Gang, but it sure looked that way. I wish we could have stayed longer. I would have been so much better off. Instead, we left separately, Frank being pulled away by his brother and me with those lousy bikers.

We cruised around town until one of them suggested we stop at the lake. We walked casually down the wooded trail until one of them disappeared behind us. I assumed he had to "take a leak" or retrieve something from the bikes, but when I found myself alone with the other biker, everything changed.

He was the bigger of the two, six feet and muscular. He grabbed me and started kissing me hard. I resisted, but he dragged me off the path and threw me on the ground. He tore at my clothes and pinned me down. I fought, but it only made him rougher.

I don't know why I didn't scream. The only one around was the other biker, and by this time the sick feeling in my gut confirmed he was part of the plot. "No, don't! No!" I begged, but I was overpowered. That big lug forced himself on me with branches and roots digging into my back and raped me.

Then he ran like a scared rabbit, and I was left to pick myself up and walk home. My hair was full of pine needles, my clothes tousled, and my emotions jumbled.

I was hurt and humiliated, dirty and ashamed. Mad as a hornet, shocked and wounded—but I never told a soul. What good would it do? Dad would be so angry he would probably have another heart attack and I'd never be allowed out of the house again. Mom had enough grief already, what with cancer treatments and all. The police would blame me, and I would have believed them. I was stupid to trust them. My hurt turned to anger and ricocheted inward.

What a day! In the span of about seven hours I had an emotional break-up, a thrilling pick-up, a sweet start-up, and then a horrible rape.

The summer sun was setting as I walked home with my hands in my pockets and a downcast face. I only told my parents the part about breaking up with my boyfriend on that fateful Friday. So when I went up to my room and shut the door crying, they chalked it up to a broken heart.

3. Free to Go

I wish I'd stayed home, or at least at the ice cream store. I remembered those sweet blue eyes, and wiped hot angry tears from my face.

Ever the free thinker, Frank decided to follow his heart regardless of his brother's opinions. Determined to find me, he talked to a musician who knew 'my ex,' and as fate would have it, he found my name and number. With a town of 60,000, that was extraordinary, but two days later I picked up the phone and heard his voice again.

"It's Frank," he laughed. "Are you the girl who gave me the cup of water at Carvel's?"

"How did you find my number?" I had been in my room all weekend wondering if I'd ever go out again, but hearing his gentle voice I was coaxed into conversation. He asked if he could see me, and about fifteen minutes later he showed up on a white scooter.

"This is a gas!" No pretense or posturing with this guy, he was more interested in getting to know me than impressing me. We talked and laughed the rest of the day, and the next, and the next...

I remembered the humble gymnast, but soon discovered other facets of Frank's fun-loving personality—humor, creativity, and a quiet sensitive intelligence. The more I got to know him, the more enamored I became with this nature-loving adventurer, artist, surfer, guitarist, anthropology student, and health food lover. I fell head over heels.

Together we explored New England's coastal towns and diverse countryside. We shared concerts on the Common, craft fairs, and Chinese restaurants. We'd drive to the Concord River with guitars, visit Harvard Square's bookstores, or fill a backpack with fruit and nuts and bike to Walden Pond. We'd discover a fiddler's contest in Vermont, a field of hot air balloons in Western Mass, or live musicians in Provincetown, taking off without a plan just to see where the road would take us.

One Saturday morning we headed to Wellfleet in my little Triumph. Weekend traffic on 128 was heavy with vacationers and optimistic beach-lovers jostling down the four-lane highway when it started pouring. I drove in the far right lane with the radio playing and the wipers beating hard, but I never saw it coming.

We were suddenly spinning in circles as though my tires were greased, with four lanes of oncoming traffic bearing down on us at eye level. Everyone around us hit the brakes and spun wildly out of control. My engine stalled just as some cars narrowly avoided our right side and hit each other. We finally slowed to a stop in the left lane. I kept trying the key, but my flooded engine wouldn't crank over, so we waited helplessly. And then, it happened.

"Hold on, honey!" Frank pulled my head down in his arms as the horrific sounds of dragging crunching metal and breaking glass engulfed us. Our seats were pushed off the floorboards, and the back end crumpled like aluminum foil as we shot down the road like a toy sprung from a jack-in-the-box. When we finally came to a stop, our necks were stiff but we were unharmed. We scrambled out of our seats and looked back at the highway.

"Look what I did!" I screamed. Cars were piled up on the median, glass and metal were strewn across the highway, and a semi was just slamming down on the pavement sideways across all four lanes. As the cab jack-knifed into the air, I thought surely that truck driver was a dead man. It looked like the end of the world.

I took off barefoot running from car to car. "Are you alright? Do you need help?" It was a nightmare. Families sat in stunned silence, clutching one another. I'll never forget the frightened faces of the little kids peering out at me, surrounded with beach balls and water toys. The piercing sound of sirens came from every conceivable direction. Soaked to the skin and shaking, I felt doomed. *This whole disaster is my fault!*

Police were first on the scene and an officer rushed toward me. "Miss, which one of these vehicles is yours?"

Here goes, time to fess up. "You see that little blue sports car in the very front of the line? That's me." I thought he would cuff and charge me on the spot.

He took down my information, then asked stiffly, "Who did you hit?" *Geesh, do men always assume that a woman had to hit somebody?*

"No, no one," I stammered. "Officer, I think we hit an oil slick. I started spinning in circles from the right side of the highway until my engine died. I couldn't get it started again and then that big black sedan skid into us from behind."

"What's going to happen?" Frank asked pointedly.

"Each impact will be treated as a separate accident," the officer explained. "Since we have no-fault insurance now, your incident will be charged to the vehicle who hit you."

My incident is separate? I wouldn't be faulted? My thoughts were jumbled.

Frank stepped in, "What do we do now?"

"Notify your insurance company right away. I've got your information, so you're free to go." Then, with a nod of his head, he rushed off.

"Free to go?" I repeated in shock.

"Do you believe it?" Frank asked. "So many wrecked cars!"

"I know! I hope that truck driver is okay."

After tilting the seats into their tracks and pulling the fenders away from the tires, my Triumph was still drivable. Though the back end was damaged, everything else was intact and the engine started right up.

"Frank, if we had stopped in any other direction, one of us wouldn't be talking!"

"I know. We could have been *killed.*" This was uncanny. So much wreckage but we were actually driving away in my little toy car, with not even a ticket to show for it.

We saw it on the news. That twenty-eight car pile-up closed the highway for eight hours while heavy equipment unloaded and removed the tipped semi. We could have died, but the true *triumph* was that Frank and I and everyone else in that tangle of tires survived.

Back at work I told my girlfriend, "We almost bit the dust this time!" and we'd compare stories. It seemed that life was a very precarious thing, more tentative than I knew before.

Elaine and I were hired at the same time to work at the engineering headquarters of the phone company. We clicked right away. I loved her laugh and her spunk, and we had a lot in common. Though working in the *real world,* we were just a couple of teenagers trying to hang on to the zany part of our youth. We'd race to the reservoir to smoke a joint for lunch or traipse around the city into the wee hours, and somehow show up on time the next morning. We thought we were hot stuff making money while other kids our age were still in school.

Our immediate supervisors were two Italian sisters from North Boston. Barbara and Jeanne knew we were living "on the wild side" and every Monday morning these precious ladies would come in saying, "Thank God you're both alright! We were lighting candles for you all weekend." I didn't understand burning all those candles, but I knew they cared.

Then one morning we came in and found everyone clutching tissues and rubbing red eyes. Barbara and Jeanne broke the news.

"Sarah fell down the stairs and died last night. She had a heart attack."

Sarah was one of the nicest people I'd ever seen—and I'd seen a lot of her since she sat between me and Elaine. The worst part was that she was due to be married in three weeks and her poor fiancé was completely derailed. They buried her in the unworn wedding dress.

We all attended the wake and mourned her short life. Yet, I realized I never knew her. Sarah was a mystery to me. She seemed so pure and at peace. I never knew why. Now she was dead and gone at twenty-three, and I sat by an empty desk every day to remind me just how quickly life can end.

Work was steady and the money good, but I was getting restless. *If I die by twenty-three, do I really want to spend it like this?* I'd already had two promotions, but I was surrounded with thirty-five-year-olds who never followed their dreams. I was taking physics at Northeastern University to scratch my itch for learning, but what's the point when you already have a good paying job with benefits? You'll still end up punching a clock somewhere.

I thought about my brother Steve, living in the heart of Alaska thanks to the Viet Nam draft. At least he was getting to see the world. He wrote home about his bungalow on the tundra in that mountain wilderness. "You ought to see this place. The sun never sets."

My senior boss sensed my restlessness. One morning with a hand on my shoulder, he launched into a fatherly spiel about my bright future with Ma Bell. "Sweetheart," he said in Humphrey Bogart fashion, "if you stay with the company until you retire, you'll get the biggest pension ever given since you were hired at sixteen." He spoke with unfeigned satisfaction, but my ears pricked at the words.

Retire? I'm eighteen! My own father hasn't talked about retiring yet! I'm sure this father of ten meant well, but while he rambled on about the benefits of a full life with Ma Bell, I glanced to the back of the room where my eyes rested on Madeline, and in those brief seconds I had one of life's great epiphanies.

With white hair and a cloud of blue smoke around her head, she furiously cranked the adding machine while never-ending streams of paper numbers spilled over the edge of her desk onto the linoleum. *That's the reality*, I thought to myself. *There's my future if I stay!*

This wrinkled, husky-voiced manager was smart and shrewd and I liked her a lot, but she had no life. Whenever I asked what she planned for holidays, she'd grind another butt into the ash tray and squint at me sideways. "I'll be right here, sweetheart. *Right here!*" I wondered how anyone could endure the same desk for thirty or forty years in a stale, smoke-filled corner, and that vision sent a shiver up my spine.

I told him I'd think about it.

Pulling into the parking lot the next morning I sat and stared at the building, a concrete block with a thousand tiny slots. Two thousand employees made their way like so many ants to the hill. My slot was in the front corner, second window by the head honcho. Would I spend the next forty years moving from one row to the next? Is this what I want out of life?

My boss was probably right about the money, but I didn't want to die crunching numbers for Ma Bell, Pa Bell, or any other

15

tinkling relatives. Look at Sarah, dead at twenty-three. *There has to be more to life.* So I went in and gave my notice.

"Where are you going?" everyone asked.

"Alaska," I announced. "If I don't do it now, when will I?" Frank sure understood my desire to travel and the thirty-year-olds applauded. Then my bosses surprised me with a big cake that read, "Alaska or bust," and I never looked back.

I was eighteen when I retired from the phone company.

4. Alaska or Bust

"The question is not what you look at, but what you see."[2]

Standing in the middle of my bedroom with an army knapsack in my hand, I pondered the life I was about to leave. After thirteen years in that little pink room I'd plastered my soul on its walls. I made a gigantic poster of the Beatles and painted it with neon colors for the black light. My shelves were lined with books and albums stacked against a record player. Surveying all my accumulated toys and treasures, I realized my duffle bag was still empty. What do you take with you?

In that holy pause my eyes fell on the black jacket of the Bible I was given by the Methodist Church when I was thirteen, but it stood virtually untouched for five years. Oh, I looked at the pictures a few times, but not knowing how this ancient history pertained to me, I'd put it back on the dusty shelf thinking, *maybe someday.*

"Now is the time. Take it." I pulled the book from its resting place and shoved it to the bottom of my sack. I covered it with clothes, fastened the clips, and tossed it by the door.

I bought round trip tickets to span five thousand miles to the Alaskan wilderness and splurged on a new Minolta camera and zoom lens. Folding a book of traveler's checks into my purse, I knew I'd have to find work when the money ran out.

---

[2] *The Thoughts of Thoreau,* edited by Edwin Way Teale, New York: Dodd, Mead, and Co., 1962, p.231.

My parents drove me to Logan Airport and snapped a few photos, standing arm in arm on the sidewalk. Then, with long hair flying in the wind, I swung that duffel over my shoulder and hugged goodbye. Soon after Boston Harbor faded into the distance, the entire landscape of my life changed.

The sun never set in Fairbanks, but rolled lazily around the horizons and turned to dusk at about four a.m. About an hour later it rose again, one day sloshing into the next with no black skies or starry nights to divide them.

I moved into the loft in my brother's bungalow on Badger Road and soon discovered it was a party house for Steve's army buddies who wanted a break from the post. I didn't mind the people and music, but it was impossible to keep food in the fridge and my money was going faster than I planned. When the guys were out playing their army games, I'd take Steve's "piss green" car and discover the tundra and glorious surroundings of Central Alaska.

The adventurer in me came alive and I met people that seemed to flesh out characters from old Westerns on TV. These were no-nonsense pioneers who loved hunting, fishing, and living off the land. Everyone had fascinating stories, like Lola who ran the saloon.

She was a tough cookie, but treated me like her kid sister. She even fixed me up with a full-blooded Eskimo and gave me her clothes for the occasion, but I felt like I was auditioning for the high school play in her frilly dress and western boots. "No more blind dates, Lola." I returned the frills, and went home to write long letters to Frank, surfing on Cape Cod.

I made a more practical connection with an old woman who ran a bakery out of her kitchen. If ever I'd felt like I had stumbled onto the set of a fairy tale, it was here.

Granny had snow white hair, a soft wrinkled face, and the tough hands of a pioneer who survived many winters. She wore long wool skirts and bleached white aprons and her hands never stopped moving, incessantly peeling or rolling or scrubbing something. Even when work was done she did needlepoint or darning in her rocker. Her eyes shone with the wisdom of decades and her stories intrigued me. She'd set her happy old tea kettle on the wood stove and invite me to sit and "take a load off while."

With my thinning wallet and waistline, I asked her to teach me about living off the land. Nodding behind our houses I prodded, "Is there anything good to eat out there?"

With her long shaky finger, she pointed out the window to a wide open field and said, "Oh, yes, honey! You see those bushy green leaves out there, honey?" I followed her gaze. "Those are lambs quarters!"

"Lamb's what?"

"Wild spinach, honey! Do you like spinach?" She smiled. "Take all you want!"

It so happens that I love spinach, and I was delighted to discover my own private stash in the fields right behind my house. I'd pick buckets of the stuff and boil it like Popeye thinking what grand fortune it was to have this vast supply of nutrient-rich produce growing right at my fingertips, but I started looking more like Olive Oyl as the weeks went by.

I found a decent job in town running the local Sears outpost. I had migrated from Metro West to the Wild West! Okay, I was punching a clock again, but the people and surroundings were so interesting, I was energized by it.

Fairbanks always held a mystique with a twist of the wild kingdom for me. Everyone had dogs and guns. The guys drove pickups and wore cowboy boots; the women wore denim skirts and calico. Street names included Gold Dust Drive or Old Pioneer Way, and towns like Dogpatch, Musk Ox, or Fox dotted the map. Even the creeks offered a slice of history with names like Goldstream and Deadman Slough.

With Fort Eilson air force base and Fort Jackson army base, men outnumbered women 4:1. I heard that the bodies of Eskimo prostitutes were found along the highways after the winter thaw, but oddly, that didn't stop me from hitch-hiking.

I went to barn parties, country bands, and mountain rivers, but underneath it all, I missed Frank. What was I doing up there? What was I looking for? Was it just a fling with freedom, a thirst for adventure, or something deeper?

One bright night a bunch of Steve's buddies were hanging out at the house drinking beers and smoking pot and someone said, "Let's go to McKinley." They looked at me. "Have you been there yet? You can't come all the way from Boston and miss that," they persuaded. "You haven't lived until you've seen Denali."

Haven't lived? I flashed back to the corner office where Madeline crunched numbers in a cloud of smoke. I thought of Sarah's empty desk and former coworkers moaning about their lives passing by. "Sure! Why not?"

So we took off on the spur of the moment for the road trip of a lifetime, as the sun surrounded majestic horizons at the top of the world. Continuous bands of rainbow colors crest mountain vistas like a never-ending sunrise on another planet. TV screens don't do justice to the mind-expanding panoramas of Alaskan skies that make you feel like you're about to see the face of God.

These spectacular memories fuel my visions of heaven to this day. Alaska's beauty drew me spiritually, and I hungered to know what *or who* was behind such grandeur. It's like standing in the museum of fine arts, enraptured with a particularly exquisite painting, then asking, "Who made this incredible masterpiece?" Alaska provided the heavenly gallery where God began *"tuning my heart to sing his praise."*[3]

Once a week, I thumbed fifteen miles up Highway 6 to collect armloads of books at the Fox college library, then venture out to the tundra on a dirt bike to study my treasures after work each day. Steve's white shepherd "Bear" accompanied me, a faithful protector while I harvested my spinach dinner and devoured books in fields of radiant fireweed.

The occult section of the college library stretched the farthest down the aisles and I thought I'd stumbled across the biggest depository of spiritual reading in the Northwest. I presumed people were more attuned to spiritual things between the green alien flashings of the Aurora Borealis and the dread of facing another long winter of two-hour days.

But why did I focus on the cults? Why not philosophy or the classics? Maybe it was Dad's fascination with the wonders of the universe, or the feeling of standing on Jupiter in Denali Park. My spirit begged to know, *what's out there?*

When I was thirteen, I got a *Ouija* board, then Tarot cards at fifteen, and got my tea leaves read on Tremont Street. That fascination with the supernatural revived, and I stayed up to three or four a.m. studying and attempting spiritual feats like astral projection. Some authors claimed diet and solitude as a means to

---

[3] From the lyrics of a hymn, Come Thou Fount of Every Blessing

achieving holiness, while others claimed yoga and meditation brought you close to God.

Almost imperceptibly, like floating on an ocean current, I was being carried to the shore by an unseen hand. Part of this flow was the realization that all the conflicting requirements in my occult readings couldn't possibly be true at once. Gurus professed to have arrived by crawling on their knees around Calcutta while others were allegedly shooting around the cosmos like miniature comets. Does standing on your head or piercing your skin really impress God, if He's up there?

Above all, the spirituality offered by these men seemed utterly unattainable except by a precious few. I was tiring of the endless whirlpools of spiritual jargon and felt the rip tide of religion pulling me further and further out. I'd drown trying to swim and save myself. Maybe I needed a good dose of reality—maybe my own personal guru—but I never expected him to manifest so soon, or in such a flashy car!

Hitching in Fairbanks one day, I was walking in the gutter when a bright orange Lotus caught my attention. *Nice car! Who is that?* It slowed as it passed me, but I couldn't see the driver through its sleek fastback window.

He went around the block and suddenly reappeared, popping the passenger door to talk. I walked up and looked at the driver, a well-dressed man in his mid-forties with tanned skin and gleaming white teeth. He looked smart, sober, and wealthy.

"Where are you going?" he asked. His eyes were coal black, like an Indian mystic.

"Oh, not far," I lied.

"Come on, I'll take you to lunch," he invited. "There's a really nice place down the road and I'd like you to join me and talk about the work I'm doing here."

I can hardly believe it now, but "lunch" was the magic word. I had the job at the outpost, but it took three weeks for payroll to process the first paycheck, and I was more waif-like then ever. *Why not? I'm starving half to death!*

This guy was different than anyone I'd met—something elusive and mystical. Maybe he was a spiritual guru?

"I don't believe in God," I said suddenly, but startled myself when I said it. He said he wanted to talk about that too.

21

True to his word, we pulled into the nicest restaurant in town where I started chowing everything in sight and he started talking. Atlas, a doctor of engineering contracted to the military, was opening a sports car dealership to showcase Mazarattis, Lamberghinis and other hot items like the one he was driving.

I couldn't believe my fairy tale good fortune. You know, cinder girl meets frog and discusses portents and princes. I was a starving sports car fanatic and story-lover with a spiritual appetite. After living on little else but wild spinach and bread for weeks on end, this lanky long-haired eighteen-year-old gorged herself on fancy foods while he piqued my interest with amazing stories. One thing was certain—the timing was impeccable.

"Years ago in 1961, I was shipwrecked in a big storm off the coast of Haiti," he began. "I had to swim to shore and washed up on the beach, exhausted. When I came to, I was greeted by a prophetess."

"Why are you telling me this?" I asked between gulps.

"She described you to a tee." In fact, he was told to watch for me, "walking in the gutter with long brown hair," and other striking details that led him to believe I was the one. "What? You're saying you know the plan for *my life*?" *The very thing I'm looking for.* "But how? Are you talking about knowing God, or Jesus?"

"Don't *ever* say that name!" he charged. "Call him *the Superior*." I tried to get a handle on what *and who* he believed but he said, "You're *not ready* to receive the answers," like a slap in the face. Anger rose up in me like the steam in Granny's tea kettle. All my life I was told to ask questions and now this spiritual acrobat was telling me I wasn't ready?

Atlas must have enjoyed watching me eat, or he had simply figured out that was an invitation I wouldn't refuse. We went to the best of places, sitting on mats on the floor and eating raw salmon served by Eskimos. We also drove onto the military bases and I attended his meetings—a crash course in possibilities.

One day, at a wide expanse of mountains and valleys displaying his projects, he said, "Pick a mountain, *any mountain*, and I'll build you the house of your dreams. I'll dress you in sealskins and you can model sports cars." I couldn't believe my ears. *Who are you, the genie in the bottle?* I just stared at him. "You can have whatever you want," he smiled.

22

Whoa, easy girl. Offers like that don't come around every day, but I was conflicted. How could this be happening to this skinny kid from the burbs of Boston? Granted, I didn't love this old-enough-to-be-my-father guru, but he was a lot more interesting than the books on my headboard. What I really wanted was to have Frank in the leading role of this fairy tale.

While Atlas tried roping me into the good life, there was a little more going on in me than being impressed with a fat wallet or a full belly. I was truly searching now, trying to understand why this unusual figure had come into my life, and find a connection to God, if that's even possible.

Later that week on my way to work, I was accosted by a fast-talking stranger handing out flyers on the street. He was a Jehovah's Witness who followed me down the road trying to lure me into some kingdom. If only he knew the key to this girl's heart was through her stomach, he could have just handed me a lunch menu and I would have talked all day!

"I don't believe in God!" I finally sputtered. "I believe in science." That did it. He stopped in his tracks and I kept going. With a twinge of embarrassment at my own hostility, I was annoyed. *Why did I say that again? Twice in one week! Do I believe in God, or not?*

I resented Atlas for denying answers to my questions, then spewed nastiness when someone professed to know. I quickened my pace and rushed off, convicted by my own words. Why was I denying God while privately hoping to find Him?

Unwittingly, Atlas became the stepping stone in my spiritual journey. I couldn't wait around for him to decide when I was ready. *IF there is a God and He has a divine plan for my life, I have to find it. If God is know-able, I need to know Him myself!*

Night owl that I am, I'd lie awake imagining the ferocious enormity of the universe Dad described in fascinating detail. If we could hop a space shuttle and travel at the speed of light, it'd take over four years to cover the 24.6 trillion miles to our *nearest* neighboring star! Our entire solar system is dwarfed by more than 100 billion galaxies in the universe, each one containing hundreds of billions of stars! It frustrates my tiny brain. So where's God?

Dad loved going into great detail about the uncanny precision of all this matter in all this space. "There is nothing chaotic about it at all," he'd say puffing that cherry pipe and challenging my mind to expand like the cosmos. "Everything is held in place and perfectly aligned in orbit, but if the earth were to fluctuate by the slightest degree in either direction, we would either freeze to death or burn up!" I'd watch the blue smoke rise in paisley curls and disappear in thin air, but those astounding thoughts left a mark on me.

I tossed and turned through this twilight of my life, sometimes going out to stare at the incredible expanse of wide Alaskan sky. Is God holding everything together? Between streaming sunsets and sunrises I agonized *to know*. Then a strange thought blazed across my brain like a shooting star.

This is like algebra homework! Whenever I was really stuck I'd go to my father. Typically, it would be 10 or 11 p.m. and I'd racked my brain trying to get the extra points for some bonus question too difficult for me to solve. *"Daaaad,* can you help me?" It never occurred to me that he was tired too, but he'd take the book from my hands, invite me to sit by his side, and start flipping back to the beginning of the chapter.

"No, Dad!" I'd moan. "I already did those pages! Just help me with number 12."

"Well hold on, honey, we'll find the answers by going back to the beginning." He was right of course, but I was exhausted, and lazy. Though I dreaded the process, it was necessary to review the steps and formulas of prior pages. "Remember, if you give a man a fish you meet his need for a day; but if you teach him *how to* fish, you meet his need for a lifetime." He smiled over the top of his glasses. "Do you want to learn, or do you just want number 12?"

"Oh, okaaayyyyy," I'd breathe a big sigh of unhappy surrender and hunker down for the lifetime version of an algebraic stumper.

"Atta girl!" he'd belt out a big laugh. "Now let's get down to brass tacks."

Now I wondered if God was waiting for me. I think He's not giving me what I need fast enough, but maybe He's more interested in my learning the lifetime version.

Like flipping pages to chapter one, I started consciously rewinding all my religious training over the years. At various times, I attended Catholic, Episcopal, Unitarian, and Baptist churches, not to mention eight years of being dutifully dropped off at the Methodist Church.

Once a month, we kids were allowed in the service to hear the black-robed reverend bellow from an elevated pulpit, *"THIS IS THE HOUSE OF GOD!"* The great pipe organ thundered out the stanzas of "A Mighty Fortress is our God," and it all felt very sacred, but I didn't understand. I used to count the 729 window panes and I knew of course that all good members expressed devotion in the velvet-lined collection plates.

At six, I was chosen to read the Christmas story to the whole church. I climbed up into that high platform like the pastor. "Make sure you read nice and loud," they directed. I was nervous, but my voice rang out in the large hall like a character in Charlie Brown's Christmas. I proclaimed the Name of Jesus to a large congregation and even "enunciated with feeling," they said. I knew he was born in a manger while shepherds watched their flocks, but I never *knew why* and I never *knew Him,* and I still lived like he didn't exist.

I even attended mass on Ash Wednesday as a teenager. The service was conducted partly in Latin which was Greek to me of course as they stood, knelt, crossed their hearts and hoped to die, but the ashes on their foreheads piqued my curiosity most. I finally leaned over and whispered, "Why are you doing this?" but received a dissatisfying response. "I don't know—it's just what they make us do." I thought about that for a few minutes and left.

The sermons seemed pointless, the voices monotone, and it all droned on under the eyes of dead statues. Robes, ritual and religious externals merely created a dark veil like a "Do Not Enter" sign to my hungry soul.

Admittedly, old European architecture is interesting, and I love organ music. In sixth grade I dreamed of going to the Boston Conservatory of Music. I saved babysitting money and walked to Hammond Organ every week to learn endless progressions on multiple keyboards and rows of big black pedals. But spiritual music and fancy buildings didn't answer the needs of my heart.

Lying awake in these gloaming hours in Alaska, my mind drifted home. I wondered if my parents were worrying and if Barbara and Jeanne were still lighting candles.

I recalled my devout Welsh grandmother and wondered if I was somehow being touched by ancestral prayers for blessing. After all, they chose me to be caretaker of the massive 200-year-old Judd family Bibles when I was about 15. The covers were worn ragged, the pages browned and brittle, but pressed inside the cover I discovered a letter penned by a great great grandmother dating back six generations, to the spring of 1812!

I always imagined a mahogany writing table with a feather quill and inkwell. In my mind's eye, she wore a white lacy blouse with pearls, her braided hair pinned up in ringlets as befits her daughter's wedding day. Being in declining health, she may have wondered if they'd ever see each other again, so despite the excited flurry in the household, she escaped to the privacy of her drawing room to capture her most precious thoughts. Here's an excerpt:

May 3rd 1812

My Dear Son and Daughter, Sibyl and William Lewis,

This being your Marriage Day, I would wish to give you something that would be of service and do you good. I don't know of any thing so valuable as the Holy Bible, and so precious as the word of God. It is all ways new—when you open it, it will be good to say, Lord open our eyes… open our understanding that we may understand what we read to our soul's good. To those who love and fear God, O, how sweet and precious are the promises, for the Lord hath said I will be a God to thee and to thy seed after thee … If you seek him he will be found of you… I pray God to make you his humble and upright and faithful servants…

May the God that has protected me to this time and is now the support of my declining days, keep you under the shadow of his almighty wings, may he be your guard and guide through life, your comfort in the hour of dissolution and your portion and happiness to all Eternity. Amen and Amen. I pray God All mighty to bless you both and give you grace, wisdom, and understanding in all things, which is the sincere wish and prayer of your ever affectionate Mother, Nbrown

When I read that, I yearned for wisdom and understanding in all things. I wanted to be kept "under the shadow of his almighty wings." I wanted to seek and find God, but how?

5. I Am

My five-year-old Bible waited at the end of my headboard in my little bedroom loft. Finally, I picked it up and held it in my hands. "Don't even try to understand the Bible," my mother was told. My Italian Catholic family assumed you needed to be a Latin scholar to understand it, but I had to try.

I went out to the tundra, flipped open to John, and got hooked on the story for the first time in my life. I read for hours as the sun rolled around the fields of fireweed until another light began to flicker, the Almighty himself illuminating my spirit.

The print was miniscule and the words simple, but the message was profound and revealed a magnificent God. Contrary to the cultic spiritists I'd been reading, Jesus was approachable, merciful, and best of all, He had answers! Without a speck of Latin, I soon discovered that the Lamb of God who takes away the sin of the world made powerful claims:

I am the Messiah with living water—to fulfill your thirst 4:26
I am the Bread of Life—that you never hunger again 6:35
I am the Light of the World—that you see truth 8:12
I am the door—that you enter freely and be forever home 10:7-9
I am the Good Shepherd—that you find peace and rest 10:11,14
I am the resurrection—that you need never die 11:25
I am the Way, the Truth and the Life—that you find heaven 14:6

Jesus spoke with authority over every earthly circumstance without being haughty or manipulative. Even to the piercing pain of being nailed to a cross, he forgave his enemies and loved to the bitter end. What kind of man would do this? *"All these things were recorded so you may believe that Jesus is the Christ, the Son of God, and that by believing you may have life in his name."*[4] Is this same Jesus alive?

I got down on my knees right there in the field and said, "Jesus, if you're God, I have to know you for myself. If you have a plan for my life, please show me... Are you there? *Are you real?"*

A soft breeze touched my face and I listened with my eyes wide open. The fireweed waved gently in the wind. Then came his sweet reply. *"I am."*

I didn't hear it from the sky, or even in my ears. It was as though the words were spoken inside me, a whisper in my soul.

That's how I met God on the Alaskan tundra and felt his presence for the first time in my life. Five thousand miles from home, I found the welcoming arms of my heavenly Father.

How do you explain something so profound to someone who has never experienced it? "Amazing," and "awesome," are overused and seem weak. Perhaps, "breathless wonder" or, "mind-boggling heart-stopping euphoria," comes close.

Why did it take me so long just to talk to Him? He was right there the whole time, as near as my breath. The living God of Abraham heard my prayer and answered me and I knew in the depth of my being, *THIS* changes everything!

God didn't answer because my prayer was polished, perfect, or theologically sound. It was simply the cry of my heart to know Him and, *"Whosoever shall call upon the name of the LORD shall be saved."*[5] That day I discovered that "whosoever" includes me, as though I'd been living in a dark house and someone came in and threw open the blinds. **"I am,"** he said, and I was filled with those two words. Yes, the eternal God is present, here and now.

I immediately sat down and wrote a long letter to Elaine to share my newfound joy, but sadly she never received it.

The phone rang at 5 a.m. with the shocking news from a former coworker. "Karen, you're not going to believe this... Elaine is dead!" Gail said.

Bolting to the edge of my bed, I started trembling. "How? What happened?"

"She was out with Keith Woods on his motorbike." I knew the name. We were in the same Sunday School class as kids. "They

---

[4] John 20:15, 29, 31
[5] Romans 10:13

were on Grove Street." I also knew about the hairpin turns on Grove. One of them nearly claimed my own life in a little mustang when I was fifteen. Five of us hit that curve near the common doing 80 and landed sideways against a tree, narrowly missing the granite wall around the cemetery. Again I knew I could have died, but walked away without a scratch. Not this time. A nightmare was coming true.

"A truck came around the corner and broadsided them," Gail said. "Elaine's helmet flew off and she was thrown into the woods. Her head hit granite and she died on the spot."

My mouth went dry. As severe as shattered glass, death puts life in sharp relief.

"Keith is in the hospital with fractures and crushed bones, but they think he's going to make it." Gayle gave me the details of the funeral and I scribbled it down and thanked her.

Then I got down on my knees and cried. "Jesus, should I go home now?" This is the first time I asked God for direction *expecting* him to answer, but it seemed the natural thing to do now that we were on speaking terms and all.

"Yes," God spoke so clearly I thought for a second someone had come into the room and said it.

I didn't know any ritualistic prayer lingo. I simply said, "Wow, okay God," and got dressed. I somehow understood I'd found what I was looking for in Alaska and now it was time to go. So I called the airline and booked the 1 a.m. flight back to Boston.

This time, my Bible wasn't buried in the bottom of my duffel bag. I clutched it like a life jacket on the *Titanic* and read for five straight hours. Watching vast glaciers and mountains in glorious sunrise, I journeyed across Canada feeling like the real adventure had just begun.

Elaine's funeral service at St. Bridget's seemed surreal. I had slipped from the majestic grandeur of Alaska into a gothic incensed world, where echoed chords of grief reverberated against cathedral ceilings.

And there lay Elaine, her slim and youthful body so pale and still, adorned in white and surrounded by flowers. Gone; that cackling laughter, and the flitting hands that waved incessantly when she talked. Gone; her wild, wavy hair and lively expressions,

29

the dancing circles of smoke around her head, and all our crazy adventures. My dear friend was gone.

Her mother rushed to embrace me, weeping. "Elaine never got your letter," her eyes spilled over. "It didn't get here in time." Little did she know, the impact of those words would remain with me for the rest of my life. She hugged me tightly and her little shoulders shook with sobbing. Nothing could repay what one truck across a little yellow line had taken from her... the life of her daughter, bright, beautiful, and only eighteen. Gone!

We followed the parade of black flagged cars to the cemetery on Grove Street, where she took her last ride just days before and our headlights brushed the stone wall that nearly claimed my own life a few years earlier.

The ground was opened and draped with cloth, and we gathered in a stiff black cluster facing her coffin. I watched it all from Elaine's perspective, imagining her commentary of quips and how she would hate the gaudy florals. We try to beautify the graveside service, but this was no joke. I feared she wasn't in heaven and my heart was screaming in protest, but I stood stiffly as the rest of them engulfed in a powerless grief. *Jesus, save us from this bad ending. I have to tell people! I have to talk to Keith!*

Rounding the corner to his hospital room, my eyes took in a maze of suspended ropes and life support tubes. Keith was covered with bandages, his limbs suspended in traction. It took a moment to recognize my childhood classmate in such critical surroundings.

"The whole thing happened so fast," he started. "That truck was way over the line and I couldn't get out of the way." Tears rolled into the bandages on his face. "I hit the brakes and swerved but the bike spun right into him... I still can't believe she's dead. If only we had gone later, or picked a different road or—*anything* but this!"

I told him about Alaska and the message of the Bible. "Keith, Jesus is alive! I heard him speak. This isn't just Sunday school stuff, He's real! Talk to him." But it seemed my words fell flat. Though he kept thanking me for coming, he wasn't ready to talk about forgiveness, and couldn't forgive himself.

Years later, Keith took his own life.

6. Jesus Made Me Kosher

Suspended in the high corner of my bedroom, a long demonic face with red eyes leered over me. The whole room got cold as he taunted me night after night. It loomed over me sneering wickedly, and I felt the chill of death in those frightful moments praying, *Jesus, take it away. Jesus, protect me.*

Was Atlas conjuring an evil spirit to haunt me? I suspected his "Superior," in effort to keep me in his clutches, but the devil's attempts to dislodge my faith failed miserably. These night visions drove me harder into the arms of a loving Savior. My appetite for God's Word only increased and that devil's face disappeared.

After months in Alaska, I was back in my little pink room trying to process everything. Why was I spared? What was God's plan for me? Immersing myself in God's Word, I made discoveries too good to keep to myself, but every attempt to share this spiritual awakening was met with skepticism or disdain.

Atlas started calling. He said he would send me a diamond, but I didn't want a ring. I'd found something worth so much more. I tried explaining my new-found faith, but his cold repulsion crept right through the phone lines. My parents didn't understand either.

"Mom, Dad, I really heard God when I prayed! Jesus is *alive!*"

"How do we know you haven't been brainwashed by the Children of God or some cult?" Dad took hold of my thin wrists. "You're nothing but skin and bones! Calm down and get some rest, honey. It'll be all right."

Calm down and rest? I desperately wanted them to understand before something else happened. I also wanted to see Frank, but no one knew his number. I only had a P.O. Box in

Wellfleet, a quaint fishing village near the tip of Cape Cod. *Help me reach him, Lord, so I can tell him about you.*

Call the General Store, the Lord whispered.

Yeah! Even if he was camping in the woods he would eventually need supplies, so I left a message for the local surfers. The very next day, Frank was walking down Main Street when a sports car sailed by. The woman who took my message recognized that unmistakable long hair and beard. He looked like Jesus.

"Call Kara--...!" her voice trailed in the wind as she whirred past him. He walked straight to a phone booth and dialed my number, and I was right by the phone.

"Are you home?" he asked excitedly.

"Frank! Elaine was in a motorbike accident and she was killed! I flew home for her funeral!"

"No wayyyy!" he said. "That's freaky."

"I know! I would have called you but nobody has your number."

"Yeah, I don't have one. So what's going on with you?"

"Well, I want to tell you everything..."

"You should come down! You'd love it." Frank had a room in a big country house near his favorite surfing hangout. "It's a pretty cool place," he said.

The next morning I started off on what should have been an easy three-hour drive. Unfortunately, traffic was terrible all the way to the Bourne Bridge and my little Triumph over-heated. The fan belt broke and I nearly burned up my engine before finding someone to service a foreign car. Then I ran over a paper bag filled with beer bottles and crept into another station with slashed tires!

It took eight hours and a lot of cash to go 150 miles, and by the time I pulled into the sleepy sunburned village of Wellfleet, I had been praying all day about how to tell Frank about Jesus. I was excited and afraid. What if he rejected me?

Someone on the third story heard my tires crunching the stone driveway and popped his head out an upper window. I saw bleached blonde curls, a red beard, and a blue bandana. When he smiled and waved I realized that colorful character was Frank!

"That night was like a date with a Mexican jumping bean," he said. "There was something different about you. You were definitely happier and your face seemed brighter than I'd ever seen. And you were jumping all over the room!"

32

I told him all about Alaska, how I read the Bible and got down on my knees and heard the Lord. "Honey, it was Jesus! He spoke to me!"

"Don't talk to me about *Jesus,*" he said, *"I'm Jewish!"*

"But... *so was he!"* I countered. "Why don't you guys... get along?"

This kicked off an entire night's discussion. We drove to the beach and watched the ocean waves crash on the shore, matching the collision of mind and spirit inside our car. In two years of dating, religion never came between us—his bar mitzvah and my confirmation had never changed how we lived.

"Honey, Jesus is real! He answers prayer! *He's alive!"* We watched a bright moon cast silvery beams across the water and I prayed God would reveal himself to Frank.

We often wished we could replay that pivotal night's impassioned conversation. Frank said, "It was surreal. I remember a lot of talk about the blood, and couldn't figure out why that was so important, but I could see that Karen was different and I wanted to understand why."

Then, much like the seafaring disciples who dropped their nets to follow Jesus, Frank decided to hang up his surfboard and move back home so we could pursue "this thing" together. He packed, threw a bag in my car and came with me, just like that.

The film, *Jesus Christ Superstar,* was released that September, 1973, and we sat in my car with the top down discussing the life of Christ afterwards. It suddenly occurred to me that the same demonic enemy whose face haunted my bedroom was also trying to keep Frank from believing.

I looked up at the sky and said, *"I despise Satan!"* A giant streak of lightning suddenly lit the sky right over us and we nearly jumped out of our skin. There was no other lightning that night and no storm brewing, except in unseen realms.

"Let's get out of here!" Frank yelled. We put the top up, rolled the windows and peeled out, but we never forgot *"that bolt* of lightning." It was one of the signs that convinced Frank I wasn't making up stories, and he was determined to study Jesus as thoroughly and honestly as he could.

"It's really weird," he said later on. "When I was living in San Diego, a surfer drowned in thirty-foot waves and washed up on Ocean Beach. Then I was walking down the boardwalk with my surfboard and met a couple of Jesus freaks. One was strumming a harp and the other asked if he could pray for me." Frank laughed at the memory. "So while one strummed his harp, the other anointed me with oil and prayed over me. I thought it was crazy, but now here you are, saying Jesus changed your life."

"Well, I don't know about them, but I'm not making this stuff up," I said. "You ought to talk to Him. He's real!"

Walking downtown a few days later, Frank asked, "So, what are we going to do for money?" As soon as those words were out of his mouth, we stopped in our tracks. Two ten dollar bills were lying on the sidewalk—one in front of me, and another directly in front of him! Dumbfounded, we looked up and down the street and even up the sides of the building to see if anyone was watching. Oddly, the money wasn't crumpled or wind-blown, but the bills were perfectly straight and flat against the concrete, as though placed by hand.

"It's the angels!" I said, "God wants us to go in here!" Instinctively we picked up the bills, and Frank followed me through the doorway to a little shop we never noticed, where we found ourselves surrounded by Bibles! Holding crisp ten-dollar bills with equally parched expressions on our faces, a warm voice surprised us from behind the counter.

"You two look like you've seen a ghost!"

At first, we thought it was all about the money, but Stu was the real God-send. That store manager was the first believer we met, and we left with a wealth of new research material and someone to answer our questions. I was ecstatic.

Frank wasn't entirely convinced yet, but he was reading the Bible and asking a million questions, weighing the claims of Biblical Christianity with everything he believed as a Jew. How did the Old and New Testaments come into being? Why are Jews and Christians divided? How does the cross come into it and why is the blood significant?

We were still looking for work but all doors were closed until a personable businessman who attended Stu's church hired Frank. Bob Fulton, or "Fulty" as everyone called him, embraced every opportunity to shower the love of God on a band of long-haired ragamuffins, but coming from the laid-back surfer scene, a paper cutting plant downtown was the epitome of everything Frank avoided.

While learning the ropes of the equipment, other employees talked to him about his spiritual life. Tony was particularly zealous, quoting Bible verses over the hum of the machinery. His passion was unstoppable—a man head over heels in love with Jesus after years of heroin addiction—but Frank felt like he was being brainwashed, and resigned.

"I'm sorry to see you go," Fulty said, "but I'm not going to worry about you. The hound of heaven will follow you wherever you go."

Craving more creative work and missing the outdoors, he joined a team of carpenters, but he never forgot Fulty's words. Meanwhile, we started attending Stu and Ruth's weekly Bible studies. They offered a wealth of Scriptural knowledge and invited us to church.

Already treading thin ice at home, this was hard for Frank. "For the first time in my life, I'd wake up with a tight chest feeling like I was betraying my family. How could a Jew just start going to church? How could I stop being who I am?"

One day he was reading his new Bible when his father burst in. "Frank! Don't you know the Bible is the biggest book of hypocrisy on the face of the earth? You're killing me!"

"There must be something powerful going on here or it wouldn't create such a reaction," he told me. Then he decided to see for himself. He wanted to go to church.

The Village Bible Chapel was about five miles away on a wooded street at the north end of town. It certainly wasn't an intimidating structure like some gothic cathedral with gargoyles carved in the doorway. The Chapel was a single-story white-sided building nestled in New England pines. Yet, in a classic case of cold feet on that beautiful autumn day, Frank didn't make it through the doors. As we neared the building, he changed his mind. "If your God is real, I can talk to him in the woods."

"Sure you can," remembering where I first connected to God, and I dropped him off at Nobscott Mountain, named after the Indians who lived there 200 years ago. So I went to the little Chapel alone praying, *Dear Jesus, show Frank that you're there. Show him that you're alive like you showed me.* And the second I saw him smiling from ear to ear, I knew.

"You wouldn't believe it!" he started excitedly. "I hiked to the top of the trail and sat on a big granite rock eating blueberries. I kept thinking about this whole Jesus debate, feeling like a tug-of-war was going on between you and my family, my dad and me...Then I just started talking to him. I said, 'God, is all this talk about Jesus true? Are you who Karen says you are? Are you the Messiah?' And I heard, '**I am.**'"

With those timeless words came a rush of peace and freedom he hadn't felt before. Now Frank believed—not because of me, but because of what he heard in his own heart. Once again, the Lord introduced himself as I am, the name He gave to Moses.[6] He is the God of the ages; the same yesterday, today, and forever!

The following week Frank decided it would be safe to "try church" again. We arrived to a packed house and the usher showed us to the front row. Frank wore his trademark leather cap which remained firmly in place through the entire service; we were two long-haired hippies fumbling with the hymnal right in front of the organist. The minute the service ended an energetic woman rushed to greet us. "Welcome! I'm so glad you could come," Sandy said, not at all put off by our non-churchy appearances. Not everyone responded as kindly.

Hannukah arrived and Frank's uncle flew in from Miami. At the dinner table, his father started the conversation with his usual, "So, what's new?"

Frank jumped right into the fray. "I believe in Jesus now."

Everyone dropped their forks and mouths hung open, but the Zionist of the family physically lunged at him. A former wrestler, as wide and strong as an ox, Uncle Albert grabbed Frank by the throat and lifted him off the ground. "Can I punch Jesus out of you right now?" The veins were popping out in his neck.

"If you want to," Frank stammered.

"Do you believe in *the virgin birth*?"

"I... I think so," He was choking, but we all just stared wide-eyed in shock.

"Then you're a *Christian!*" he accused, throwing him to the floor. "How can you do this?" He stormed around the room with his arms flailing in the air. "Don't you know that Christians marched around the burning bodies of Jews in the Crusades? Christians have persecuted us for centuries! How can you turn on your own people like this?"

---

[6] Exodus 3:14

Frank was on the floor rubbing his neck. He couldn't believe his "loving uncle" would turn on him like this. *You're not exactly treating me kindly for my faith either, uncle.*

Uncle Albert pointed at me. "If *she* was Buddhist, would you be Buddhist?" There it was. They were pinning me, assuming he would only profess Christ because of "some girl."

"No," Frank was surprisingly soft-spoken, more hurt than angry. "I don't know why you're so upset. None of you are orthodox, and you don't even attend temple. I could be standing on my head and smoking pot and you'd laugh. But I'm trying to tell you I've found God and you're ready to kill me. It doesn't make sense."

He did his best to explain, but Jesus brought explosive reactions. They tried dissuading him, but Frank would never change his mind. He knew he'd heard the Lord in the woods that day, and no one could convince him otherwise.

Our adult class at church was led by a Jewish teacher at the time. Frank confessed his struggles and he quipped, "Oi vey, I used to think God was Jewish, Jesus was Catholic, and John was a Baptist. What did I know? But don't be afraid to ask the hard questions, Frank. Keep studying and God will teach you." Frank took that advice to heart.

Meanwhile, our relationship grew stronger than ever. In three years of dating, we never felt ready to commit, but with God as the anchor of our lives, it seemed right.

Frank spotted an ad for a loft apartment in a historic colonial. With five spacious rooms and fully furnished for $250, we rushed over to see it. "This would be perfect for us. How long can you hold it?" we asked the landlord.

"Why? How much time do you need?" they asked.

"Well, we have to get married first," we confessed sheepishly.

Amused, they asked, "What date did you have in mind?"

We pulled out a calendar, "Two weeks should be enough... How about June 8th?"

They looked at each other smiling. "June 8th is our anniversary, too. Okay!"

We planned our entire wedding around that house. We went to the mall to pick rings, a long chiffon dress off the rack for $40, and a suit for Frank. "Well, that was easy," I said. "Why do people make such a fuss about weddings?" Then I thought of a few more *little* details. "Oh honey, we need to book the church and ask the pastor to do the ceremony!"

"Oh, that'll take two minutes," Frank said, and called the pastor. "Chuck, hi. Are you free on June 8th? We want to get married... Can we use the church?"

Chuck is a Dallas Seminarian, a highly esteemed Biblical scholar and elder of the church. "Well, I, uh, normally recommend six months of pre-marital counseling," he started cautiously. "I should pray about my answer before I agree."

"That's cool," Frank said, but he had never heard an answer like that in his entire life.

"I'll call you back Thursday," the pastor assured.

Frank shrugged it off. "That's fine. God will show him."

The pastor turned to his wife, "Whatever is their *bodacious haste?*"

Two days passed and he called back as promised. "I can't explain it, but I have complete peace about marrying you two on June 8th, and yes, the church is free."

Good thing, it was only nine days away! My biggest worry was my brother's safety and my parents were a nervous wreck about him coming home. He was wanted by the FBI!

It all started with a downed plane. Steve went head to head with his CO about a plane he found unfit for flight, but the CO insisted it fly, with Steve on board. Incredibly, the engine failed and the plane crashed in grizzly country, its wings snapping into Alaskan pines and stranding the entire crew which had to be rescued. The embarrassed CO consequently had a personal vendetta against my brother and made life intolerable for him. Steve sought help from the Chaplain, applied for transfers, and scoured military law to no avail. He was at the mercy of a CO who hated him.

Six months shy of finishing his three-year term, Steve decided to kiss his college tuition and MIT dream good-bye. He outfitted his van for the Alkan Highway and drove off base, joining the ranks of thousands of AWOL troops during the Viet Nam War.

"The only thing that'll stop me is a bullet through my back," he determined. This explains why we didn't dare publish our nuptials in the paper. Dad read about one soldier who came home from Canada for a funeral and the FBI was waiting for him with handcuffs.

This situation became a great faith lesson for me. One day, a picture of the Apostle Paul in my Bible caught my eye. His enemies watched the gates in hopes of arresting him, so friends lowered him over the city wall in a basket.[7] *Yes, God is able to make a way of escape!* I got hold of that idea and prayed for Steve's miracle day and night. *Turn this around, Father. Provide a way of escape for Steve. You're the only one who can help him.*

Frank and I were sitting at the kitchen table with Mom one night when the subject came up. "I'm praying for a miracle to help Steve escape," I said hopefully.

"Oh, Karen, this is the army and the FBI we're talking about! How can he escape?"

"God is greater than the army! He's bigger than the FBI! He can make a way."

"I wish I could believe like you," she said.

"You can!" we chimed. So we bowed and prayed with her to put her trust in the Lord not only for Steve's circumstances, but for her own salvation. The Lord used my brother's dreadful situation to bring my mother to that huge step of faith.

On Saturday evening, June 8th, 1974, Pastor Chuck officiated at our simple candlelight service at the Chapel, adding eloquently about our faith in Christ as a Dallas man is apt to do. There were a few muffled gasps from the Jewish side of the aisle, but Robbie gave a comical champagne toast about his brother and the Sax-gang girl, Frank's mother clung to my Dad's arm, and everything turned out fine.

Best of all, there were no arrests, though a scruffy freelance photographer showed up in jeans and a scraggly beard. Afterwards, he disappeared into the anonymity of the open road while I kept praying, *Safety and escape, Lord. Help him escape!*

---

[7] Acts 9:25

7. Promised *Land*

"Wouldn't it be fun to move to Oregon?" Frank asked. Soon after the wedding we were dreaming about moving out west like it was the Promised Land.

Frank's Dad hollered, "You don't know a soul out there! What are you going to do so far away from family? Is God going to rain money down on you from heaven?" He opened his wallet and started throwing twenties and fifties around the living room carpet. I thought about picking up a few, just to make him feel appreciated, but Frank didn't flinch.

"I want to build log cabins, Dad."

"You couldn't build your way out of a paper sack!" he laughed. "And you'll never make it past the Mass Pike in that old jalopy of yours!"

Nevertheless, a little phrase from Genesis stuck in our brains. Determined to, "leave and cleave," we quit our jobs, packed Frank's old pickup, and hit the dusty trail to begin a new life. With God's help we would find our way.

Our cross-country trip was exhilarating, camping across the Rockies, picking up hitch hikers, and sharing the Lord with anyone who would listen. Frank drove and I read Exodus and Acts until my voice was hoarse each day, comparing our travels with Biblical history.

Somewhere across Iowa the sky grew dark with an ominous black cloud. It dropped into a gigantic tornado that swirled and danced its way through buildings a few miles away. Frank floored the accelerator while we prayed it wouldn't come in our direction, but we were scared to death.

Is this how Israel felt passing through the steep walls of the Red Sea? Finally, it dwindled down until it resembled a thinly twisted bed sheet of wispy cloud, but we kept driving. In fact, we drove 700 miles until we hit mountains in Colorado.

We fell in love with the Northwest. Yosemite and the Grand Tetons took our breath away. We bought cowboy hats, went horseback riding, camped at Snake River, and roped a 14-point rack of elk antlers to the roof.

Reaching Oregon long after dark, we splurged at a dinky motel right across the northeastern border. Then early the next morning, we stepped outside expectantly to survey the great land of our hopes and dreams.

Instead, hot dry wind blasted our faces and tumbleweeds blew across the parking lot right in front of us. Our Promised Land appeared to be nothing but a desert wasteland! How would we even find work in a place like this?

Frank stood with his hands on his hips. "Maybe we should keep heading north and see what British Columbia is like?"

"Great idea!" Just like that, we abandoned our Oregon dream and headed for Canada.

Parenthetically, I should mention what happened a few years earlier on a weekend jaunt to Montreal. We cruised over the border and toured around the city for a day, slept in the car, and headed home. Unfortunately, we were halted by customs at the Derby Line of Vermont, a couple of disheveled long-hairs in a sports car without baggage. Certainly we were up to no good. The customs agent took one look at us and snarled, "Pull into the second bay."

They separated us for questioning and body searches while agents raked through my car and found marijuana seeds in the upholstery. We forgot about the little baggie in Frank's boot. He rolled it up in his sock and tossed it aside, but the officer flipped it inside out.

"Aha, you found the magic bag of tricks!" Frank snickered, but the agent wasn't laughing. They impounded my car and detained us with just twenty-two dollars in our pocket. "You're going to need a lot more than that to get out of here!" the officer laughed.

"How much are we talking here?" Frank asked.

"$500 for the car and fines before you can be released," came the shocking reply. "And if you don't have it here by 6 a.m., you're both going to jail!" Jail? We only had a few ounces, but it wasn't open to negotiation.

"Don't we get a phone call or something?" Frank asked.

"Me too?"

"Yes, you can do that," he growled.

Frank called his wealthy aunt who helped her own kids in similar situations. Thankfully, she was home and agreed to help. Now, my turn. Let's see, who would be crazy enough to drive to the Canadian line to get us out of jail by 6 a.m.?

"Elaine! It's me. I'm so glad you're home! Frank and I were busted with a bag of weed on the Derby Line in Vermont. We need $500 by 6 a.m. or we're going to jail!"

"You gotta be kiddin me." She said, and started howling.

"No joke! Frank's Aunt has the cash, but we need someone to deliver it by morning." I gave her directions and then we slept on the floor in the barracks under the eye of a few ornery guards. We tossed and turned but didn't breathe freely until Elaine pulled in at 5:50 a.m. Ironically, she took speed to keep awake and drove her Mercedes like a madman all night. "If I crossed the border, I'd be busted too!" she laughed, but we were cleared to go.

Now, two years later, we were trying to cross the Canadian border on the western side. This time, we only wanted to visit a Bible College and start a new life, but as fate would have it, we had camped out the night before and didn't look much different than the first infamous crossing at Derby Line. A stiff agent eye-balled Frank's long hair and beard and started drilling us.

"What's your destination?" he demanded.

"We want to go to Regent Bible College."

"Have you been accepted?"

"Uh, not yet."

"Have you applied?"

"Well, not exactly.... We wanted to see it first." That sounded lame. We were obviously packed to move.

His eyes narrowed. Then the agent hit us with the million dollar question, "Have you ever been arrested before?" He looked right at me.

"Yes," I blurted truthfully, "but that was *before* we became Christians."

Frank darted a surprised look my way, as if to say, was *that* necessary? He knew I'd just blown our chances of ever seeing B.C.

Our first border crossing in Vermont taught us the stiff penalty of the law. Washington taught the cost of our words, but God used it all in spite of ourselves.

Plainly, my little proclamation of faith didn't impress the agent. "Turn around" he said curtly, "and *don't even try* to cross at any other border point. I'm sending your photos down the line to every other crossing... *Canada doesn't want you.*"

"Imagine, *a whole country* not wanting us!" I vented on the long trek back through Washington. "What a waste of time and miles!" Any ideas about claiming Canada as our Promised Land fizzled.

"Didn't Paul have to change directions a couple of times?" Frank asked. "Didn't the Spirit forbid him from entering some country in Acts?"[8] Remembering that great apostle being bound, stoned and left for dead, we realized we weren't so bad off, and kept praying all the way down the Pacific Coast for God's help.

Seattle was beautiful and coastal areas tempting, but we hadn't given our original Promised Land a very fair chance. "Maybe God wants us in Oregon after all," Frank said thoughtfully.

Reaching Oregon's northwestern border, we pulled into the Navy port of Astoria and stopped at the Chamber of Commerce. Frank wanted to get a layout of the land. Standing over a table map of the state, a spunky clerk approached, "May I help you guys?"

"Yeah, if you could live anywhere in Oregon, where would it be?" Frank asked. I gave him a sharp look. *What a stupid question. Who cares what she thinks?* Imagine my surprise when she snapped, "Right here!" and planted her finger in the center of the state. We nearly bonked heads leaning in to look at the spot.

The chatty clerk raved about Bend, an open, friendly mountain town with snowy peaks on the west and high desert on the east. "You guys would love this place," she oozed. She made it sound like the Swiss Alps with ski resorts, mountain lakes and waterfalls, cool people and a wonderful culture. "It's the best place to live in the whole state."

---

[8] Acts 16:6-10

"Do you think the Lord would lead us through a stranger's opinion?" I asked, climbing back into the truck. All along the Oregon coast, people saw our Mass. plates and discouraged us. One old man said plainly, "Don't live here unless you like rain every day!"

"What about Bend?" we'd ask.

"Oh, it's beautiful there!" No one had anything bad to say about the place.

We kept studying Israel's Exodus wanderings, cravings, and foibles, envious of the pillar of cloud and fire that marked their way so plainly. "Oh, if only God would give us a big cloud or a red arrow we could understand!" I whined.

Despite so many glorious reports about Bend, we resisted the interior, clinging to dreams of living near the ocean. But by the time we reached the border of California, money and morale were nearly gone. We had missed our so-called Promised Land the second time through. Pulling over to camp for the night, road-weary and discouraged, we could practically hear Frank's Dad laughing. Maybe he was right. What were we doing wandering all over the country?

As darkness fell around our tent we confessed everything we could think of and prayed, "Lord, lead us where you want. It doesn't matter what it looks like. Direct our lives as you did with Israel. And please Lord, give us a sign we can understand."

The next morning we climbed out of the tent and stood up to stretch our sore backs. I was just about to ask Frank what he wanted for breakfast, when I realized I was staring at a wooden sign nailed to the tree behind our tent.

"Hey Frank, look at this! We pitched our tent at the head of Damnation Trail!" The arrow on the sign was pointing south. "What kind of a name is that? I mean, that's like saying, this is the road to hell right here!"

"That's it!" Frank said resolutely. "We're turning around and going North!"

God had given us just the "sign" we needed—complete with a red arrow! We scrambled back into the truck and headed for Bend, and it felt like God was smiling at us, "Way to go, kids."

As if to test our prayer about appearances, our course from Damnation Trail on the California coast led us directly through a

45

few hundred miles of charred land and lava beds. This time, we determined not to veer off course no matter what it looked like.

What a great sense of humor God has! As we reached the city limits of Bend, our tired old pickup gave up the ghost as though God was saying, "This is the place, kids! And just to be sure you stay put, I'm pulling the plug right here." Then, that pillar of cloud I wanted literally shot out the back end of our Chevy!

We had traveled five thousand miles before rolling into the Motel 6 on Hwy 97. We were broke, but right where God wanted us. Best of all, the girl in Astoria was right. From the minute we rolled into town, we absolutely loved it.

I went to take a hot shower and Frank met a man named Woody, who *just happened* to have a newly vacated, furnished rental two blocks away. "Karen! I found our apartment!" Frank hollered when I came out. A contemporary ranch in the pines fit our style and wallet perfectly, and we moved right in.

The next morning, my enterprising husband went for a walk and passed a log cabin under construction. He befriended the workers and they hired him on the spot to join the crew on his dream job. Then I heard about a secretarial job at the courthouse that had *just* become available and I was hired by the county commissioner. Wow, God!

As we drove around exploring, we passed an old stone church, "Chapel of the Cascades. "Let's go there!" I yelled, and from that first Sunday, the Chapel was home to us. We ate, played, and worshipped together. Bible studies in our houses, volleyball at the college, and witnessing in the park. Hippies were flocking to the area at that time, and many were being saved.[9]

It took us awhile to get there, but then everything fell so quickly into place with a home, great jobs, and a wonderful church family. We had seen God do *exceedingly above all we ask or think*.[10] We made it to the Promised Land!

While I attended public hearings and worked with county commissioners, Frank built log cabins and slab pine furniture. A couple of Siberian Huskies rounded out our homestead, and Bear and Grizzly rode in the back of the truck when we went cross-country skiing or camping in that alpine wilderness.

---

[9] Our teacher later became pastor and they've grown to about 4000 members.
[10] Reference to Ephesians 3:20, KJV

My brother was still AWOL from the army, so Bend became a safe haven for him, too. He came to live with us, and we often stayed up late nights talking about faith. We didn't have all the answers, but told him about the One who promised, "You will find me when you seek me with all your heart."[11]

It was a cool September day when Steve hopped into his van and headed back to his nomadic lifestyle. I understood his need to keep moving, but I cried when he left.

During this time, John White's *Daring to Draw Near* began expanding my view of prayer. I knew it's not about reciting memorized phrases or mind-numbing chanting. The prayer that honors God is faith-filled and specific like Abraham pleading for Lot, but does God really act *differently* when we pray?

My answer came in the form of a promise. "Until now you have not asked for anything in my name," Jesus said. "Ask and you will receive, and your joy will be complete."[12] God not only welcomes participation, but He promises results! I was challenged.

After Steve left, weeks rolled into months and we didn't hear a word, but my prayers were fervent for three specific things: *Wherever he goes Lord, draw him to yourself. Even in a bar, send girls that will talk about you. Don't let him rest until he finds his rest in you, and please bring him back for Christmas!*

On Christmas Eve I spent the day baking and wrapping gifts, but every time a car came close, I ran to the window to look. Surely God would answer my prayers! It was nearly midnight when Frank tried to coax me to reason. "Why don't you blow out the candles and come to bed? Maybe he'll call tomorrow."

I looked at the candle wax and smoldering wicks sadly. "Remember Elijah with the little cloud on the horizon? Let's pray one more time!" I pleaded.

"Okay, but you have to let God work in his own way," he said. "Go ahead. You start."

"Lord! I asked in your Name for you to bring him back by Christmas! I asked in faith like you said. Now, how can I go to bed until we hear--?"

Tires crunched to a stop right in front of the house. Then, after three months of praying, my brother was standing in the doorway at 12:02 on Christmas morning!

---

[11] Jeremiah 29:13
[12] John 16:24 NIV

He had wandered around doing odd jobs but couldn't settle down. "Whenever I tried talking to a girl, *even in a bar*, she turned out to be a Christian and started telling me about Jesus!" He couldn't deny it any longer and decided to come back to Bend.

On the way, he was in an accident and his arm was tied in a make-shift sling. People tried to detain him overnight, but he felt compelled to keep driving. "I just had to get here by Christmas," he said. "All my excuses are gone and I want to accept Jesus. Would you guys pray with me?"

Incredibly, what came out of his mouth was almost word for word as I had prayed and my JOY was certainly full! Then God answered abundantly for him to resolve his military record, and fulfill his dreams. (He later went to MIT on full scholarship!) Faith multiplied through the power of prayer. Not only for Steve, but we also grew to appreciate the impact of prayer to move and anchor our lives.

Sundays in Bend often included dinner at "Gramma O's." Retired doctors Sam and Mary lived on the outskirts of Sunriver and often invited "young people" for home-made gooey rolls and God stories. One day Mary surprised us as we talked about our latest encounters around town. "You guys would be *wonderful* missionaries!"

"What's that?" We knew about Paul's missionary journeys two thousand years ago, but, "Hasn't the world been covered by now?" we asked naively.

"Oh no, missionaries are still going all over the world to places where the Bible has never been translated."

"There are places still waiting for a Bible in their language?"

"Thousands of them! In fact, there's a missionary training camp only a few hours away." Frank's curiosity was aroused.

We talked awhile, then they went back to their knees. This dear couple prayed for us on their knees *every day* until the Lord called them home.

It should come as no surprise then, how the Lord began to move. We heard it in sermons and started noticing a call to serve on every page of the Bible. The cover of a magazine showed a giant trumpet blaring from heaven. "Do I have to YELL?" blazed across the sky and the great commission, "GO YE!" across a sacred scroll. That did it, but considering Osgood's prayers, a bubble gum wrapper could have knocked us down.

The following Saturday morning we hopped in the pickup with our dogs and headed to Baker about 200 miles away, where a military base had been converted to a missionary training center. We had no idea what to expect with real-live missionaries, but we asked non-stop questions including some deep and profound concerns like, "Can we bring our dogs?" which made a huge impression on the staff.

More substantial issues were also addressed. What countries do you go to? How do you qualify? How do you support yourself? And the big one, how do you know if it's God's will or not? We left with a head full of ideas, and impressions of a group of sold-out believers ready to change the world.

Lo and behold, a week later a missionary came to the Chapel for the Sunday night service. It was a clear cold February night with a full moon, so we bundled up and walked to church to hear a southerner named Dun Gordy. With a ten-gallon hat and a passion for God, he showed slides of villagers with grass skirts and bones in their noses. He talked about ordinary people like us bringing the Word of God to those who never heard it.

Then he told about five missionary martyrs speared in the jungles of Bolivia in 1942. [13] If you go into a place like that, it makes sense that you'd be shishkabobbed, I thought. How can you expect tribal people to understand?

Frank's response was on a higher wavelength and he made a bee-line to Dun afterwards. While I yakked about potluck menus and socialized with the ladies, Frank collected pamphlets. Then the Lord gave me a nudge so clear I thought someone tapped my right shoulder. I turned and caught the look on Frank's face from across the room. *Karen, look! If he goes, you go. Pay attention to this.*

I reached Frank's side just as Dun put his hand on Frank's shoulder, "Brother, I'm going to South America next week and I'd love to take you with me. You'd love it!"

"I know I would. I majored in cultural anthropology in college," he said with a laugh. He had a natural fascination for

---

[13] Dun's message from Lk 24:45-48, forgiveness will be preached to all nations. You are witnesses. For history of the 5 martyrs, you can see also http://www.christianhistorytimeline.com/DAILYF/2003/08/daily-08-12-2003.shtml .

primitive cultures and I could practically feel his heart tugging for the plane.

We walked home from that meeting grappling with the great commission. Could this be God's direction for our lives? Did we travel 5,000 miles, get turned out of Canada, halted at Damnation Trail, and broken down in Bend... *for this?* Scenes from the tribal slides flashed through my mind. *But Lord, I'm just a city girl!*

Will you go? the Lord prodded.

Weighed with conviction, I looked at the clear full moon as we walked through Riverside Park. That radiant messenger gazed with a pure white face like an angel, but I knew the true Son was waiting for my answer. *How can I say no to the One who died for me? If this is your will for my life... who am I to question where, or how, my life should be spent? Okay ... I will die for you at the tip of a spear... if that's what you want.*

Every thought formed like little dominos tumbling one into another as we walked. Something lovely and pure transpired between me and my Creator, the moon is my witness, and I'll never forget it. Warm peace flooded through me and then I felt completely free.

"I'll do it," I told Frank, and we marveled how the Lord had been putting this in our path for weeks. "I always wanted to know God's plan for my life, but I *never* expected *this!*"

Frank dropped the pamphlets on the kitchen table, and I sat down and filled out an application. In my mind, it was a done deal, but Frank developed a sudden case of Gideonitis, like the man who fleeced the Lord.[14] So we got down on our knees and Frank asked, "If this is your will for our lives Lord, give me a dream—*three nights in a row*—so I know it's not just my emotions at work. I have to know this is coming from you, Lord."

I thought it was ludicrous asking God for *three* dreams! Sure, He's big enough to answer the needs of our quaking hearts, but isn't *one dream* enough?

I slept soundly until Frank grabbed my arm and yelled, "Karen!"

I jumped straight up in the bed. *"WHAT?!"*

"You wouldn't believe it!" he yelled, "I was just there!"

---

[14] Judges 6:37

"What?" I glanced at the clock. 6:00 on the dot. *"Where?"*

"I was surrounded by a circle of black faces! We were beside a river. Everyone was sitting on the ground and I was holding a Bible and teaching them. Honey! I was speaking *fluently in their language* and they were understanding! It was *so real!"*

I was wide awake now. First of all, Frank never *ever* remembered anything he dreamed. *Surely, this was a vision from God.* I was astounded at the clarity, amazed that he had somehow 'traveled' to a distant tribe and seen into the future! Was an angel standing over us at that very moment?

We got up and knelt by the bed. "Lord, I know I asked for three dreams," he started, "but you can cancel the other two. I know this is from you."

Cancel the order? Is God a short-order cook? We were funny in our prayers but it highlights God's incredible grace in answering. Frank marched straight to the kitchen table to fill out his application to Bible School. We dressed and took them to the post office, and never looked back!

The acceptance letter came right away. They had one small guest room left on their Michigan campus, but we had to move fast. Orientation was only four weeks away.

After one fun-filled year, it was hard saying good-bye to our "Chapel family." We didn't really want to leave, but we wanted to *follow.*

So we took off believing that the same God who led us to Bend was able to lead us to the tribesmen of Frank's dream.

First stop, a little log cabin in northern Idaho to see my brother and his girlfriend Debbie amidst crystal lakes and national forests of Priest River. On the way to the swimming hole, Debbie picked up the mail and had a letter from a girlfriend who had just been saved.

"It's not the first in recent weeks," she said. I thought of the similarities between the letter she held and the one I wrote to Elaine. The big difference being, of course, Debbie was reading hers. *Show her that you're real, Lord.*

Suddenly she yelled, "Steve, stop here! They sell fresh eggs at this farm."

The farmer came out with his wife and started friendly conversation, asking where we were all from. "We're moving to Michigan," Frank said.

"Whereabouts? We know people there," and then we were shocked to learn they had just hosted 30 students from the very same Bible school! "Do you all know the Lord?" they asked.

"Yeah," Steve said, but Debbie answered, "No, I don't."

By the time we left, there were hugs, gifts, and promises to pray for us. Debbie commented that though we had never met, we left like we were "like family." She had never seen anything like it.

That night we were in bed praying for her when we heard the stairs creaking. Steve rapped on our door. "Are you guys still awake? Debbie wants you guys to pray with her so she can be saved."

We lit a lantern and prayed, and jumped around in our jammies. Then they announced that they want to get married, and we jumped around some more!

What a great way to begin our missionary journey!

8. Take My Yoke

We finally rolled up to the sidewalk of a run-down city block and hopped out of the truck in the doorway of the old Otsego Hotel. The five-story building sat like a big ugly brick on a busy corner where it had served as housing for city drunks. Unlike Central Oregon's natural beauty, there were no snowy-peaks or flowing river. Here, the cold gray horizon was lined with spewing smokestacks while ambulances and fire trucks roared by.

"What on earth did we get ourselves into?" Before we could answer, a group of buttoned students with Colgate smiles flooded out to unload our truck. We stared as if faced with Martians. "If they hadn't emptied all our belongings so fast, we might never have made it through those doors!" Frank laughed.

Inside, the first floor was a massive marbled lobby with a long reception desk. Corinthian columns flanked high ceilings and grand balconies from the upper floors. We were whisked to the elevator and led directly to the Dean's office. Later on we learned why.

With long thick hair down my back and short shorts it almost looked like I wasn't clothed. Frank's beard and hair were still long, and after three days driving we looked so shabby the Dean yelled, "Get those hippies out of the lobby!" We were bad advertising.

Minutes later we were seated in front of his massive desk, facing native spears, animal skins and a python head with bared fangs in a jar of formaldehyde. Mr. J was also an imposing figure of about 300 pounds with forearms the size of melons.

"Not long ago," he began, "I had three young men from California *sitting right where you're sitting. They looked just like you* with long hair and beards and said they were committed to serving the Lord. But then when they heard about our rules they wouldn't even sleep in the building." *(Note to self: find out about these rules!)* "They camped in the park and then hitched all the way back to California!" He leaned forward. "Those guys sold out over a beard and their hair! Can you *imagine* having to answer to Almighty God for something *so trivial?* I need to ask you two, are you *ready to live for Him?"*

The python's fangs looked menacing and his piercing yellow eyes seemed to be looking straight at me.

We must have answered well, because we were shown to our little room where Frank swiftly found a razor and cut and shaved everything in sight. In fact, when Mr. J passed him in the hall a few hours later he held out his hand. "Hi, have we met?" Frank was unrecognizable without the long hair and whiskers.

For me, however, my hair was the only thing that fit the dress code! Everything else was too short, too low, too something or other. Jeans weren't allowed and the required length of two fingers above the knee outlawed every skirt I owned. Blouses had to reach below the hip in a style we labeled CC's, for "crotch covers."

My mind was already rebelling, and I fumed on the bed of our tiny room. "These styles look like Amish people—in the 1950s! I don't want to dress like that!" Plus, after enjoying a sprawling three-bedroom house on the river, we now had one sooty window overlooking the dreary landscape of downtown rooftops and belching furnaces.

We picked up the rule book and nervously started reading regulations covering things we'd never even thought about, like PDA. "Public display of affection" seemed extreme, with demerits assigned if you touch someone of the opposite sex. Even to tap someone's shoulder, you needed a pencil.

I appreciate staff attempts to resist counter-culture and establish boundaries for an "untamed generation," but that rulebook presented more restrictions than the Mosaic Law. How could we ever live like this? We were so disheartened.

Orientation started the next day, and I joined an assembly hall with 150 scared young women from around the globe before the Dean of Women. She talked about her own arrival from California, then said, "Even though we have established rules to guide us while we're here, just remember, it's not forever. You can put your jeans in a box for now." She admitted it would be hard at first, "but there's just one question I want to ask," and her voice softened. *"Will you do it for Jesus?"*

Joannie's gentle question sliced through my cranky complaints and discomforts. We had gone from the pristine mountains of Oregon to the musty corridors of an old city hotel. I had been obsessing over the rules and styles, grimacing at the taste of the water fountains (one was called Coke and another was Pepsi with an awful taste) and the high carb diet in the dining hall.

I remembered how I'd told the Lord I would go to the ends of the earth and die at the tip of a spear, but now all I could think about was diet, fashion and the landscape? How terribly shallow!

I would have to learn what it means to follow, to eat what was provided and wear what He asked. I might not always like it, but we did believe the Lord led us here. How could I refuse Him? Tiny tears tickled the corner of my eyes, but to me they were huge. *Okay, Lord, I'll do this for you.*

As soon as that session ended, I ran to the "mission barrel" on the fourth floor and rummaged around in that attic until I found things that fit me *and* the dress code. My hip-huggers, hot pants and tie-dyes were piled neatly on the bed by an open box and I wore a button down dress when Frank came in. He was clean-shaven and his hair was shorn above the collar. "You look *so* different!" I giggled. "I've never seen your whole face before!"

"I feel like I've joined the military." Frank laughed.

"Yes sir, we're in the Lord's army," I said, stashing my jeans in a cardboard box.

Classes began the next day and we were soon immersed in Bible teaching. Before long, it seemed far less important what we ate or how we felt in Quaker fashions, than what we knew and believed. We were being liberated in far more significant ways, learning God's Word from people who loved it and lived it wholeheartedly.

We were benefactors of a wonderful staff who dearly loved God and poured their lives into ours. Frank's favorite was Larry Harris, tall and thin and brimming with passion. I confess, I was often lost in class as overhead sheets slid to the floor or he'd lose count on his outlines. "Mr. Harris! Mr. Harris, what happened to the last two points?" we'd plead, worrying about exams.

"Oh, I'm sorry folks, but I really don't care how you write it down, just as long as you get this point..." and he'd expound on the unconditional love of Christ. He literally lost his breath at the lectern preaching with all his heart and soul.

Larry may have had trouble sticking to an outline, but he was so full of the love of God, it oozed from him. It was rumored that every time he walked around the block people would get saved—one night alone he led eight people to salvation! He was a dynamo for Christ and we esteemed him highly. This dear man was certainly focused on pressing toward the heavenly goal. In fact, we sang his favorite song at the beginning of every class, which said in part:

Wonderful, wonderful Jesus is to me!
Counselor, prince of peace, mighty God is he!...
Heaven is a wonderful place, filled with glory and grace!
I want to see my Savior's face!
But until then, with joy I'll go on singing,
Until then, with joy I'll carry on
Until the day my eyes behold the Savior,
Until the day God calls me home!

When we heard Mr. Harris had cancer, we went right to the hospital and he grasped our hands in his. "You won't throw in the towel will you?" He wanted everyone to press on and preach the glorious message of God's grace no matter what. We prayed and then he broke into the song that expressed the consuming love of his heart, *Wonderful, Wonderful!* His sweet wife Nancy had tears streaming down her face, but he said, "Sing, dear, *sing!*"

Larry sang with such gusto the halls filled with the sound of his deep voice. Nurses gathered in the hallway amazed that this booming tenor was coming from a terminal patient, and I wondered if the Lord answered our prayers for healing. I'm sure angels paused to listen to this man worship.

Two days later, Mr. Harris experienced what he loved to sing about. God called him home, and that must have been a *wonderful, wonderful* home-coming. I can only imagine.

We struggled to understand why God would take him. Wouldn't the world be better off with more men like him? But I know if Mr. Harris could talk to us today, he'd say, "Don't waste your time on that, kids. Just tell everyone about Jesus! And please, sing louder!" At least one thing would be different. Mr. Harris wouldn't lose his breath any more.

"The righteous perish... devout men are taken away, and no one understands that the righteous are taken away to be spared from evil. Those who walk uprightly enter into peace; they find rest... in death."[15]

Second term, a young missionary family on furlough from New Guinea moved in next door to us. Don and Becky had been living in a jungle tribe and night after night we'd sit in the hall or cram into our tiny quarters to hear their stories. Becky was also pregnant and I got to feel the baby kick, sharing the wonder of pregnancy and the joy of all her little "lambies." That stirred me.

We had been married two years now and in mid-February I went into my little room, got down on my knees and asked God for a child. I called it my Hannah's prayer.[16] "Lord, bless me with a child and I'll raise him for you." Then, in a childlike moment of unguarded sincerity I remembered the little girl in the nursery. "And God, would you give me a daughter with beautiful eyes like Amy's?" It is a miraculous mixture of emotion and design when God puts a dream in our hearts so that he can fulfill His purposes. I conceived that very week.

Meanwhile, our entire lives were absorbed in the confines of that big ugly building. We ate in the dining hall on the 1st floor, did laundry in the basement, and attended classes on the 2nd. We systematically studied the Pentateuch, prophets, and kings of Israel. We learned church history, hermeneutics, eschatology and the Pauline epistles. We ferociously wrote papers, mastered doctrines, and memorized 100 words of verses every day—all with the admonition, "Don't let the Bible become a text book!"

How do you do that?

There was only one activity that forced us onto the streets to use what we were learning: Evangelism. Even in Michigan's

---

[15] Isaiah 57:1-2 NIV
[16] I Samuel 1:11

bitter cold, we traipsed through icy slush to hippie houses in drug-torn neighborhoods or knocked on brick-faced homes on tree-lined avenues. Nerve-wracking at times, but it was worth it all whenever we bumped into people who welcomed the message of the cross like a life jacket to a drowning soul.

One time we went to the hospital to visit terminal patients. We entered the room of an old man hooked up to life support and offered to read the Bible, but his wife took offense. "Oh, no, not now." She started pushing us away, but the old man's eyes opened wide as though begging us to stay. His wife thought we were agitating him and made us leave, but I'll never forget that haunting look of desperation in his eyes.

In the very next room, an old woman lay alone, dying of emphysema. We offered to read to her and she welcomed us gladly. As we read she squeezed our hands, and was greatly comforted. We led her through the Romans Road,[17] introducing her to the One who came to abolish the fear of death that holds us captive.[18] Soon after, she met him in Paradise face to face.

You never know when God will allow you to present someone's very last chance to meet their Savior on earth, "as though God were making his appeal through us."[19]

In fact, a friend of ours was going door to door in a nearby neighborhood. At one house, an old man came out with a loaded gun. "If you don't get off my property, I'll shoot!" Our friend apologized for disturbing him and continued a few doors down the street before hearing the ambulance. It stopped at the very house where he had been threatened, and he watched them carry that man away. Oh, if he knew how little time he had left, he might have responded differently and asked to understand the way to heaven.

We were learning that God leads every encounter. We just need to be faithful, even if only to raise a question. "If you were to die today, do you *know* where you would go?" That critical reality should bring us to our knees and remind us who God is.

As much as we may try to deny it or put it off, death forces us to face the infinite. So does birth.

---

[17] The Romans Road points a sinner to salvation by grace. Romans 1:16-17, 3:23, 6:23, 10:9, 10:13.
[18] Hebrews 2:14-18
[19] 2 Corinthians 5:18-20

My labor started Friday night right after the international potluck so of course everyone blamed Mrs. Snure's Thai curry. Saturday we bundled up and walked for hours in the wintry air, committing our child to God. I was learning to rest in the shepherd's arms with Psalm 23, and those precious verses anchored my mind all day. *"The Lord is my shepherd. He leads me, he guides me. I will not fear…"*

The delivery room felt like New Year's Eve waiting for the ball to drop, and when our precious baby girl made her entrance, she was radiant! Dr. Petersen was also beaming. He had never performed an all-natural childbirth. And Becky, our nurse who was saved after one of our Lamaze classes, whispered, "Karen, this is the second amazing birth we're sharing!"

We named her Naomi Faith— the Hebrew *No' omi* means pleasant, and *Faith,* for the transforming reality at the center of our lives. God is good! He answers prayer!

Every parent knows you can be swept away by one glance of your child—the tender glow on their face, or the tiny curl of a smile on such dainty lips. *But those eyes!* God went beyond my wildest dreams. Everyone would comment about her eyes.

Holding her in my arms, I was overwhelmed. If this is how I feel about my child, how much more does God who put this powerful emotion within me? "How great is the love the Father lavished on us, that we should be called children of God!"[20]

I got my first glimpse of the force of it when they tried to take her from me—like a she-bear that would kill for her offspring. That too, was instructive. Now, *"I am convinced that neither death, nor life… nor height, nor depth, nor any other created thing, shall be able to separate us from the love of God which is in Christ Jesus our Lord."*[21] In the end, this may be the most profound thing I learned in Bible School.

---

[20] I John 3:1
[21] Romans 8:38-39

9. One Red Cent

*"God delights to increase the faith of his children. We ought,
instead of wanting no trials before victory, no exercise for
patience, to be willing to take them from God's hand as a means.
I say, and say it deliberately, trials, obstacles, difficulties, and
sometimes defeats, are the very food of faith."*[22]

Driving over the bridge into boot camp in the Pennsylvania woods for the first time, our sore eyes soaked in a glorious landscape. An old white farmhouse, barns and outbuildings were flanked by a patchwork of snow-covered corn fields along the rippling Susquehanna River. Compared to the city block we called home for the past two years, it was heavenly, but similar questions loomed in our minds.

Not only had we heard rumors about the rigors of the program, but financial concerns were mounting and outside employment was forbidden during this phase of training. How could we survive? Physically and spiritually, did we have what it takes or would we be booted out of boot camp as soon as they realize how stupid, stubborn and stilted we were?

The purpose of boot camp was to take all the academic knowledge we'd crammed into our heads at Bible School and align our feet. Sure, we could quote the book of Ephesians in 12 minutes and recite the rules of hermeneutics, but now, under the personal supervision of staff, we would get down to brass tacks.

Here, training would imitate life in a third world country, from isolation to deprivation of comforts we'd taken for granted our whole lives. For instance, our living quarters weren't equipped with phone wires or indoor plumbing so we would haul water in

---

[22] Diary of George Mueller

61

and tote "slop buckets" out. Community bathrooms were centrally located, campground style. It wasn't too bad except in the cold winter months when you were sick, or pregnant. Waking in the middle of the night "to go" involved bundling up to run with a flashlight in ice and snow. We did enjoy the luxuries of electricity, a stove, and a nice big fridge—however bare.

So was our apartment! In a step of unnecessary zeal, we had given away everything we owned that was breakable or ornamental. Even the set of hand-thrown pottery and the last of our wedding gifts were deemed impractical when we left Bible School. What wasn't sold to pay bills was individually wrapped and given away as Christmas gifts. "What was I thinking?" I moaned. "This place feels like army barracks!"

Like the army, boot camp curriculum was more mission specific in this phase. There were practical skills to acquire, such as learning how to take a chicken from the barnyard to the kitchen table with our own hands. We had to chop off the head with an axe or twist its live neck in our bare hands! For the farm boys among us it was a snap, but for us city gals who never had to kill for a meal in our entire lives, some were literally bent over vomiting at such atrocities. I admit, it was brutal for my poor chicken. I couldn't even look when my axe found its mark, but God had mercy on it.

These 'momentary trials' paled compared to the rigorous summer course known as jungle camp: six weeks of isolation in simulated jungle survival training. We had a few weeks to prepare in advance, so we tucked our baby girl in a backpack and headed into the woods to build a house out of poles and plastic by hand. Frank and I worked side by side to wrap the frame with screen wire, the roof with plastic, and construct furniture—table, bed and chairs, even a bucket shower. The greatest effort went into our mud oven with a sheet of iron for the stove top.

What you didn't complete by D-day, you would have to live without, so we worked hard. We would forego other amenities such as power, phones, radios, supply and mail runs, but we canned our meats and veggies and carried everything uphill to "jungle camp" on time. When it was done, we had erected a small community of about eighteen rustic shacks with a meeting house in the center. Amazing, what you could do with a few rough-hewn logs and rolls of plastic, slapped together with mud.

We women then had opportunity to face the lions, tigers and bears without our husbands. First, the men went into the mountains on a rigorous three-day hike and then we had to endure our own three-day.

That involved making fires and carrying all our gear on our backs. We women faced scary moments and aching muscles, but a lot of laughs, too.

One night, we had to string mosquito netted hammocks on an incline over running water. Janice had such trouble with the knots that her hammock somehow slid down the tree in the middle of the night. "Whoa! Oh no! *Help!*" She was lying in water with her legs kicking wildly to get untangled from the mass of ropes and zippers. Scrambling to her assistance with flashlights, we nearly split our sides laughing and trying to retie the ropes over the water while she changed into dry clothes in the dark.

After the three day expedition, we returned to camp feeling like accomplished outdoorswomen. We had conquered fears and blisters, crossed log bridges, scaled steep inclines loaded down like pack mules, and managed to cover the entire course without injury. Enough to make you want to beat your chest and bellow Tarzan style!

Another Tarzan talent I acquired in boot camp was the ability to cook and eat almost any kind of meat, including bear. State rangers called after 'thinning the herds' of wild deer, and donated the meat to our camp provided we would butcher it. So, the men were called to an all-night butchering party of 40 deer in the barn, filling our deep freezers with free venison.

It reminded me of the quail God rained down around Israel, providing fresh meat for his people in the wilderness. By God's grace, we often dined like royalty from the fat of the corn-fed land. Then, there were leaner times.

Stretching the occasional ten dollar bill, I learned to limit groceries to staples like oats, dried beans and flour, saving two dollars for gas and church. But after weaning my baby, I faced a new and costly need. Baby formula was exorbitant, but money wasn't the only thing I needed to stretch. My faith was taking baby steps, too.

When I got down to one bottle of formula, I dumped my purse and drawers on the bed and scoured for money on the verge of panic. Since the age of nine I always had some stashed envelope of bills or coins for the "rainy day," but I could only find one penny! One red cent to my name! I held the solitary coin between my fingers and started to cry. "Lord, I don't care if we eat mush every day, but please don't let my baby starve! Jesus, I need formula, fast!"

I quoted Hudson Taylor in my journal, *"Now is the time for God to show Himself!"*[23] *My baby is on her last bottle, insurance is due this month, and today we got the bill for rent. I've become Mother Hubbard in the nursery rhyme, only this isn't funny. Where is my faith? Since God is capable of sending fire from heaven, raising Lazarus from the dead, or parting the Red Sea... Why do I think He's limited now? What circumstance is not subject to Him? I have to trust His ability to supply, and witness His faithfulness once again!"*

But while I was crying to God in our room, Frank and the guys finished work and headed down to the showers. Dan called, "Hey Frank, I've been meaning to tell you, if you're ever short on baby formula, come on over. We've been getting it by the case. Don't let me catch you letting your baby starve!" he teased. Little did he know, that's exactly what I was thinking.

With no other resources, I had no choice but to muster up courage and knock on my neighbor's door. "Your husband said you have baby formula. Could I, uh, borrow a can?"

"Oh sure," Nancy said sweetly. "Why don't you take a couple, just in case?"

"Oh no, that's alright. Maybe we'll be able to buy some tomorrow." But this little scenario continued for two solid weeks! Like an extended version of trick or treating, she'd open the door with a smile and graciously share another day's supply. Thank God for their willingness to help me learn that His provision sometimes comes in the form of "love your neighbor as yourself."[24]

The lyrics from one of our chapel songs helped hammer home the message of grace.

He giveth more grace when the burdens grow greater;
He sendeth more strength when the labors increase.

To added affliction He addeth His mercy;

---

[23] From *Spiritual Secret* by Hudson Taylor
[24] Mark 12:31 one of the greatest commandments according to Jesus

To multiplied trials, His multiplied peace.

His love has no limit; His grace has no measure;
His power has no boundary known unto men.
For out of His infinite riches in Jesus,
He Giveth and Giveth, and Giveth again!

When we have exhausted our store of endurance,
When our strength has failed 'ere the day is half done,
When we reach the end of our hoarded resources,
Our Father's full giving is only begun! [25]

We were learning to abound in times of plenty and abase in times of God-ordained testing.[26] Like manna from heaven, God demonstrated his faithfulness, and Naomi thrived while I grew in grace.

As a young mother I constantly drew parallels between my faith lessons and my baby's physical development. Whether trying to balance on the icy driveway, cut teeth, or sample solid food, she mirrored my spiritual learning. And though my spiritual legs may be wobbly, God admonishes me to press on, holding his hands out constantly.

The green bridge over the Susquehanna became a symbol of quitting. Chapel messages often ended with the admonition, "Don't go back over that bridge! Don't turn back from the Lord's calling when things get uncomfortable." And they certainly did.

A prime cause of discomfort was an emphasis on "personal ministry" or PM, which was more like PMS, causing a great deal of aggravation in the "body." We were taught to address issues that might hinder our service and exercise faithfulness, a gift of the Spirit. "If someone is caught in a sin, you who are spiritual should restore him gently... and carry each other's burdens." [27]

The object was spiritual growth and commitment to one another in brotherly love. Great concepts, but that little phrase about 'you who are spiritual' was difficult to gauge. Most of us

---

[25] *He Giveth More Grace*, by Annie Flint
[26] Phil 4:12-13 Whether well-fed or hungry, Paul claimed Christ's strength and learned the secret of contentment despite circumstances.
[27] Gal 6:1, 22

lacked the maturity to function constructively, but representing a wide assortment of age groups and cultures, we gave each other a lot of practice with PM.

For a sampling of our diversity, fellow students included a state cop from Baltimore with teenagers, an industrious farmer with nine kids from Wisconsin's cheese country, a native Hawaiian, hippies from Chicago, and a Cadillac salesman from DC. We had a big Italian family from Boston's North End, a soft-spoken pastor from Canada, and a family from Amish country.

Imagine, 30 couples bombarding each other with spiritual advice and interpretations about how to live, raise kids, or spend money. It was said that if someone doesn't like the music you listen to or how you part your hair, you're going to hear it. One friend confided, "I'd run into the bathroom and lock the door when I saw people coming. Oh God please, not another 'faithful' brother to tell me what's wrong with me!"

I knew the feeling. PM could be about as pleasant as being choked, convincing us we'd never be able to toe the line. We teetered from one ditch to the other like imbalanced toddlers, sometimes pulling one another down in our efforts to stand. We gave each other some bad examples, but thank God for the good ones.

I was shy in jungle camp—okay, inhospitable is more like it. I viewed people as intruders, like the time town folk wandered up to visit all us lunatics in the forest and I sat studying the Bible. My baby was napping and this was my quiet time, after all.

I didn't really want company. I couldn't cook well and many meals flopped royally, like the pizza that slid into the fire. We ate a lot of ashes and charcoal while I learned to regulate the firewood in those days, and I was embarrassed. Besides, we didn't have food to spare, and I had my hands full with a baby...

That's what I told myself anyway, but those reasons didn't fly with the chairman's wife who brought the visitors past my house. Jean is a seasoned missionary who raised four kids in the jungles of Brazil.

"Hi Karen, how are you today?" I always enjoyed talking with her. This time, the subject turned to having an open heart and home and she brought up the visitors. "Karen, I was hoping to bring them in to meet you. When God sends someone to your door, you should always be open to what He might want to do regardless of your agenda. It took me a long time to learn this, but people should always come before projects."

Bam! I knew she was right and her words would come back to me a thousand times over the years. To this day, I smile when I remember Jean, proving the power of kind words to soften a hard heart and melt excuses. Love motivates change, like Zaccheus shimmying down from a sycamore tree. That was one of my sycamores, and I started down after Jean's visit that day. That was good PM!

Then news filtered back to camp about a missionary wife prostituting herself to tribesmen at a remote outstation in New Guinea. Obviously, something of this magnitude jeopardized the reputation and work of the whole mission. One woman, whose problems weren't recognized, sent tremors around the world that shocked and discouraged staff. "Where are we going wrong?" the leaders asked. "How could such serious needs escape us?"

It was time for extreme measures. Staff had to impress us with the urgency of "dealing with sin in the camp." We knew about Achan's sin and the devastating consequences on the battlefield.[28] We were acquainted with Nathan's confronting King David,[29] and we knew about Jesus making a whip to drive merchants out of the temple.[30]

Sure, sin is serious, but we just wanted to live our own habitual lives, forgetting that God called us to oneness. Merely trying to live around each other and not step on toes is a far cry from being knit together as Paul described. "Speaking the truth in love, we will in all things grow up…the whole body… builds itself up in love, *as each part does its work.*"[31]

We came unsuspecting to practical class the next morning and Mr. J began abruptly. "Take out a piece of paper and write your name at the top. Then, list the names of everyone in this class." He paced the room with a pointer. *What's this about, some new game?*

"Now, check off which ones, if any, you would NOT want for partners in a tribe."

---

[28] See Joshua 7 for the story in the Valley of Achor, the story we call Achan's sin.
[29] 2 Samuel 12:1-13 KJV
[30] John 2:14-17
[31] Ephesians 4:15-16 NIV

We were shocked, but if we didn't answer honestly we might regret it. Everyone squirmed in their seats making little check marks here and there. "Now, if you've checked any names on that list, write the reasons why..."

Oh boy, the test was getting harder. We had to itemize reasons we wouldn't want to spend the rest of our lives joined at the hip to everybody around us? We mulled over names, taking furtive glances, struggling to assign labels to all our imperfect classmates. I scribbled a few uncomfortable notes—too legalistic, argumentative, or insensitive.

When pencils grew still Mr. J said, "Now, turn your papers over and leave them at your seats. You're dismissed." As we started gathering our things, he called, "Oh, if you wrote anything about anyone in the room, I trust you've *already* been faithful."

Ouch! Frank and I saved PM for the "big stuff", trying to avoid confrontation. We certainly hadn't met with everyone to dole out opinions on marriages and personality issues. Now Mr. J made us accountable and we felt compelled to clear our consciences.

The next few days were PM mayhem as a constant stream of people wound their way around camp for the dreaded knock at the door followed by a slamming session to unload the guilt. No doubt, there were damages in that onslaught, but there was also good as we made an effort to get honest with each other at last.

Mr. J had been with us from the beginning in Bible School (remember the python on his desk?) and then followed us to boot camp, relocating his four kids off the city block and into the country. Despite the history, I still had a hard time with his tough guy personality. One day Mr. J stopped by our apartment.

"How are you guys doing?" he asked. "How are you finding the teaching?" *He needs to hear the truth too, but we could go sailing over the bridge with this!* He looked right at me.

"Well, I have a hard time, uh, with some of your... um, teaching methods."

"What do you mean?" he asked.

"I think you're too, too... *strong* at times." *Wimp!*

"Really?" Mr. J seemed glad I was opening up. "You're strong too," he said. "What is it in particular? There must have been something I said or did that made you feel this way."

Yes, it was true. I thought him to be too hard on people, intimidating. Good friends had been dismissed and... *Oh dear, I have such a long list and I haven't even been faithful **to him!***

He was still waiting. I looked him right in the eye and blurted, "I *hate* you, Mr. J!"

So much for diplomacy! Frank let the air out of his lungs and it sounded like deflating a tire. "Oh boy!" he said under his breath. I'm sure he was planning to start packing.

Mr. J's eyebrows flew to the top of his head. "I'm glad you're being so honest!" Maybe his marriage to a woman like me and four kids provided ample experience for handling my verbal free style. Over the next hour we talked it out and ended up praying, hugging, and saying how much we appreciated one another!

"Don't let the devil get a foothold, alright? Let's keep the doors open between us." In those moments, Mr. J went from being "staff" to brother, and after that, we felt a lot less stress. We had broken through the sound barrier.

Nevertheless, when we were called for our final review, we didn't know what to expect. Either we'd be released to language school, or asked to leave. "This could go either way," Frank said before walking nervously into the little wood paneled office.

Mr. J cleared his throat to break the news. "Frank and Karen, it's been a real pleasure working with you and getting to know you in the last three years. We've had our ups and downs, but we've agreed that you're ready to be released to language school."

"Really?" we chimed.

"Really. Congratulations." They all stood up smiling and hugged us.

Boot camp had been an intensely challenging and life-changing 18 months. Out of 30 couples that started the course, only eight were released that term, heading out to such remote places as Senegal, Indonesia, the Philippines, Mexico, and the Amazon. One couple even went to Siberia, and great things have been accomplished for the kingdom of God. How awesome!

When I remember boot camp days, I think about the cost of discipleship. Then I remember my dear friend Reneé, a bubbly Spanish single from Chicago. With big brown eyes and a wonderful laugh, she was a joy to me—even working in the dirt. She loved being with us and holding our bright-eyed baby girl. Most of all, she loved talking about the Lord and we discovered a lot of truth together.

We corresponded long after crossing that bridge—after she married Mike and moved to the jungles of Venezuela to work with the Yanomamo Indians; and even after they had three darling little boys who all got her chocolate brown eyes. She wrote about making bricks by hand and trekking through the jungle and we reminisced about jungle camp days.

Years later, a letter arrived from her husband Mike. He was going through her address book to let her friends know that Reneé had cerebral malaria and slipped into a coma. She died in a matter of days leaving three precious sons at 9, 7 and 5 years old.

On her headstone, Mike engraved the years of her brief sojourn followed by a quote she loved: *"Not only is Christ worth living for; He's worth dying for."*[32]

Oh God, keep me heavenly minded! Help me to remember it will be worth it all when we see you face to face!

---

[32] You can read about Reneé in Mike Dawson's book, *Growing Up Yanomamo*, WinePress Publishing, 2006.

10. My Father's Love

"I'm so glad I found you," Mr. J began. "Karen, there's been an emergency at home. Call your mother immediately."

We were enjoying Sunday dinner at the Hartman's after church when the call came. I dialed the familiar numbers with a trembling hand and Mom got right to the point. "Karen, Dad died this morning," she said. "Steve and Debbie are here and Danny's flying back from North Dakota."

"What happened?" I stammered.

"He had another heart attack."

"We'll get there as fast as we can," I promised, but hanging up, I thought, *how are we going to do that? We don't even have gas money!* Our tank was already running on fumes.

I hung up and told everyone what happened. Fred opened his wallet and gave us forty dollars on the spot. "You'll need this to get home," he said firmly. That was a small fortune to us.

"Can we pray for my brother?" I asked. "He's not a Christian yet." So we joined hands and asked the Lord to comfort mom and show Danny His loving presence. Then we threw some bags in the car, and drove 400 miles through wintry New England, while 23 years of memories of my father flooded my mind.

My Welsh ancestors settled in the hills of Pennsylvania in the 1800's where life revolved around the coalmines. Grandpa grew to be lead engineer in the mines until his health started failing. Then he moved to the Delaware River and became the first police chief of the town before dying of black lung at 55, leaving my father fatherless at the tender age of ten.

Tough times meant that young Vaughn had to shovel coal for fifty cents per truckload to put "a little more substance in the soup." He shoveled until his hands were raw and gave all his earnings to his mother. No wonder he hated complaining and ungratefulness. If we turned up our noses at the kitchen table, even for sour kraut, he would blow a gasket. "Don't let me *ever hear you complain* about the food your mother puts on the table!"

He'd retell the stories about having to go to bed hungry, and we kids rolled our eyes, but grew to appreciate what he endured through the Depression years. That's where he developed work ethics and a knack for finding joy in simple things, and he had a life-long soft spot for the underdog.

Dad was a born storyteller. I credit his entertaining tales for giving me an early appreciation for words. When he saw me writing in diaries, he'd quote Sir Francis Bacon: "Speaking maketh a well-conversed man; reading maketh a well-rounded man; *but writing* maketh an exact man."

Dad's stories also inspired me to wonder from an early age, laying a foundation for my faith. One of my favorites involved a couple of snakes in the Panama jungles where he served in WWII as a radio technician. Lying on his cot one day, his buddy noticed a huge black snake dangling over his head.

"Judd, lie still!" his partner called. In those spine-tingling seconds, his buddy reached for a gun and slowly took aim.

"Don't shoot," Dad whispered.

"Are you sure? I *think* I could get it..."

"What if you miss?" he reasoned.

Then they noticed movement higher up in the trees. Another snake, white, and longer than the black one hovering over my father's cot, plunged first. It killed the black snake and slid silently into the jungle. *Miracles do happen!* That impressed my young mind that I might not be here if they didn't, either!

As a ham operator, Dad's hobby was a custom-built short-wave radio where he followed BBC broadcasts and contemplated the world's woes with a pipe full of cherry tobacco and a glass of white wine. "*Think* about it. Ask questions. Shoot for the stars!"

Dad was a kind-hearted man. I was about twelve when we headed to the store in a snowstorm. Streets were plowed, but conditions were frightful when we saw a frightened woman stranded on the side of the road. I watched his thin coat whipped by howling winds and gasoline spill on his freezing fingers as he siphoned and tested, but he wouldn't quit. "Let me try another wrench," he said, fishing through his tool kit.

I was so worried about him, but he kept checking on me. "Are you warm enough, Karezee?" Classic. His hands were a horrible icy-blue but he kept at it until he had it going. The appreciative woman tried to pay him but of course he refused, just happy to see her safely on her way. Yes, Vaughn Judd was my hero and I cry easily when I think of him. Thank God for a father whose example helped me understand my Heavenly Father's love.

In all my memories, one consoling thought kept bubbling to the surface. Dad trusted Christ before it was too late. Coming to faith had been a long process for him. He believed in the Creator-God, but Christianity reduced the incomprehensible to a mere man. How could GOD Almighty become human and how could Jesus be fully God? With a great philosophical intelligence, he grappled long and hard.

We lived at home between Bible School semesters and Frank and I would share what we were learning, but faith is counter-intuitive, contrary to everything we can understand with the natural mind.[33] "God wants your heart first. It has to start with faith," I said. "We don't have all the answers, Dad. *Ask Him* to show you."

Shortly afterwards, on a hospital bed in the ER, he did. When I visited the ICU after his second heart attack, the sweet expression on his face tipped me off. He was at peace.

"Honey, I'm not alone anymore." He pointed heavenward and gave me a thumbs up with a little wink. He was extremely weak and tired, but for the first time in 40 years he had a living Father! I don't know how I could have handled the grief if that hadn't happened. If he hadn't *told me* that it did!

We finally reached Massachusetts at 1 a.m. but my younger brother Dan beat us all the way from North Dakota on the plane. He couldn't wait to tell us what happened.

---

[33] I Cor 2:14, Isaiah 29:14

"When Mom called this morning, I couldn't believe Dad was gone without being able to say goodbye. All I could think about on the plane was that I've lost my best friend in the whole world." He choked up. He had a copy of Chuck Colson's book *Born Again* with him, and right there on the United flight halfway to Boston, he prayed and found what Dad meant when he said, "I'm not alone anymore."

Danny became a child of God in the clouds—possibly passing over us while we were praying for him on the ground in Pennsylvania! It was a scoop of joy in the midst of sorrow, like ice cream on a hot slice of pie, and we talked until 4 a.m.

Mom also filled us in. Dad's condition had grown much worse since we last saw him at Christmas. His legs and ankles swelled so he couldn't wear shoes and he groaned with pain, but he didn't want us to worry. He slept on the couch so not to disturb her, but that morning, she heard him groaning.

"Are you alright?" she called.

"No... I'm going..." She heard a thump and found him on the floor with his eyes open.

"Judd! Judd!" she called frantically, but there was no answer. She dialed 911, then rushed back to his side. "Judd, can you get up?"

"I'm trying," he said, but he wasn't moving. EMT's carried him out on a kitchen chair and by the time Mom got to the hospital, Dad was in shock and he had no pulse. Minutes later, he was pronounced dead.

Dad's viewing was the hardest thing I'd ever faced. My brothers and I went in and looked at the shell of the man we had loved since birth. The makeup made him look artificial and he was wearing a new suit. I imagined him asking, "What's wrong with my old shirt?" *Oh, Dad!* I longed to look into his blue eyes again. I reached out to touch his hands but recoiled at the cold hard feel of death. No, this lifeless mannequin was not the man I loved.

I thought about heaven and the resurrection. "To be absent from the body is to be present with the Lord."[34] *He's not here! He has passed from suffering into glory!* In my spirit, I knew he was already with the Lord!

---

[34] Phil 1:23 Paul desired to depart and be with Christ; 2 Cor 5:8 to be present with the Lord.

Just like the man who hung on the cross beside Jesus, Dad turned to Christ before his time ran out. And though that man couldn't lift a finger to change his life, he looked at Jesus and believed and Jesus promised, "*Today* you will be with me in Paradise."[35] It's so simple, yet baffling to our earth-bound minds.

Over and over I relived the memory of his thumbs up from that hospital bed. This is the only comfort you can find in the loss of someone you love. I knew his ailing heart was at rest at last, and the questions of his vast mind could be fully answered by the One who created him.

At the funeral, I tried telling everyone, "Dad found peace with the Lord. He's in heaven now." They listened politely, but most probably thought me deranged from shock. They hadn't seen the heart transformation or how deeply Dad wrestled with his decision.

I learned a lot about my father in those few days, like how much he was loved. His coworkers were so torn up they couldn't serve as pallbearers. Then Dad's dear friend Alan called. "Oh, he loved all his children, but *you!* You were *the apple of his eye!* And your baby girl! Oh, how he loved her!"

Listening to him describe my father's love, I felt the awful pain of losing him like a stabbing wound. I went upstairs and cried the hardest tears of all. I lost my father!

Oh Dad, I loved you so much! Why wasn't I here? I'm so sorry I wasn't here to say good-bye to you!

Once again, I experienced some of life's extreme ironies. In this solitary day, my hero died and my baby brother was saved. The first man I ever loved met death, and the other found eternal life.

Just like that! One gone, the other secured. It was incomprehensible, like my heart in the ER getting slammed with electric paddles.

Funerals are impossible to absorb all at once. I think it takes a lifetime.

---

[35] Luke 23:42-43

11. Hands and Feet

The final step of training led us to a backwoods Missouri campus in the Ozarks. Beginning with the extreme humidity of August, Language School provided technical preparation and some authentic exposure to jungle living conditions. I was six months pregnant and especially noticed the sticky heat in our little classroom with no fan, but thankfully, it cooled off by October.

For six months we studied phonetics and phonemics, literacy, and translation principles. We looked down each other's throats with pencils in hand. We goggled and gurgled, learning how to record every conceivable human utterance. We had a crash course in field medicine and culture. With shaky hands, we stuck each other with injections and sat face to face with Dobu Indian informants.[36] Frank's anthropological interests resurfaced and he thrived at this hands-on phase of final prep for the field.

Soon, we'd be on our way to a tribe to begin using these tools, but we still had no idea where we were going. We'd heard about dozens of countries in four years, and corresponded with the Meyers since Bible School. In a stream of descriptive letters, Becky shared the struggles as well as the marvels of life in Papua New Guinea. One of their long standing requests had been to pray for partners.

Meyers opened the tribe with a sweet Iowa couple who loved the people and excelled at the language. Sadly, their youngest son struggled with such frequent bouts of malaria they were advised to leave the country when the little boy's liver started shutting down. We prayed for them regularly—but it never occurred to us that the Lord might be preparing *us* to answer these

---

[36] An American Indian language called Dobu served as a sample for language learning on the mission field.

prayers until Becky's little blue mailgram arrived inviting us to join them. After three years of praying for Meyers' partners, *we* were heading to Papua New Guinea to become their partners.

Meanwhile, I grew fatter and my ankles swelled and we prepared to receive another child by Thanksgiving. I found a clinic that would accommodate natural childbirth, but it was twenty miles into the boonies through rolling goat country.

My contractions kicked into high gear in the middle of the night and we left camp at three a.m. The roads swirled with thick fog as we meandered through the countryside for an hour, and our firstborn son arrived at 6:30 a.m., healthy and glowing with long black hair. What a beautiful child! We chose regal names from the Messianic lineage. Jesse, from the Hebrew *Yishay* meaning "gift," and David, derived from "beloved." Our *beloved gift* arrived by Thanksgiving, and I was ready to feast!

"How is mother doing?" the doctor asked kindly.

"I'm starving! How soon can we get going?" The little clinic had no provisions for meals, so I showered and we were released right away.

Frank was ecstatic carrying his newborn son out the door. "Let's celebrate!" He said. Another student had pressed a twenty into his hand and we decided to splurge at the big country restaurant down the road. So, minutes later, with our handsome son laying on the seat beside me, the waitress came to take our orders.

"Good morning! Oh, what a cute baby!" she exclaimed. "How old is he?"

Frank looked at his watch and answered, "One hour and, um, fifteen minutes!"

The waitress nearly dropped her teeth, calling everyone to see this newborn child like a mini Christmas pageant. She looked at me again. "What are you *doing here?*"

"I'm starving!" So they brought me the "lumberjack special" with bacon and eggs, biscuits and gravy, grits and coffee, and every morsel vanished.

On the way back to camp we stopped for supplies where the Walmart clerk leaned over and remarked, "What a beautiful baby! How old is he?"

Once again Frank consulted his wrist. "Two hours and twenty minutes!" Again, she called everyone over to see the new baby, and we marveled at God's blessing.

The next day, I bundled up my little beloved and took him to class, but I couldn't stop smiling on his perfect peaceful face. At two days old, he was already in school. *What will the rest of his life be like? Where will these tiny hands and feet go, and what will they do? Dear God, I pray my son will love you with all his heart and soul.*

Much of language school was technical in nature, but there were testimonies that will be with me forever. Our Bible translation teacher Bob Gustafson served in the Philippines and inspired us with colorful tales of tribal life. He told of a morning stroll through the village that rattled his understanding of the missionary's role.

"Good morning, God!" the tribesmen called. "Good morning, God!"

"Oh no, I'm not God!" he corrected, but he couldn't stop them.

One of the old men explained, "Your voice teaches us God's words. Your face shows us his face. You are the only body we see. You are God to us."

Bob challenged us, "You will literally be God to the tribal people. You're his hands and feet wherever you go."

Another elder missionary from Thailand described a Bhuddist ritual attended by 200 saffron-robed priests. He hoped to observe culture but was overwhelmed with spiritual oppression the moment he arrived. Retreating to the privacy of his tent, he got on his knees. "What's wrong with me, Lord? I feel so useless and outnumbered. What can I do here?"

Much like God's answer to Joshua, the Lord said, "Get up, and go in *my name!*" [37]

He confessed he had been carrying the burden of ministry on his own shoulders, but Jesus warned, *"I am the vine; you are the branches... apart from me you can do nothing."* [38] By the time he finished praying, priorities were rearranged and he was comforted. So, he headed back down the hill.

This time, as he left his tent, they heard "a sound in the trees like a mighty wind" and the chief priest approached him. "All

---

[37] God told Joshua, "Stand up! What are you doing down on your face?" Joshua 7:10
[38] John 15:5 NIV

our spirits fled when you came out of your tent just now. Who is your God? He must be the most powerful Spirit of all!" That priest was clear. Nothing happened the first time he left his tent—it was only the second time. Same man, different approach. Power of prayer and adjusted perspectives.

"Remember, you go in Jesus' Name!" he said. What a privilege to be his feet and hands, his face and voice, bearing the Name of the living God to those who never heard!

Four years of training ended in January of '79. We packed up and prayed the old station wagon would climb the icy hills once more. Our next assignment: a jungle tribe off the Sepik River, somewhere south of the equator!

Our to do list included applying for passports and visas, getting shots and x-rays, shopping for equipment and packing and shipping crates to the field. The "recommended shopping list for the tribe" included such big ticket items as a boat and motor, generator, and kerosene fridge. Air fares for a family to Southeast Asia, shipping costs, and funds for house-building in the tribe all seemed laughable, considering we had NO money.

We were also concerned about establishing a prayer base, and oh yes, that final little detail—*raising support*. We had attended churches from Oregon to Massachusetts, but how do you ask people to promise support and sell your ability to do a job you've never done before? What if no one believes in you? What if nobody cares? We felt like Moses, battling our shortcomings on our way to speak to Pharoah.[39]

Our old station wagon was loaded to the gills as we headed to Kansas for our first church meeting. Suddenly, our car sputtered and died! There was no breakdown lane, so we were stopped in the right lane when Frank hopped out and lifted the hood. He stood in front of the car, but our roof rack stacked with luggage blocked the view of him from behind. Heavily traveled by logging trucks barreling 70 mph, the narrow highway made me frantic that someone would plow into us before realizing we were stopped. *"Oh Jesus, help!"*

Just then a motorcycle stopped beside us and a blonde biker with a chain around his neck hopped off on the driver's side. "Hi

---

[39] Exodus 3-4 gives the story of Moses with all his "who am I?" doubts and 'what if' questions.

there, need a hand?" I watched intently from the front seat. "I see your trouble," he said with certainty.

He walked all the way around to the right side of the car and touched something. *How could he have seen that from the other side?*

"Here. This will get you started so you can get on your way." He squeezed something in the palm of his hand, then said to Frank, "Go to the first exit a mile down the road. Pull off into the first store on the right and ask for one of these," showing Frank the little wire.

Oh no, I thought, we can't afford mechanical trouble now!

"Don't worry, it will only cost a dollar," he smiled at me.

"THANKS for your help!" Frank called as he jumped back on his bike and disappeared.

Frank hopped in and turned the key and the car started perfectly! We drove a mile to the next exit, pulled up to the first store, and Frank went in. Sure enough, one of those little wires was hanging on a peg. The price tag, you guessed it, exactly one dollar, no tax. And we never had car trouble again.

I still can't get over how God sent roadside service that day. He knew we needed a good boost to get going, physically *and* spiritually. He showed up the second I prayed, "saw" the problem from an unnatural angle, and somehow fixed it in his hands. He knew where we'd find the part and its exact cost. God can energize our engines and re-supply our feeble souls. He sent a member of the Heaven's Angels to remind us of His presence and power. *"Are not all the angels ministering spirits, sent to serve...?"*[40]

That hair-raising breakdown on the logging highway turned into an incredible boost to my faith. If God would do something like this, we needn't fear what lay ahead. We could go to these meetings and stand up and speak. The Lord is with us!

Though our needs were great, we determined never to ask for funds. It would be by faith alone, and the Lord went out of his way to do the opposite of our expectations until we quit trying to plan it or even gauge responses. God has a wonderful sense of humor. (He made us, didn't He?)

Before speaking at our first big church in Ohio, our hosts asked us to join them for devotions. We took turns reading

---

[40] Hebrews 1:14

Proverbs 4 and God touched us with a very personal word of encouragement for the long road ahead.

Frank and Karen, don't let these life-lessons go unnoticed. Hold onto everything I taught you in training and everything I am showing you now. Don't swerve to the right or left. I will protect and keep you in every detail. Don't worry about the cost—keep walking in the paths I set before you. On every highway I will keep you safe just as I did on the way here. Keep your hearts in faith and focus on what you know to be true. But don't give up![41]

The people at church were fantastic, but we were surprised when such a large congregation gave us a check for only $40 afterwards. "My goodness, it's going to take an awful lot of meetings and an awful lot of driving (we had traveled 700 miles) to get to New Guniea at this rate!" Yet, we clung to what we had just read in Proverbs 4 and determined not to swerve right or left.

Back at the house that night our host asked, "Hey, would you guys be able to visit one more church before you leave? It's a smaller church, but they love to have missionaries."

"Sure," Frank said, and the next night we attended the little country church prayer meeting. We noticed many with white hair and walking canes. "Maybe God brought us here for prayer support," Frank whispered. We shared our hearts, sang our songs, laughed a lot and closed in prayer. Someone in the back called, "Let's pass the plate for our special guests!"

We were still talking in the parking lot when a deacon quietly handed me the sealed envelope. *Oh, that's a sweet gesture,* I thought. Honestly, I expected twenty dollars from this retiring group of elderly people, but twenty times that fell into our hands! $400, which was ten times the "big church" gift, and more than we received from anyone in four years of training! These elderly saints gave a small fortune, and a tremendous faith lesson for us.

From that day on, we never asked for money or pre-judged results. We accepted invitations, spoke from the heart, and God demonstrated His ability to provide all our needs. We would practice the motto, "faith plus nothing," to get us to the field.

Frank played beautiful acoustic guitar and we sang together often, especially the minor keys of Jewish songs. We loved *Hineni*, saying "here am I" to God, and *My Beloved* from Isaiah 5, which

---

[41] Assorted excerpts from Proverbs 4 in my own words

spoke of God's broken heart over his vineyard. Over and over, these lovely lyrics knit the messages to our hearts as we determined to be available to God and *"press our lives into his hands so he can drink the wine."*

Interacting with people was our favorite part of these church meetings. Frequent questions revolved around day to day jungle living such as, "Where will you get your food?" and, "How will you learn the language?" Occasionally, we were shocked by bizarre confessions.

A heavy-set young woman came up to me one Sunday at a buffet luncheon. "Oh, I think it's wonderful that you're going to the mission field to help all those poor natives, but *I could never* do that! I can't leave my make-up," she said.

Perhaps her fears went deeper than cover-up. Truthfully, I wondered how I would be able to live *like that too,* but at the moment I was dumbfounded. Imagine, looking into the Lord's eyes and saying, "Lord, I know the harvest was plentiful, but I just had to paint my lashes and nails!" Someday, we will *face* the One who went to the cross for us, taking lashes and nails of a more gruesome nature. *God, help us rethink our priorities.*

Another time, an old man admitted he carried guilt for decades. "The Lord spoke to my heart about missions when I was a young man, but I never responded," he said sadly. "All these years I've known that's what He wanted." The poor man felt he had wasted his life, but Frank gently encouraged him, there's no condemnation in Christ.[42] Let's just live for Him while we can.

The Lord used all these meetings and encounters to reinforce our calling and convictions. We spoke at conferences, home groups and area churches, and reconnected with precious people at home who became our lifeline in years to come.

Our visas finally arrived, stamped with a deadline for arrival in PNG by March 16, 1980, so by faith we booked flights for the 10th. There was still so much to do, but the Lord was weaving every tiny detail. My own mother presented our largest gift *ever* for building a house in the tribe and I was floored (pun intended). Even more than the dollar amount, this gift spoke volumes about Mom's faith and a parental blessing over my chosen path.

---

[42] Romans 8:1

Step by step, God provided every item on the list through the generosity of his people. We rented a storage space for the fifty-gallon drums Frank found for $5 and stenciled our new address in bold black letters: East Sepik Province, Papua New Guinea. With every label it became more of a reality. *We're moving to the jungle!*

Despite everything God was doing, I privately wondered how I would raise a family in a jungle tribe. One night in particular, maternal emotions flared in a most unusual setting. Before the shipping deadline, my final mission was to scramble to Toys R Us and pick out gifts for our kids for the next *five* years. *What was I thinking?* I had such limited time and cash in hand before the drums and my kids' fate would be sealed.

At 11 p.m. I was still trudging around that cavernous store with an empty cart wishing I could buy a tricycle or a pogo stick. Nothing matched the space in the drums or the bills in my wallet except crayons and teaching tools. I roamed up and down those aisles until my heart ached as much as my feet. Scouring enormous shelves and equally staggering price tags, the sheer impossibility of what I was trying to do hit home with a wave of incredible sadness.

My poor kids! What will it be like on birthdays and Christmas? They'll never have the things I wished for them. No bicycles, baseball teams, or merry-go-rounds. What will life be like *for them?* It was prime time for the devil to add to the mental slop bucket. "This isn't fair to your kids! They'll be deprived of every good thing!"

It was a horrible mix of parental guilt and fear of the unknown. Tears filled my eyes and I was glad the aisles were empty in this post-Christmas season, because anyone seeing me in Toys R Us that night would know I was off my rocker. I imagined headlines in the local paper, "Missionary Loses It on Midnight Shopping Spree!" They'd post a photo of me drooling cross-eyed in the corner with hoola hoops dangling around my neck.

Maybe it was that inner sense of comedy that helped me snap out of the doldrums and rebuke myself soundly. *This is ridiculous! Kids don't need all this stuff to be happy. I don't think Dad **ever** had toys! We'll make what we can, or make do without. My kids are part of God's plan and if He could care for the* *children of Israel in the Sinai, he can meet their needs anywhere, anytime. So get behind me, devil!*

I went home with school supplies and board games, but truly scored a spiritual life lesson in those aisles. It's far more important to seal our hearts than our drums.

Early the next morning, my darling Frank picked up a Want Ad. "Look! Someone's selling a life-time collection of Lego!" Although this sales magazine covered a wide radius from New Hampshire to Rhode Island, the seller lived right down the street.

Amassed over eight years, their collection included castles and rockets, police cars and cranes—the entire set at a bargain price even we could afford. Lego blocks are perfectly suited to jungle conditions. Bugs don't eat them and moisture can't affect them. They're durable, educational, entertaining, and capable of holding kids' interests as far as their imaginations can go. They even serve as excellent packing material. God gave us the grand jackpot of all toys!

Not only so, but the Jewish father took an interest in Frank's faith and it was evident that our visit was orchestrated for more than building Lego blocks. It turned out to be an opportunity to build eternal connections as only a Master builder could do.

Those amazing little Legos illustrate God's supreme ability to solve every dilemma and answer every concern of our hearts. The timing, cost, and over-abundant provision of such a perfect solution proved God cares about the little things. Truly, when we trust him we need never worry about our lives, what we will wear, eat, or even what our kids will play with! This is basic Sermon on the Mount 101 [43] and you'd think I would never forget it.

But then another *little matter* came to light during our final weeks in the States that helped explain the flood of emotions. Just as we were preparing to leave for the great unknown, I discovered the news with a home test. *You gotta be kidding me! Expecting, again?* This time, I felt trapped, *already* forgetting the lesson of the Lego!

Sudden fear brought a lasting empathy toward frightened young women who resort to abortion. I admit, that crossed my mind, a momentary insanity exploding in a wave of panic. I also

---

[43] Matthew 6:25-34

felt a deeper kinship with Mary because of this uncomfortable-trip-to-a-foreign-land-at-the-worst-possible-time thing we had in common. Only in my case, I wasn't saying the humble, "behold your handmaiden" to the Lord. Oh no, not I. I could better play the braying donkey in that manger scene.

Why now, Lord? This is the worst possible timing! Did you forget that we're going into a tribe in the middle of nowhere? How can I move into such a rugged environment in this condition? Oh Lord... not now! My stomach was doing flip-flops, and the hormones—those little unseen culprits that make a woman's head spin out of control—were raging. We had no idea what God was planning for this unborn child, but I would laugh for years to come.

For now, it was crunch time!

On a frigid January day, a team of men from church came to help us load the truck for the docks. They estimated six months for the container ship to shore in the South Pacific, but if we missed the boat, it'd be months before another sailed.

All the details were in place, the lists checked off, and amazingly, money for shipping had been received in our account. I should have known by now, God moves mountains. All we had to do is drive to Boston Harbor.

Our friend Bryant borrowed a twenty-foot truck with a hydraulic lift from work. Frank and his dad hopped inside and I followed in our car with Bryant. We cruised into the city onto Storrow Drive along the choppy Charles River.

All of a sudden, catastrophe struck. Frank's truck headed down into an underpass while my eyes measured the lesser distance of the arched granite tunnel from afar. I slammed on the brakes as their roof peeled back like an accordion. With a horrific screeching sound, the company truck was wedged against stone!

"We ain't goin' nowhere fast!" Frank said with his hands on his hips.

"Honey! Do you think everything's damaged inside? How will we ever make the docks on time?" My faith shines at times like this.

Sirens careened down city streets and police diverted traffic. We were embarrassed but an officer said, "This happens all the time. People just don't read the clearance sign."

"What clearance sign?" we asked in unison.

"It's at the top of the ramp," he said. "It should be bigger though." We strolled to the top of the ramp to look, and sure enough, a tiny sign read simply, 11'10".

"That explains it.," Bryant said. "We have a 12'6" truck!"

They let the air out of the tires, eased the vehicle out, and incredibly, we made it to the wharf in time.

Afterwards, I started thinking about the damages. "Oh no, there goes our plane fare!" I said dejectedly, but we all prayed while Bryant called his boss.

"A couple of missionaries on their way to New Guinea just installed air conditioning in your truck for free," he explained. "You have a refrigeration truck now." What a relief to hear laughter. His boss said he'd take care of it, and another mountain moved that day.

These five years of training were certainly memorable. The things that seemed devastating then are the very things I laugh about now... like toy store melt-downs, biker-angels, and air-conditioned trucks. Nothing was insurmountable and nothing derailed the plan, even in the crunch time. Hormones calmed down, the Lord sent help when we needed it, and we learned some great life lessons on faith that remain with me to this day.

12. On Eagle's Wings

"As the eagle stirs up its nest and hovers over its young, spreads its wings to catch them, carrying them on its pinions... So the Lord did lead them."[44]

March 16, 1980, was a bitter cold day in Boston when a small group of friends came to see us off at Logan. It had been a rush of last minute packing and jittery nerves, and the final moments went too fast. All of a sudden the loud speakers called our flight, and it was time to board families with small children. Where are those boarding passes? Zip up that diaper bag! Everyone lined up to say our good-byes and Mom waited for the final hug.

"Well, this is it! Don't forget to write," she said.

"I won't, Mom," and we traipsed down the ramp. She knew we would never meet again this side of glory. She had been fighting cancer nine years, but she held her composure and waved us off with a brave smile to fight our own battles. *Oh my heart!*

Before I could fully absorb it, we hustled on board with our kids and carry-ons. We buckled in and I craned my neck to see if everyone was still in the terminal. There they were! It was so dreamlike; all our friends were lined up along the railing, waving!

They couldn't see which of the tiny windows of that 747 held our faces, but they hoped we could still see them. And there was Mom, surrounded by that smiling, waving, loving little bunch. It didn't occur to me at the time, but they had come for her more than us. That makes me happy now.

---

[44] Deuteronomy 32:11

The doors slammed shut as if punctuating the closure, and the plane started rolling back. I clutched the kids and cradled my growing belly. "This is it kids!" and then my eyes spilled over. All the little hands fluttered in the terminal. All the prayers ascended. We drew a big breath and slipped away into the clouds.

We were soon jetting across the nation and across the Pacific to Hawaii where sweet floral fragrances and balmy air embraced us. After all the hectic packing and rushing around, we enjoyed the beaches and a pool at the little mission guest house. We read our Bibles, basked amidst palm trees, and treated the kids to our "last McDonalds" and ice cream cones. Best of all, we slept like babies. *"The Lord is my shepherd... He makes me lie down in green pastures. He leads me beside quiet waters."*[45]

We were up before dawn for the ten-hour flight to Sydney and another long jaunt to the capital city of PNG. It was a long day, but excitement mounted and we had crew members from New Guinea on the last leg. Now we could see faces and hear the rolling sounds of the Pidgin tongue spoken by natives for the first time.

The minute we landed in Port Moresby, the scene changed drastically. No more Hawaiian luaus here! We pushed through sweaty crowds of half-naked bodies carrying their cargo of coffee beans, live roosters and even nursing piglets in their arms. One tired ceiling fan did nothing to move the air or relieve the smelly press of heat and flesh as we made our way from room to room to stamp visas and collect luggage.

Finally, we were discharged to the street with all our gear to find a phone. I clung to the kids, trying to keep their hands clean and their feet out of the odd puddles of urine and splotches of red spittle. "Stand close to me, kids." At 15 months, the baby was too heavy to carry and our backs were stiff. "Hold my hand honey, I can't carry you."

Poor, elderly and disadvantaged people loitered along the streets. Beggars and cripples in rags clamored around us. Mothers nursed babies and kids with snotty noses hovered around their skirts. Flies were everywhere. Men holding hands wore knit hats despite the heat. Women and girls wore thick bands of multi-colored beads around their necks. Colorful string bags hung from

---

[45] Psalm 23

their heads. It was a fascinating parade of humanity, but difficult to absorb in our tired state.

Frank called the mission office, hoping for a rest stop before continuing to the interior. We looked forward to meeting coworkers, but the office manager hadn't been informed of our arrival. He griped about the lack of proper notice and said he didn't have room for us. After saying that we were keeping him from his Sunday nap, he did offer that if we had gas money, he'd pick us up and let us "use the shower" before flying out of the capital city. We were at his mercy. "Of course we'll pay for gas," Frank said.

Dismayed at such an inhospitable welcome my mood soured. *Aren't there plenty of retirement communities in places like Ft Lauderdale for people who want a Sunday nap?* After all we'd been through in five years to get here, that was the last thing I expected. "I think I'd rather sit it out at the airport," I said sadly. But oh, a shower sounded so good after 24 hours! First impressions were shattered, but the Lord was way ahead of us.

There were exactly four seats left on the next plane to Goroka, so Frank booked them right away. It just so happened that a Tennessee couple was en route to furlough with their troop of handsome sons. These gracious folks overheard our mission rep and offered to pick us up. If not for them I probably would have spent our first day in a puddle of exhausted tears.

I remembered my own apathy toward visitors, like the time I sat in my jungle camp hut and ignored the people outside. *"Lord, it's so sweet to be welcomed when you're road-weary and a stranger—no wonder you talked about it so much. Help me remember this."*

We hated saying goodbye to Jack and Janie, our sweet Tennessee heroes, but it was soon time to board a smaller plane for the last leg of our journey. Just a few more hours and we landed in the lush green mountains of the New Guinea Highlands, at last.

In the bustling town of Goroka, our restless eyes fell on more pressing crowds of sweaty bodies, babies on every limb, and long breasts flying. (The first time I saw this, I though a child was suckling his mother's elbow!) Our noses filled with pungent aromas and the sounds of garbled languages filled our ears.

I tensed on crowded streets with kids and luggage—not a short family vacation bit of bags, but a permanent-relocation-around-the-world-with-toddlers caravan. We had fourteen pieces including brief cases, camera bag, diaper bag and backbreaking suitcases *without* wheels. I felt vulnerable, and we stuck out like cotton balls against a sea of velvet.

Enveloped in a tide of smoking, crying, bare feet shuffling, men spitting, dogs peeing, noses spraying mucous into hands and wiping, and a thriving population of flies on festering sores, my tired eyes struggled to absorb it all. Tattoos, red-stained mouths, pierced septums, stretched ear lobes, and the flapping breasts hit us with a visual onslaught of raw third-world humanity. Truckloads of singing passengers flew by, leaving a chorus of song in their wake.

It had been a very long haul from Hawaii through Australia and from Moresby to the Highlands without sleep. Just as a fresh wave of nausea was taking hold, Frank said, "Hey honey, look!" and we recognized the faces of our new partners weaving through the crowd.

Don and Becky were scheduled to fly out but bad weather prevented them. Maybe that explains the missed messages and the mess in Moresby. The Lord held them back by storm, then rushed us through, even holding the last four seats so we could be together. That put a different light on what I had merely seen as one man's bad day.

Meyers drove us about ten more exciting miles down the Highlands Highway on the left side of the road. Passenger trucks called PMVs barreled around blind corners, making it easy to verify claims for one of the most dangerous highways in the world. Winding around the countryside, we came to a large sloping tract of land called Numonohi, our mission headquarters.

This thriving little community had grown over several decades to include its own store, print shop, gymnasium and soccer fields. I didn't know it yet, but the tiny radio shack at the top of the hill would gain great significance to our family in years to come.

Assorted teachers, mission leaders, pilots, and support workers lived in a smattering of bungalows around a field office and school. The whole base was fenced and gated, surrounded by a beautiful spread of mountains and valleys where cattle and horses roamed.

They dropped us at a guest house at the top of the hill, a most welcome end to our transcontinental journey, where sweet New Zealand hosts showed us to our private room. At last, we could unzip our suitcases and lie down, but our eyes hurt and our heads were pounding. Our confused bodies couldn't decide if we were more hungry or tired, and with a fourteen-hour time difference we were falling asleep when everyone else was rising.

Despite feeling disoriented, we were delighted to be there at last. It was more beautiful than I imagined. Hardwood floors and glass louvered windows in the guest house surprised me. Another wonderful discovery was flushing toilets and running water supplied by water tanks. Laundry lines and rows of flowers lined the property, with long-horned steer snorting at us across a wire fence. The view at the top of the hill swept across rolling mountains draped with bands of cloud and fog.

Early mornings were crisp and cool but it quickly warmed into the 80's. At the main gate in the mornings, we could buy fresh fruits and vegetables spread out on tarps. Local villagers loved to peddle their goods market style. They carried net bags on their heads called *bilums*, laden with plantains and pineapples, papaya and tomatoes. Lemons, greens, cabbage and sweet potato were plentiful. You could eat pretty well for a few dollars a day.

This field orientation allowed time to meet leadership, get national drivers licenses, and order supplies. We started language study, stocked up on malaria medicine, reviewed field policies, and started using the shortwave radio. There was a lot to learn.

Best of all, we started making life-long friends, bonding with missionaries at the guest house. Bob and Noby invited us to town to show us local hot spots and customs. For example, we city slickers just wanted to point to what looked good and ask, "Em I kostim haumas?" in our book-learned trade-speak for "What does it cost?" But in PNG, half the fun of selling is bartering.

It took awhile to get the hang of the currency and coins, too. Some pieces are distinguished by crocodile or possum faces or holes in the center. Shuffling around in the muddy well-beaten trails of the market place, I felt awkward, but managed to buy my first colorful *bilum* net bag. Then I didn't know how I ever managed without one.

In the same way people want to ask an astronaut about body functions, our friends answered the all-important question, and introduced us to the best bathroom in town. The Bird of Paradise, a European hotel on the edge of town, became a favorite stop not only for toilets and washing hands, but ice cold lemon "squash" drinks, and fish and chips.

At the main entrance, we encountered two old men dressed in native garb with bird feathers and headdresses. "Piksa, piksa," they smiled with big toothless grins. [Take our picture.] But after posing proudly with spears in hands, they demanded payment. Nonetheless, the Bird was a favorite stop for every annual visit to the "big smoke."[46]

With its gleaming floors, restaurant and swimming pool, it was one of the only places in the country that made you feel civilized. Waiters wore flip flops and gardeners wore skirts, but we were assured it was the cleanest place around outside of the Australian Bank. So when I went inside the tiled ladies' room, I was taken back by a big black bug crawling along the floor. I kept my eyes on it the whole time I was in there, as it scampered around my sandaled feet.

"Did you see that cockroach in there?" Noby asked, "They fly too!"

I had no idea cockroaches were so big, and I certainly didn't know they could fly. *Good grief! If they have bugs that big in the cleanest place in town, what on earth will they look like in the jungle?*

We would soon find out. We were cleared to move to the Sepik to begin bush orientation the following week. Once again, my stress levels inflated, partially fueled by many who felt it their duty to offer advice. "Oh, you're headed for the SEPIK! If you think this is hot, you ain't seen nothing yet!" Or, "Say goodbye to veggies! You won't be getting any fresh food down there." And my favorite, "The mosquitoes are as big as helicopters! Hang on to your kids! *Ho, ho, ho!*"

Speaking of hanging on to my kids, the hardest comments came from teachers and dorm parents asking my daughter (not me), "When are you coming to school, Naomi?"

Give me a break, she's only three for crying out loud! That's what I wanted to say. Of course, what came out of my mouth sounded more like, "Oh, that's a long way off yet. We'll

---

[46] A favorite term for describing a town or city, more populated than our village of a few small fires.

cross that bridge when we get to it." I was most definitely hoping to put that off as long as possible.

Unthinking people didn't realize the awful effects of their words and I wanted to plug my ears before they could fill my head with more dreadful sounding obstacles. In the country one week and my family and sanity were already under threat—not from wild natives, but from the untamed tongues of other missionaries. *Oh Lord, help me to take it one day at a time.*

The Highlands was lush and beautiful, but if unguarded, I could see how headquarters could become an enclave of comfortable and cloistered Europeans. One of our mission reps even compared us to manure. "Piled up in one place, we stink! We have to spread out to fertilize a field or do any good," he said. Another missionary compared the mission base to a chicken coop. "We have to beware not to peck each other to death!" The same is true of churches, companies, and any human gathering and roosting place. Of course, not every encounter was negative, but this is what stuck in my craw during our initial introduction period.

After two weeks in Goroka, we booked our flight and spent a small fortune on supplies to fill the pod of a Cessna, shopping to meet a firm weight allowance in kilograms. The cost of our first Sepik flight was offset considerably by sharing with another family returning to their tribe at the midway point.

It seemed the skills of three Chinese magicians and one marvelous Houdini were prerequisites I hadn't heard about. These are essential skills for utilizing every gram of weight allowance, cramming it all into a five-seat aircraft, and still leaving room for your bodies.

It was a chilly morning, somewhere around 50 degrees when the airport van arrived and we loaded for the hangar in the dark at 5 a.m. A wiry Aussie pilot named Dave personally managed all the details of the flight, fueling, loading, and logging reports. As soon as the fog lifted, we were cleared for take-off.

Jammed in with five adults juggling four toddlers on our laps, jostling egg cartons and mail bags around our feet, we bounced down the single runway and rose above the mountains into the early morning sun. The other family was all smiles with little girls bouncing happily on their way home. Frank was high energy in the front seat with the headphones on, talking with the

95

pilot the whole way. I, on the other hand, was full of uncertainty; a bundle of nerves ready to puke.

After 90 minutes, our altitude dropped and the temperature rose about fifty degrees. As we circled Maprik airport our three-year-old started throwing up. We approached a dirt runway surrounded by trees. No signs. No lights or parking lots. A few gardens and village houses speckled the lush surroundings. "Downtown" was a few miles away, comprised of a few meager trade stores and a market place.

My face felt red hot and my kids looked green when we finally emerged and stood under the shade of the little wing. I paused to see if I would keel over in the heat wave that swallowed our bodies and we quickly peeled off socks and sweaters and stuffed them in my new *bilum*. We probably wouldn't need those items for a *very* long time.

Then, as soon as our cargo was unloaded to the ground, our spunky pilot hopped back into the driver's seat and zoomed off leaving us standing in the middle of nowhere. We watched him shrink into the cool blue sky. *Oh God, now we're stuck here!* "Let's get into the shade," I suggested, wiping the kids' faces.

We had announced our arrival by "buzzing over base" before landing, so a mission van soon arrived and a tawny veteran of about sixty stepped out. Dale reminded me of a long tall Texan, his skin dark and leathery from so many years on the equator. His zeal was unparalleled, and he welcomed us with a wide smile.

Everyone was dripping by this time, but we were soon bouncing along deep ruts in the dirt. The moving air felt wonderful but Frank kept checking back to be sure nothing was bouncing out on the road, including me and my bladder. We arrived at the base just in time.

13. Vile Emotions

"You guys will be living right there," Dale pointed to a long house with a corrugated aluminum roof. "You can take the left side and make yourselves right at home."

The narrow duplex stood on a slab concrete floor with a tin roof to collect rainwater. Walls consisted of woven bamboo mats, yellow plastic and screen wire for windows. Both end units were identical and shared a central porch area where a couple of wringer washers and sinks stood. Rows of laundry lines hung out the back and a few coconut and sago palms offered some welcome circles of shade in the front.

We stepped cautiously inside and looked around our new flat. Approximately 600sf of concrete floors "fully furnished" with a home-made picnic table, stainless sink, kerosene stove and a small refrigerator in one main room. Two small bedrooms opened off the main room, offering a wood slat crib for our one-year-old son, a twin bed for our daughter and a double bed frame with sheet of foam for us.

It had electricity and running water but with an austere simplicity that felt like a wilderness adventure on an African safari. Peeking into the little bathroom, I made the happy discovery that indoor plumbing included a flushing toilet and a little shower stall. And, since all our belongings were still floating somewhere in the Pacific, an assortment of plastic bowls, melamine dishes and utensils were going to help immensely. *Thank you, Lord!*

Though metal roofs are great for collecting rainwater, they're swelteringly hot, so I brought the kids outside to play in the afternoon shade. But we no sooner sat on the grass when I noticed a big black rhinoceros beetle clambering toward their tiny white feet. The long black horn looked ferocious to my new American eyes, so I quickly scooped them up and rushed them back inside. "We'll play outside another day, kids."

Hanging clothes on the laundry line one morning I felt something smack onto the back of my leg that wouldn't let go. It felt like a big hand grabbing the back of my thigh. Barbed legs entwined in the cotton folds of my skirt and the more I waved the fabric the harder that tenacious bugger held on.

Frank heard me screaming, and ran out to rip it off with his bare hands. *My hero!* That was my first run-in with a giant walking stick. Enough outdoor fun.

Inside, geckos chirped happily and their droppings fell everywhere. I dreaded the thought of some long-tailed reptile falling on my head and everything made me jumpy for some time. Eventually I began to relax and develop a routine of home-schooling and studying Melanesian Pidgin. Then on Sundays we had *lotu* [church] in a nearby village, about twenty minutes' walk down the dirt road.

We befriended one pleasant young man named Moses[47] who became a regular guest at our dinner table. At 22, we were close in age and he could read and speak three languages. Our three-year-old Naomi called him "our friend with the different hair" because Moses wore dreadlocks.

Since he was very friendly and eager to talk, we loved having him over and our language ability took off. Moses would *stori* freely, teaching language, local history and customs about the Sepik people we had come to reach. As an added benefit, we started taking him through the book of Romans verse by verse enjoying the opportunity to make the time count for eternity. That was our favorite part of orientation.

Frank put in half-days working on the director's new home overlooking the jungle, while I put equal time into the kids' daily schooling, a source of grounding normalcy no matter where we went. Keeping them comfortable in the heat was the hardest part. It was still winter and thirty degrees in Boston, but now their little faces were flushed bright red and sleeping was difficult.

Thank God, water was plentiful due to heavy rains. We found relief taking several showers a day to fight heat rashes and prickly heat, and I hosed the kids in a washtub. Some adjustments

---

[47] Biblical names were commonly assigned in gov't schools. Thomas, Peter, James and Joseph were common.

were harder for me than for them, like the day I cut Naomi's beautiful ringlets because her scalp and neck were so irritated. I loved her long curls and now they were falling to the floor, and my tears fell with them. Am I a total wimp?

Maybe it was hormones, but I felt terribly estranged and irritable from the heat. I heard someone comment on the "spoiled young Americans coming to the field these days." Maybe a little shopping expedition would get me out of the doldrums.

"The truck leaves at 8:30 sharp," Doris said. "If you want to come, get some boxes."

"That sounds fun," Frank said encouragingly. So I hung laundry before the sun was high, dressed the kids in rubber boots, grabbed my *bilum* and a cardboard box.

Doris, a tough old Californian pioneer, was already in the driver's seat and ready to go with her sunhat tied on and the engine running. Two older women were in front, so I helped the kids over the back gate and climbed in wondering how I would hang on to the kids and carry a box of groceries. I wished Frank could come, but he was working on their new house.

"Have fun, honey!" he waved from the rafters as we pulled out.

We bounced along the bumpy dirt road while moving air refreshed our prickly-heated bodies, but I hoped the kids wouldn't fall off the benches. "Hang on to the bars, kids! Stay on the seat!" At one and three years old, they thought it was a great bouncy ride, but I felt like a mama kangaroo over the back tires.

When we finally parked at the marketplace, I was shocked at the size of the milling crowds. Hundreds of black bodies in colorful clothes jammed into an open air market area. This was more than a shopping day. It looked like the social event of the year. Gangs of young men exchanged smokes and eyed the women. Mothers clutched their babies and everyone tried not to step on scrawny dogs and kids. An assortment of other curious creatures such as *kapulis* [tree possum] rode around wide-eyed clutching people's heads.

By the time I climbed out of the flatbed with the kids and an empty box in my hand, the ladies had taken off, swallowed up in a mass of sweaty flesh and curly heads. Oh, for a shopping cart to put my babies in! In no time my back was hurting from carrying the one-year-old.

We waded around in the gunk, weaving through the maze of tables and displays of produce. Was this the same stuff we'd seen in the Highlands? Between the smells and the heat, my stomach was turning. I already had to pee, but this town didn't have any public bathrooms. We were wading in the stuff.

Sloppy red betel juice was everywhere. The equivalent of drinking beer in PNG, *buai* or betel chewing[48] is all part of the feel-good social event of the marketplace. On the down side, it makes their teeth black and produces copious amounts of red saliva which is splattered all around your feet while you're "shopping."

Pungent aromas combined with the muck and mud from the evening rains, and it was a mess. The bright Chinese rain boots we bought the kids in the Highlands helped, but food shopping is for the birds when such horrific smells shoot your appetite to smithereens.

Mucky paths, language issues, bartering, and health concerns weren't the only challenges of the day. Most of the sale items were foreign to me. What were my options here? There was sugar cane but I really didn't know what to do with it, let alone the challenge of adding long spikes to my busy arms.

There were plump green spiny fruits the size of melons, but I passed them by in ignorance. How do you compose a meal out of these foreign objects? The hard skinned tree tomatoes looked like spicy peppers. The green leaves tied up in bunches are probably tobacco. There were betel peppers, roosters and grub worms. *My goodness, I still don't have anything for dinner!*

I smiled at people and greeted everyone in my best Pidgin phrases but my box was still empty. I finally stooped down next to an old woman, asked the price in halting Pidgin, counted out the coins in her hand, probably overpaying, collected bananas and lemons, and got back to my feet without spilling anything. That was my big accomplishment of the day.

Now the baby needed to be changed. No, maybe I stepped in something from a dog, or a kid. My sandals were amuck. I wonder if I'll get pinworm from walking on this ground, or hepatitis from eating this fruit? Finally, I realized the *unfruitfulness* of continuing.

---

[48] Buai acts on the central nervous system giving a general feeling of well-being, and lessens hunger and fatigue much like nicotine.

I looked back at the truck to get my bearings and saw the other women already sitting inside. Oh my, it was probably just a few hundred feet but the entire way was an obstacle course. Wouldn't it be nice if one of them would come back and help me? No such luck. There they sat with their hats tied on tight, looking a little disgusted that they had to wait for me.

"Come on kids," I said in my cheeriest voice. "Let's go home and tell Daddy what we did!" What troopers—obedient, trusting, and pleasant—my great kids! Despite feeling like a wrung out wash cloth, they made me proud. We made our way back to the truck with our meager acquisitions and climbed in the back.

"We have to go to the bank," Doris announced. *There's a bank here?*

"Okay," I answered weakly. I certainly didn't want to sound like a missionary wimp, but I was sorely uncomfortable. *Maybe I really am spoiled.* I wiped my brow and bit my lip while they tended to what they needed. I stayed in the back of the truck with the kids to "guard" the stuff as they did their errands.

Seriously, if anyone of these cannibals tries to take something I'd say, help yourself, buddy! Meanwhile, I just had to endure hoping I wouldn't get a migraine from dehydration. Didn't these women remember having toddlers or being pregnant?

We finally tumbled out of the truck back at the base and I went straight into the bathroom and started to cry. "Lord, I thought missionaries were compassionate people. I thought they were supposed to love their neighbors. I can't do this, Lord!" It was a royal pity party and I was the queen of it. Then the door creaked open. Frank saw our truck return and came home to see what I got. He saw my measly harvest and found me crying on the toilet. "What's wrong, honey?"

"I'm never going to town like that again!" I sobbed. "If you want fresh food from that market you're going to have to help me." I was blessed with a wonderful husband. From then on, we made family adventures of market days, exploring every new sight and sound like the Maprik birds with their unique cries echoing over the treetops. We tasted new foods and I learned to use them. I began to relax and acclimate to Sepik culture.

Doris later admitted she thought young missionaries were unwilling to work. "We did everything the hard way," she boasted. "You have to toughen up."

I didn't argue. I was wet behind the ears. She thought she was doing these spoiled Americans a favor by letting us schlep through the mud, but then again, would it be so terrible to lend a hand now and then?

Maybe she forgot what it was like. I saw pictures of her arduous trek into the tribe, seated on a bamboo rickshaw, hoisted on shoulders like an African queen, and I wished I had one of those—especially on market days.

I suppose I expected tribal people to exhibit strange or hostile customs, but not this. For me, it wasn't the strange smells, unfamiliar foods, or new ways of cooking. The most bewildering adjustments were relational disappointments from the very ones I expected the most encouragement. So far, fellow missionaries presented the toughest single challenge.

Many missionaries were an absolute delight from the moment we met, like an Aussie couple living at base to help with construction. A wiry builder Ted was pushing sixty. Despite extreme heat and hard work, he was one of the happiest men Frank ever met.

He worked tirelessly from morning to night, usually singing songs of praise. One day he turned to Frank from the top of a rafter and said, "What a privilege it is to serve the Lord like this! I want to die swinging a hammer for the Lord."

Dear God, help me grow in grace and serve you joyfully like this dear man.

In June, Frank flew to May River to start working in the saw mill. High water season is the perfect time to float felled trees for house posts. They actually landed in a few inches of water, Frank jumped out, and then the airstrip flooded to four feet deep. Frank was "stuck" in the tribe, and I was stuck with getting to May River by boat! Lord knows, a one-hour plane ride would have been a lot easier, which reminds me of that little notion of spoiled Americans.

Waking early to pack while the kids slept, I was surprised when the Lord broke into my thoughts. "Get Jesse," he said.

"But he's quiet right now," I protested. *How does the Lord put up with me?*

"Get Jesse, *now.*" I knew the Lord's gentle voice like a sheep knows his shepherd,[49] but I wasn't always quick to obey it. *Why on earth should I take a quiet baby out of his crib?*

Thankfully, I tiptoed in and scooped him up in my arms and waited, curiously. Then, my eyes landed on a very good reason why you should never, ever, did I say, *never* question God's leading. An enormously creepy, spine-tingling centipede dashed across the crib sheet right where he had been lying!

I rushed out of the room with my baby, grabbed my daughter, and sat them on my bed. "Naomi, hold your brother and *don't move!*"

"Okay, Mommy." Thank God for obedient kids... *Hmmmm, point taken, Lord.*

Understand, these centipedes look nothing like the scrawny half-frozen insects we have in the North. This one was science fiction sized with blue-black legs wiggling in every direction.

It was eight inches long and half an inch wide and hands down, the ugliest fastest moving thing I'd ever seen. It could have wrapped around my baby's arms or legs stinging repeatedly from its head and tail, filling him with poison—even risking his life. Vile emotions welled up in me, a killing instinct far beyond the norm for this New England suburbanite.

I grabbed the longest weapon I could find—a two-by-four from the corner. Flipping the mattress and sheets, I chased that venomous creature to the concrete, hopping around nervously in my bare feet. I must have looked like a raging lunatic with bulging eyes and a big stick in my hand. *I wish Frank was here now! Help me, God.*

I finally caught it with a good smack and didn't stop until I crushed its head and tail, pulverizing it with visceral satisfaction. Seriously, I crushed it. My heart didn't slow down until its creepy carcass was scraped into the burn barrel and I was holding the kids in bed. I felt like a mother bear who saved her cubs, Rocky after the last punch.

What a way to start the day, I thought, *and we haven't even started the trip yet!* We were about to truck to the Sepik River and then proceed by boat to a little village and—*Oh no!* An oversized

---

[49] John 10:3-4, 14, 27 The sheep hear my voice and *follow,* Jesus said.

caution light flashed neon letters across the billboard in my brain—
Oh God! I'm going to be living in a jungle!

Now, one would think this would have crossed my mind by now. We had just finished FIVE YEARS of preparation, after all. How can I explain the convoluted workings of that gigantic delay switch in my brain? But in this one lucid moment it switched on and a big dose of reality kicked in.

I can't do this!

Fear ripped through me like fire through kindling, and the devil seized the moment. "You think this was bad? There are much bigger creatures lurking out there! What if your kids fall into the croc-filled river? You don't belong here, city girl!"

But the Lord called me to get the baby *before* that little demon surfaced. I'll be alright if I listen and trust Him. I can't let the enemy get a foothold now. I remembered Dick Sanford telling us in boot camp how to face fear. "How big is the biggest crocodile, 23 feet? Ask yourself, is God bigger than 23 feet?"

Okay Lord, you're bigger than all my fears. *"I will fear no evil for thou art with me and I can do all things through Christ."* [50]

For the next two hours, I cleaned and sealed everything in cardboard while the kids giggled with glee. They weren't thinking about that ferocious beast in the crib sheets, or how far it would be to the next bathroom. We were going to see Daddy and he'd take care of everything.

No wonder Jesus used children as an example. [51]

---

[50] Psalm 23:4, Phil 4:13 KJV
[51] Matthew 18:3

14. Becoming River Rats

Piling into the truck, we headed south to the shores of the Sepik River. That two-hour trek felt longer with unfamiliar terrain and kids' elbows jostling around my extended belly. Nevertheless, we had a clear sky and the added benefit of traveling with another family.

Beth and her young sons were heading to their tribe, and she was also expecting her third in three months like me. We'd meet our husbands at the Sepik, then women and kids would be loaded into the fast boat with freezer meat. Yessiree, we rated #1, right up there with the perishables!

As soon as the kids spotted Frank coming downriver, they started jumping up and down. "Daddy! Daddy!"

Wind-blown and with ears throbbing from the engines, we had a joyous but brief reunion on the riverbank. Frank had been in the tribe for weeks by now. His beard was getting thick and he was brown from the sun. He had lost weight and I wondered what he'd been eating, but there was no time for chit chat.

"Let's get this show on the road!" they called. The guys rushed around to balance our loads and pack our cargo into two john boats. I sat with both kids in the first and Frank hopped in the second. Everything went according to plan, at first.

It was too noisy for conversation, but my eyes soaked in our lush surroundings on my first jungle cruise. Periodically, I'd catch a flash of floral brilliance like red streamers cascading from the treetops to celebrate our arrival. "Look at that, kids!" Frank couldn't fully appreciate the breathtaking "jungle flame." He was color blind to reds and greens from birth, but it was one of my favorite jungle flowers.

A muddy sandbar littered with fallen trees sprang to life as our motor approached. The "trees" sprouted legs and slipped into the murky water! I didn't even want to think about the length of crocodiles lurking beneath us, but I pulled my kids a little closer and rehearsed promises from Isaiah.[52]

We rode as far as Ambunti and hiked to an old mission house that had been vacant for many months. Our group shocked the groaning floorboards of that two-bedroom house and sent a host of indwelling creatures into a flurry. We ate a light meal and slept very little. At 5:30 a.m. we zipped up our bags for another day on the river, and arrived at Aumi Village before sunset.

The village clearing quickly filled with people and our things disappeared into a mob of clutching hands. I glimpsed our big yellow suitcase bouncing up the trail and all our earthly belongings swallowed in greenery. My ears were ringing, everyone was jabbering, and all I could do was smile and shake hands, trying to hang on to my kids on the muddy slope.

Then Becky rushed down the hill and we hugged with our toes digging into the clay. She was so happy to have partners after three years alone.

We started picking our way up the trail in a mass of black skin, runny noses, and curly heads. Excited kids grabbed my hand and kept asking about the plane. "No plane, moto-canoe," I explained in my most elementary trade-speak. Becky said the Iwam people can't pronounce "f" or "r." They were asking about Frank not the airplane, but his name on their lips sounded like "plen." I was already confused!

My eyes darted from side to side noticing the thick jungle growth and very narrow trail for our tender white feet. Everyone else's bare skin slapped up the narrow muddy lane without a care, but for me it seemed a chore to stay upright. Somehow, we were carried along in the commotion, but I was huffing and dripping sweat by the time we reached the top. *Humidity must be about 150% here.*

We passed a three-foot boulder on the side of the path, the only stone I'd seen, and some graves stood nearby. "Hey Becky, we have to pass through a cemetery to get to your house?" I

---

[52] Isaiah 43:1-3 provides great assurance in fearful moments such as these.

laughed, glad to know none of our companions understood English.

"Actually, our houses are built *over* ancestral graves!" she informed me.

"Are you kidding?" *Isn't that nice?*

We leveled off at a rough-hewn gateway opening to a little grassy yard. Their old lab Smokey met us with a wagging tail, then hobbled back to the front step, too hot do any more. Two simple slatted houses with palm thatched roofs stood surrounded by fruit and floral trees. A hedge of pineapple spines poked upwards and long banana stalks draped down sleepily. Behind a few rows of laundry lines, bright yellow hibiscus bloomed.

Each structure stood about two feet off the ground on tree posts. The larger house on the left side was occupied by our partners, and the smaller place belonged to Brams, that wonderful Iowa family who returned to the States. Three long years had passed since then, but the sight of that darkened shanty made me sad. The wood was rotting, the water tank rusting, and the bamboo fraying, but that would become our village home.

The river lay beneath us now, turning lazily into the horizon with a few dotted villages on the sides. Glancing back at our little entourage, I noticed the sun was dropping quickly. *How far away is Frank in that mass of greenery?*

I couldn't linger on the thought. Hungry mosquitoes swarmed our ankles, so we danced around like we had to go to the bathroom. (Well, that too!) Thanking everyone who carried our bags and boxes, Becky paid them and we scurried inside to her country kitchen.

We were incredibly blessed to be taken in by Becky. The sister I never had, nothing was too much for her loving heart. To this day her tireless example remains untarnished in my mind. As an added bonus, our kids hit it off too, entertaining each other endlessly.

Don trimmed and filled the hurricane lamps and we ate our first of many candlelit dinners. We sat down to an ample chicken dinner, scalloped potatoes, hot biscuits and a fresh fruit salad! It would have felt like Thanksgiving if only Frank was there.

Still, no sign of him. Even though they were in a slower rig with heavier cargo, they should have arrived by evening. It was the first time in six years of marriage (except for the three-day hikes in jungle camp) that we couldn't say goodnight, even by radio… but the worst part was not knowing what happened to them.

It was pitch dark by the time we did dishes, heated water for baths, and tucked ourselves into a big mosquito net, the kids with me. I was hot, tired, and sunburned and my back was killing me from two days on aluminum seats without a back rest. This is the state of road weariness that gave birth to the term, *river rat*, which became part of our working vocabulary in the Sepik.

Yet, here I was, lying on a foam mattress listening to the high-pitched whines of mosquitoes *outside* my net, and the sheets smelled like a sunny day. We were clean, fed, safe and dry, and I thanked God for these things, but—

"Mommy? When is Daddy coming?" Even at three, Naomi knew life wasn't the same without him.

"Probably in the morning," I answered as positively as I could. "Let's pray and ask God to take care of him."

My personal passenger on board did somersaults and my ears strained at every sound in the dark. Several times I imagined the whine of a distant motor and then realized it was all part of a host of buzzing, flapping things in the night.

The eerie sounds of the rainforest formed an unfamiliar symphony that I would grow to love in time. When I got still, I listened to the soft chirping crickets, and I was finally lulled to sleep with my mind replaying the twists and turns of the river. God is with us every step of the way.

The next day we detected a sound like katydids in the distant trees. It would grow loud and then fade around the spaghetti bends of the river. Finally, one constant humming sound rose above the rest and the village kids scrambled to the riverbank for the excitement of yet another visitor. *Moto! Moto!* What a great feeling when the tiny form of a jon boat appeared in the distance, its aluminum seats reflecting hot sun like mirrors.

The minute they shored and cut the motors, everyone started talking at once. *"Are you guys okay? Did you sleep in the boat? Did you get eaten by mozees?"*

Bit by bit we learned that their motor conked out a few hours from Ambunti and they were forced to drift back down the Sepik. "Don't worry," Brad assured, "I took the OMC course in training." Unfortunately, OMC didn't help. They had inadvertently taken diesel fuel from a poorly marked drum and all they could do was float back to swap tanks.

Brad looked at Frank and asked, "So, how did you get here, big guy?"

"Oh, it's a long story," Frank said.

"Well," appraising their situation with a smile, "You may as well get started. We've got a *lonnng* day ahead of us." So the guys bonded while drifting in the hot sun, and remained dearest friends from that day on. You never know how God will use detours and breakdowns to direct or build something new. Even our "mistakes" are part of His plan.

I definitely believed God led us to this place, but my faith was tested in regard to trusting Him once we got there. There were charming aspects and pleasant moments, but it was one rude shock after another in those early days. Lots to learn and lots to fear.

Our little one bedroom house in the sago swamp was elevated above ground for some separation from the wild animal kingdom. Floors were made of *pangal*, a black palm hammered into thick slatted floor boards. Everything bounced, rattled and rolled, and I was getting heavier by the minute.

Rough-hewn poles formed a frame with screen windows. I was grateful for the galley kitchen with linoleum counters and a small stainless sink. We even had cool running water from a small tank that filled nightly with rain off the roof. The bathroom was another redeeming feature.

Although dinky by American standards and I had trouble squeezing into the narrow stall, that bucket shower was well used and we had an honest to goodness *flushing* toilet, not just a hole in the ground. It all had the feel of an old hunting cabin in the wilds of Alaska—only hotter.

The kids' tiny bedroom more resembled a pantry than a playroom. It was functional, but complicated by the discovery that we weren't the sole occupants. The place was crawling with lizards, beetles, mice, spiders and other surprise guests so I paid more attention to the mosquito nets, giving new meaning to the phrase, "tucking in the kids."

Speaking of unwanted occupants, the little pull-knob drawers nearly stopped my heart every time I opened one to see a blur of hairy little varmints scurrying away! Cock roaches were the worst. These filthy wretches lay eggs and chew holes, and I couldn't get rid of them.

One day I opened a box of supplies from the top pantry shelf and to my horror, dozens of them scrambled over my arms and leapt to the floor around my feet! I took off my flip-flops and started smacking, screaming and dancing to keep them from running up my legs. (Mental note: burn all cardboard and start collecting flour drums!)

What a sight I was, whacking ferociously like a mad woman armed with footwear. Every time I hit one, I'd shriek, and the village kids would laugh, like daily reruns of their favorite cartoons. Providing entertainment for local villagers was not what I planned, but I was pretty good at it.

The worst run-in I had with a roach was the fatty on my kitchen floor. I smacked it, then watched in horror as a host of white worms started dancing the hula out of its guts! Like a disturbed nest of baby snakes the white strands reached nearly two inches, waving around looking for something else to devour. My stomach convulsed and my appetite was in revolt for some time after that.

There were other times a flyswatter or thong were inadequate weaponry, even in the relative safety of my kitchen. I was kneading bread one morning when I sensed a shadow hovering over me. Glancing up I saw a black snake reaching toward my head right out of the rafters! I dropped the bread and screamed, "Frank! *Haiku hainani! Mapu! Mapu!*" [Get the bush knife! Snake! Snake!] Of course, he came running to do the honors for this maiden in distress, *again*.

The director's wife was right. I really was a spoiled American. I had to get tough! Even our winter-white skin had to toughen up. Being unaccustomed to bug-bites, our bodies reacted vigorously. Riddled with infections and rashes and being the size of a small cow made me uncomfortable in those early days. Turns out, jungle camp was a piece of cake compared to this.

Daily routines revolved around little things such as treating sores: heating water to soak in salt baths, tapping antibiotic powder into every sore, and bandaging with gauze to keep flies at bay. The kids developed itchy prickly heat collars that I smeared with Desitin ointment and baby powder. I had it on my neck, forearms and stomach, and taking a few showers a day helped cool down.

110

Bigger concerns were fungus, ringworm and diarrhea. Soon after moving into the tribe, Jesse was sick for the first two months and I had to boil all our drinking water. Worst of all was watching our kids shake with fever, chills, and throwing up from repeated attacks of malaria parasites delivered by countless unstoppable mosquitoes.

My kids rotated in three-week cycles with attacks, one right after the other. All we could do was hold the bucket, sponge their foreheads, and pray. *Oh Lord, how much of this can their little bodies handle?* In time, our bodies adapted quite well and all that diminished, thank God!

Of course, we weren't just there to fend for ourselves. We had villagers with similar woes and treated "standard" infirmary issues like burns, pneumonia, infections and assorted wounds. A regular flow of ringworm and malaria came to the door, too.

Then there were the unordinary issues such as machete gashes, children with detached fingers after playing with a knife, or split toes from an axe. With limited resources and training, prayer and a call for evacuation was sometimes the best we could offer.

One of the worst things I saw was a young man carried to our door after falling out of a tree impaled, with the jagged branch protruding from his neck! How they hacked that man free and carried him two hours without killing him was as astounding as the ghastly sight of the branch going into his armpit and coming out beside his head. He waited hours for a plane and two days to see a doctor, but amazingly, he survived. We have no idea how much tribal people endure without so much as an aspirin for pain.

Life was full of surprise and mystery, and the daily demands constantly cast us on the Lord for strength and wisdom. One night we heard strange crying like the sound of a banchie in the rain. We strained to identify its muted howls. What kind of creature is it?

I remembered a night in jungle camp hearing a mouse being eaten by a snake in the wood pile, and guessed this to be a *kapuli* [tree possum] in the clutches of a python. Frank checked under the house with a torch and couldn't see anything, but it continued howling, crying in the wind.

Frank went out again with an umbrella and hunted until he traced the sound to the garbage pit where we buried tins and non-burnables on the side of the hill. Imagine his surprise when he shone the light through the tiny doorway and saw the frightened eyes of a naked little boy!

Neno Whai was a deaf mute who loved fishing shiny treasures out of the pit and waving them around in the reflected sunlight. How long had he been in there? How did he manage not to cut his bare feet and legs in that heap of broken glass and jagged aluminum? Frank lifted him out and brought him home safe and sound to his anxious father.

As I thought about that, I realized a wonderful illustration of Jesus seeking us out of the refuse of this world. That boy was enticed to his doom chasing so many shiny things when he fell into the trap. Incapable of "saving himself," he was found and rescued from the pit by the long arm of a savior who carried him to his father. Then the happy ending of the story is when his father threw his arms around him... even though he smelled like garbage.

Our Father loves the lost and is waiting for them to be brought safely home, which is why He sent us to May River.

Before that could happen, we had a lot to learn.

15. Snakes, Quakes and Other Things

Life slowed and focus narrowed. No phones, TV, restaurants or movies to divert your attention. No stores, schools, churches or doctors to share the load; just us in our little black shanty, and our partners across the yard.

Our time zone was fourteen hours and about six months from the rest of the planet. That's how long it took to send a little blue air gram to the States and back, or to process film in Hong Kong. I felt more isolated than ever, living at the ends of the earth.

It's not just what we did, but how we had to do it that required such adjustments. A simple task like food shopping required a small army of buyers, shippers and aviators. Several families combined efforts to fill a plane with 450kg, or nearly 1000 pounds of cargo. I had to learn to order in bulk and make everything last, averaging one flight in about two months.

The key factor in the whole process was timing. Orders went out on one plane, then allowing several weeks for purchases and available cargo space, returned on a later flight. In cases of prolonged floods in about six high water seasons per year, we could arrange an air drop and hope the packets wouldn't explode on impact or get lost in the swamp somewhere. Or, we could always hike out to a neighboring tribe.

Hiking was a breath-taking adventure through the wilds of virgin jungle. The nearest airstrip involved two or three hours by boat followed by several more hours on the "trails." We'd hike over rocky sandbars, ease by thorny hanging vines, or balance like barefoot trapeze artists across slippery log crossings. In one place I grabbed onto roots as the trail tipped sideways or trekked down into pools of foot-sucking slime and emerged with leeches streaked across my legs like long lines drawn by a black marker. The hardest place for me was wading through waist-high rushing water clutching the kids with a death grip.

Usually, it was peaceful listening to the wild bird calls high up in the trees. We'd dream about stopping to eat and drool over flavors of ice cream. Our feet tired and backs ached, and all the while we knew the same ground we covered in eight hours could have been glided over in ten minutes by plane!

Thank God for the aviators. When the airstrip was dry, we'd count the days until our Sepik pilot would sneak up behind the mountain, appearing with a roar over the roof to give us a thrill, sending a host of unwanted critters scampering out of the thatch. His 'buzz' was like a superhero sighting and school would recess so everyone could run outside to wave. It's a bird! It's a plane! It's Dave Rowe our hero pilot!

We had the highest respect and admiration for our Aussie pilot Dave. He entered a flight contest in America just for fun one furlough. Pilots competed by flying loops over a target, tossing a roll of toilet paper out the window and seeing who could splice it with a wingtip the most times. Our pilot won hands down, slicing the long white ribbon seven times before it hit the ground! He was Superman to us, able to "save the day" on every appearing, bringing much needed supplies, mail, visitors, or kids home from school. It felt like a holiday whenever he arrived, and then we'd feast on fresh food for dinner.

Of course we tried to get food from the locals, but that was sporadic at best. Bananas were most plentiful. There were several types, but we usually bought the small sweet *susu yano* (milk white inside) and the long familiar yellow brand known as "China" bananas. I'd pay the equivalent of ten cents per "hand" and a full stalk would have about ten hands or bunches. Hanging from a looped rope over the rafter on our porch, villagers, parrots, and even fruit bats helped themselves to the ever-present stalk by the front door.

Occasionally someone would have a surplus of *nesu* (fish) and sell us a few of their catch, or they might spear a wild boar and bring us *hu kap* (pig meat). In low-water, we'd buy *hamsu* (crayfish) and save them for a battered shrimp dinner. On occasion we could get a strip of *ai* (croc tail), quite possibly the best white meat ever.

114

In season, I collected a type of spinach we called *aupa*, which was excellent. Local women brought button mushrooms, limes, or eggs from the little chickens assigned to damage control on the village insect population.

Some foods just seemed better out in the elements, like *kulau* (green coconut) cut in the heat of day and sloshed into your thirsty mouth out on the river; or *pitpit* which grew along the river's edge and waved their stalks like ladies dancing with white feathery plumes. It's beautiful for the eyes, but the long pithy fruit is bland and dry.

Am (breadfruit) on the other hand, is especially suited to roasting in an open fire. You splice the melon-sized fruit open and pick about twenty baked seeds from the pulp. Dipped in salt on a banana leaf they taste like little baked potatoes or soft Spanish peanuts. Perfect for river trips!

One Sunday after *lotu* (church) Frank's informant joined us for a family day on the sandbar in low water season. We built a huge fire out of driftwood on our 'private beach' and the kids were enjoying breadfruit and smoked fish on banana leaf dishes. Tomas dove down in the brown river and surprised us when he came up with a big snapping turtle.

My son was in the middle of asking if he could keep it as a pet, but Tomas had just one thing in mind. "I'll show you what you do with this," he said. Before we knew it, he flipped it onto the hot coals! Its legs paddled wildly but within seconds it was too hot for anything but our dinner plates. Poor Jesse was horrified!

"Don't worry kids," Frank said. "He's gone to turtle heaven now."

Then Tomas cracked it open with a swing of his machete. "Look at this! *He* was a mommy!" he said happily, adding ten cooked eggs to the menu. Getting past the fact that a potential pet had landed on our plates, the meat was delicious and tasted like lean veal.

Pwi (sugar cane) was another picnic favorite. Instead of decaying your teeth, chewing the barky stalks cleans your teeth and massages your gums while you're refreshed with sweet juice. All you need is a bush knife to hack the stalks and strip some of the outer bark and the rest you can do with your teeth. Afterwards, you toss the scraps and peelings in the river. No fuss, no muss!

I couldn't stomach all the native foods. Taro soup made from the large white root and greens was a favorite, but I usually suggested their kids would enjoy the fat sago grubs, crayfish legs, heads, eyeballs and anything that was still wiggling more than me. Come to think of it, they didn't like all our food either. One girl tried a tomato and threw up under the kitchen table! Imagine that.

As much as I avoided certain village entrees, there were some I craved, like red papaya. Try to imagine a peachy plum cantaloupe the size of a loaf of bread. A bowl of ripe papaya covered with homemade yogurt and a slice of fresh bread with Vegemite is a perfect breakfast. Vegemite is an Australian yeast extract used like peanut butter and I miss it terribly!

Whenever we visited the coast or the Highlands, there were some exotic savories we would rush to buy like tree tomatoes (tamarillo), and *galip* nuts, and my mouth is watering just thinking about them. Tree tomatoes are a cross between a tomato and passion fruit. You cut them in half and scoop out the succulent red insides with a spoon, seeds and all, like kiwi. *Galip* nuts are like big roasted pistachios.

I was convinced there were wonderful varieties of buttery cashews and delectable edibles growing in the bush, so I challenged people to bring me new foods. One day, my literacy helper Jackson showed up with a bag of nuts for me. "It took me weeks to find these," he said. "Just be sure to cook them for a long time first."

How can I foul up such a simple recipe? I boiled them all day until they were soft as little white potatoes, then salted and dry roasted them in our propane oven for hours. Frank and I sampled a few and waited to see if we'd suffer any allergic reaction. Nothing. An hour later, nothing. Our stomachs were fine, so we ate some more. They were delicious! We went to bed talking about how this new discovery would add protein to our diet and generate income for the people, but we spoke too soon.

The next morning, I woke up with my eyes swollen shut, and I was covered with red patches of itchy bumps like poison ivy!

"Sori tru, sori tru," (we're so sorry) everyone said. Some were afraid I'd suspect deliberate poisoning, stirring innate fears of pay-back, but once assured I meant no harm, Jackson came to see me. "Oh, *Kaden,*" which is the best he could pronounce my name, "you better stick to the prying weel from now on." He knew that the Chinese nuts we bought in tins were called "Flying Wheel Peanuts."

Besides an interest in sampling native foods, we acquired a hodgepodge of living creatures. We had dogs, outside cats for the rat population, an assortment of parrots, cockatiels, a *kapuli* and a white owl on occasion. The boys even brought a baby crocodile home and put him in the washing machine to keep, but that's where I drew the line. "No way, I'm NOT feeding a crocodile!"

"Awww, Mom!"

Our family favorite was a white lab named Daisy, a loyal companion for years. Oddly, every time she had puppies there were always ten, all black, and her little flock followed at her heels like a cloud of exhaust.

I was especially fond of a rainbow parrot we named Rambo. He actually lived outside but followed us faithfully. Every time the front door opened, he came in to eat bananas and when I walked outside, he swooped down out of the trees to ride on my shoulder and chatter. He played with my dangling earrings and licked the salt off my cheek.

Rambo would lie on his back and play soccer with his feet! He was not only more playful than I ever realized a bird could be, but incredibly intelligent. When we were in the school room singing or laughing, he would land on the screen window and mimic our sounds, cackling and crowing in perfect sync. Some kids had a lamb follow them to school. We had Rambo!

Home school provided a nice routine and learning environment for the kids. They just hopped out of bed in the morning, ate breakfast and came to our schoolroom at 8:00. They had the added benefit of learning from one another's materials in our one-room schoolhouse, which may explain why they were all reading at three and four. I loved it. No bullies, no buses, no peer pressure at recess.

The greatest challenges were faced outside our schoolroom, and I have nightmare memories that still make my blood run cold.

One time over the holidays, Frank's folks were visiting and we went tubing down the river in a nearby tribe. Two passengers per tractor tire, and I had a baby nestled in my arms. We set out to float around the end of the airstrip in what was to be a restful drift of about fifteen minutes. The water was only four feet deep, but it rained the night before so the current was faster than usual.

We spread out in the current, bumping into rocks and spinning gently as our friends waved from the riverbank. Then as we approached the bend, the current picked up. Frank's Dad bumped a rock and five-year-old Naomi bounced right off his lap! We were all frozen at a distance that couldn't be bridged as the current carried us faster around the bend.

I tried paddling, but with a baby on my lap it was useless and I panicked. Naomi's wide eyes were facing me as she gulped water, frantically trying to swim, but being pulled under. *Jesus! Save Naomi!*

I'll never know how, but our dear friend Ed saw it and miraculously reached her in time. When we climbed up on the stony beach I couldn't stop shaking. I very nearly watched my beautiful daughter drown right before my eyes, a living nightmare in slow motion, but thank God for the saving arms that lifted her above the tide!

Another time Jesse was climbing the stairs to our loft at about three years old. He fell over the edge and landed in the fetal position with his temple smacking the hardwood floor.

"I can't see! I can't see!" he kept saying. Is it possible to hit your temple so hard you do damage to optical nerves or cause a brain bleed behind your eyes? I carried him to the couch.

Dear God, please save his eyesight! I put a cold cloth on his head and ran to the radio. "Break, break! This is a medical emergency. Is there a doctor or nurse on the air?" Barb, an RN with the most reassuring phone presence, *just happened* to turn on her radio. Others started praying and he fully recovered from the concussion, with perfect vision.

There were dare-devil feats and frantic moments. Visions of such stories could keep me awake at night, but provided plenty of opportunities to thank God for His protection. I know the Lord rescued us from many dangers.

We also had a lot of free entertainment to liven things up. I still laugh when I think about the night I was proudly retrieving a pumpkin pie from the oven. Someone opened the back door and a fruit bat darted into the kitchen and started flitting from room to room. We ran around swinging rackets and brooms, nearly whacking each other and endangering the kero lamps in our mad attempts to get it.

Finally someone smacked him and we all watched, horrified, as he did a nosedive landing spread-eagle into my fresh pumpkin pie! Since fruit bats are notoriously smeared in feces, that pie was tossed to the dogs despite its rare and coveted ingredients. It's hilarious, now!

So were the flying ants. They'd swarm in and we'd arm ourselves with fly swatters and brooms for an impromptu indoor Superbowl. Afterwards, I'd sweep up big piles of dead bugs, the majority having flown kamikaze-style directly into kero lamps and lanterns.

At times it felt like life was a battle against the elements in a constant stream of rodents, bats and insects—but all these were nothing compared to snakes. One night, my fleet-footed husband opened the back door of the kitchen to run up to his office, and, "Whoaaaa!" leaped over a thick black fire hose draped over the plank step.

That python measured six inches thick and twelve feet long, its head and tail extending under our kitchen and along the rain ditch—and our kids were lying in their beds just a few feet away!

Frank put the torch in my hands. "Here. Hold this on him! I'll get my bush knife."

"Uh, Frank? What do I do if he—" but he was gone.

To this day, the thought of standing in the dark grass in bare feet with nothing but a flashlight between me and that slippery monster, still gives me the heebie jeebies. I prayed vigorously as sweat trickled all the way to my ankles in a stare-down with Goliath.

I hoped my beacon light wouldn't provoke him like one of Becky's stories. Sitting in the bathroom with a torch in hand one night, she had heard a rustling sound above her. Sure enough, a black rat appeared and she kept her light on him, afraid to move.

"I thought I blinded him," she said, but the rat did the unthinkable and dove straight at her! Flying through the air like a ninja to attack the light of her torch, he landed directly in her lap and her screams filled the night air of the village.

Now, standing in the dark grass holding my torch on a far more formidable enemy, I hoped he wouldn't have the same reaction to my light. But Frank ran back with a big bush knife and attacked it before that could happen. *My champion!* What we didn't know is that the rest of the family would show up looking for him!

"How *big* do these things get?" I asked, after we measured the next one at a full thirteen feet.

"I hope we never find out!" he said, but we knew size isn't everything in the realm of deadly snakes. The bite of a two-foot adder can kill you in ninety seconds, for example. Some call it the "two-step snake," because they say that's all you get if you're bitten. Again, we hoped we'd never find out.

One day, Naomi and Jesse were walking down the trail to 'deliver mail' to our partners together. Naomi stopped to check on her little brother. "Come on Jesse!" His eyes got as big as breadfruit as he pointed to the ground behind her feet.

"Snake!"

A golden brown death adder lay sunning himself on the trail. Just one more step and our beautiful daughter might never have made it home.

The tribal women dreaded snakes as much as me. They wouldn't even come near the carcass to admire the results of our prowess on the grass the next day. I expected them to walk up and whack it with their bush knife or spit over it in disgust, but these hearty souls would scream and climb straight up a tree! Must go back to that Eden thing, when God said he would put enmity between the woman and the snake,[53] but God is always stronger.

Soon after arriving in the tribe, I made this entry in my journal... *The day started out with a bang at 5:30 this morning and sent us scrambling to grab the kids. It sounded like sonic jets zooming overhead and the earth was still trembling as we huddled together. Cans fell off the pantry shelves, furniture shifted, and the whole house was shaking on its posts. A coworker's water tank crashed to the ground and water pipes split. In the cities, damage to stores and streets was reported. That quake measured 6.8 on the Richter scale. Psalm 46, 121*

We got used to sonic rumbles, but I hated to think about a roof rafter breaking loose and falling on the kids. So the drill was to run outside until the earthly whiplash finished. Usually, the house shook for a few minutes, water sloshed out of the tank, and trees fell in the river, and minutes later it looked like nothing happened. Once we were walking up the airstrip when a big one

---

[53] Genesis 3:15

120

hit, and with that vantage point over such a wide stretch of cleared land, we could see the ground rolling toward us like waves.

In just a few years we had 18 big ones between 6.8 and 8.0 on the Richter scale—not including tremors! Considering a 7.0 is the equivalent of the largest thermonuclear weapon known to man,[54] and an 8.0 is ten times bigger than that, this was another area to lean on God.

Every fearful challenge and awkward adjustment on the road to becoming river rats stretched our faith and reminded us who's in control. Whenever we felt the rumblings beneath our feet, it was good to remember, *"The Lord will keep you from all harm—he will watch over your life; the Lord will watch over your coming and going..."*[55]

---

[54]http://earthquake.usgs.gov and http://www.geophysik.uni-muenchen.de/~igel/downloads/seditectonics.pdf
[55] Psalm 121:7-8

16. Jungle Madness

"Don't look in that freezer," the shopkeeper advised in a hushed tone.

"Why? What's in there?" Frank asked.

"Brain," he whispered. "And a heart."

"*Bilong man?*" we asked in unison. Human?

"*Em nau, pasin bilong graun,*" meaning, that's it, sorcery or witchcraft. We knew it was widely practiced, but didn't expect to find it the meat section of our supermarket! Frank got him to show us—you know, just to be sure we didn't take the wrong thing. That same curiosity may have been what got my little boy in trouble.

In our tribe, it was believed that if a child fell down he'd lose his spirit and a specific ritual was required to guide his spirit back into his body. One time this spirit ceremony was being performed right next to our house. The shaman asked us not to go outside or even look out the window or we would disrupt the ceremony, but my three-year-old son peeked.

That night, he woke up crying. "The red king is coming to get me! The red king!" he cried. A dark figure with red eyes had appeared in his room and he wouldn't settle down until we prayed together, assuring him that Jesus is stronger than any other king.

I don't profess to fully understand the workings of the spirit world, but the Bible openly discusses angels and demons, and Jesus and his disciples drove evil spirits out regularly. In fact, when they were unsuccessful, they asked Jesus what was wrong.[56]

Curiously, our people's rituals wouldn't work if we were present (a little fact that should have brought them in droves to the Lord for protection), but I also witnessed men possessed when the

---

[56] Matthew 17:14-22 and Mark 9:14-29

whole house shook and their voices changed. I was just sitting around in ignorance most of the time.

One afternoon I sat on a log in a distant village with an old woman, and asked if she was married. "Oh," she nodded, fumbling in her *bilum*. Assuming she was fishing for her tobacco tin, I continued with polite American conversation inquiring about the family, the kids—all the proper introductory chatter. "Is your husband here?"

Producing a full human skull out of the clutter she thrust it in front of my face. *"Kani kam siren!"* [My husband indeed!] She smiled with her dark eyes and bright red teeth. She spat a juicy wad of betel nut juice on the ground and looked at me as if she had handed me his photograph. In her 'frame of reference,' she had.

"Oh, I see!" I stammered, wondering what Emily Post would offer as proper etiquette when being introduced to someone's skeletal remains. Do you pat his head? Admire the shape of it? You can't shake hands, although many women preserve the memory of children by wearing their severed fingers around their necks like a beaded necklace. Perhaps you could shake hands in that case. That seems gruesome, especially the acquisition of such a memento, yet I can appreciate a mother's desire to keep her children close to her heart forever.

When I'd ask women about their children, they'd start counting backwards. Holding their pinky finger down in a closed fist for number one, they'd grunt, *"Mmmm,* this one died." Then they'd clasp their ring finger and hold it down, "This one is over there." Then to the middle finger, "this one died, this one died," and on it would go as I wondered how much pain one woman can endure.

Infant mortality explains why children aren't named until weaned. It's believed they don't even have a spirit until then. Since ancestral names are protected to be summoned for their powers, they preferred taking our 'impotent' names for their kids. Consequently, we had miniature versions of *Pren Lo, Kaden Lo,* (Frank and Karen Low) and all our kids running around in the villages.

Village kids are named late and aged quickly. I was amazed to see little girls married at eleven or twelve, have babies, and turn into women overnight. They led such hard lives. If anyone asks,

"Why don't you leave them alone? They're happy as they are," we would try to enlighten them with the harsh realities.

Women are treated like property, like pigs or dogs that have no rights. I never understood how they could even endure their own wedding. After a bride price is decided, (usually a combination of dog's teeth, shell necklaces, pig tusks, and currency), she's taken by her brothers to be delivered to her new family, but the entourage is ambushed along the river so relatives can stage a tug of war over her.

The husband's family tugs the new bride into their canoe to be taken to her waiting husband, while the bride's family holds out for more money. The poor girl's arms practically tear from the sockets. Throwing rice or blowing bubbles seems so much nicer.

I struggled to understand a lot of things and language learning was exhausting. The rigors of daily life sapped my energy leaving limited resources to grapple with so many inexplicable riddles. The task surpasses mere academic challenges such as learning physics at sixteen. At least Northeastern University offered text books and professors to outline the formulas, but tribal jargon taxed my brain without rules or dictionaries to fall back on.

Particular linguistic challenges included five counting systems. Whether male or female, small round, long abstract, flat or large items such as talk, there are different terms. It sounds easy at first, but I stumbled regularly, even over something as simple as, "a fence." I tried the flat term used for counting leaves or money, but was laughed at. "Why?" I asked. "Isn't the fence flat like your hand?"

"Oh no," my friend howled at my preposterous notions. "A fence is round. It has to circle the garden so the pigs can't get in and eat everything!" Silly me.

Another hurdle was directional markers. You can't simply say, "I'm going." You have to specify whether you're going uphill or down, with the current or against it, in addition to the usual plurals and tenses. Even toddlers in the village spoke circles around me.

Familiar cultural cues were also absent. If someone shakes their head up and down and says "no," or wags their head back and forth and says, "yes," which is it? If they look at the ground instead of answering, what does that tell you? Or if someone stamps their foot a few times while you're talking, is that significant, or is a horsefly chewing their ankle?

What if an airstrip is closed due to sorcery? Missionary life is full of such unpredictability and what-do-we-do-now circumstances, like the time we were flying home from meetings with a plane full of cargo and discovered our airstrip had been transformed into a 2,000 foot swimming pool from flooding. We had to divert to another tribe and start hiking.

In the midst of such undecipherable and uncertain happenings I often felt confused, anxious, or unsettled. This sense of awkwardness is *culture shock,* a familiar term in this age of global travel, but about as comfortable as hypothermia.

Think of it like waking up to a big bang followed by bright flashing lights and dogs barking. You're on high alert, straining to hear, and more anxious to understand what's going on than if you woke up naturally in a calm familiar environment. Your senses are in overdrive to decipher your surroundings.

What's this mean? Did I do something wrong? Are these people mad at me? You're shaky and unsure of yourself, like a blind tight-rope walker without a balancing beam because all your norms and cues have vanished.

"Jungle madness is setting in!" we'd say.

One troubling aspect of village life that accentuated early culture shock was begging. Some days the constant trickle of people asking for handouts left me feeling like I was running a dispensary. I wanted to be generous, but how much can we do?

As a suburban girl, I'd been accustomed to having a car parked in the driveway and a metropolis of malls to go to. Now, month after month, I was stationed at the top of the trail with people coming and going to the door asking for food, soap, matches, medicine... I had virtually *become* a mall where people shopped for specials! And if you give to one, how can you refuse the next?

I was conflicted. Compared to the village people, we were millionaires, but we were sorely outnumbered. Sometimes, though I had what someone wanted, I didn't *want to* give it away and rebelled, obsessing over precedents.

126

One night, I was listening to Keith Green sing, "Jesus came to your door, but you've left him out on the street..."[57] and I broke down confessing a hard heart and asking God for a fresh dose of compassion. Frank read the passage about the unjust servant and using our worldly goods to win people rather than create barriers.[58] *Oh Lord, keep my heart tender.*

At 7 a.m. the next morning a weeping woman arrived from downriver with two little kids. Her house burned down in the night and she didn't know where else to turn. To my shame, my first thought was, *Oh brother, now we're going to become the home insurance company too?*

I was already imagining how people would start burning down houses just to "collect" new goods from yours truly! Then I remembered my prayer from the night before. *Oh Lord, I'm sorry! I asked you to melt me with your compassion and now I'm hardening my heart again just a few hours later! Help me find things to help this woman.*

The more I looked, the more I found to give her and her kids, and with such joy that I was singing all day! I gathered clothes, towels, kitchenware, sleeping mats, linens, fish hooks, soap and food. God used that situation as a test of obedience, to *open my hand* and bless me. And here's the clincher, *no one else* ever came to "collect."

I felt culture shock when I recorded my first *singsing* like a rookie journalist at a tribal dance ...

The people prepared for days—women made grass skirts and ornaments, and men made elaborate headbands and armbands of feathers and shells. Preparations were extensive.

On the big night, bats swooped over the river darting back and forth around our boat. Shrimp were jumping out of the water on the sandbar, and the screeching sounds of the night added to my suspense. I had never been on the river at night and nervously scanned the darkness for the red eyes of the crocs or anything else that moved in the shadows.

Something was wrong with our motor and we drifted in silence, but we were at least floating in the right direction. (Getting home will be a lot harder if it won't start again!) By the

---

[57] Keith Green song, *Asleep in the Light*
[58] Luke 16:8-9

time we arrived, the men were getting dressed and painted. I wasn't sure if I'd be allowed down the trail (tribal women were waiting in canoes), but I was waved on to witness this magical world. Shrouded by a thick evening mist, we crept down those dusky trails, then crouched in the grass with the crickets feeling like an intruder in an ancient world.

Their headdresses were made of white feathers and shells with fur caps on some. Chest decorations were made of sewn shells in bands, criss-crossed around their shoulders, and some hanging around the neck. Faces were painted red and black in varying designs. Some had bones in their noses; the curled pig tusks hanging down over their mouths making them look fierce like tribal warriors. Many had green and white striped fern leaves hanging alongside of their faces and over the ears.

On their backs were large ornaments made of bird beaks, orange fruit, striped leaves, and straw skirts hanging underneath, swaying from side to side. They were straw colored, with the mud-red dyed stripes. Most of the men wore straw leg bands with red painted calves. As the sky grew darker, all you could see was these outer ornaments and the whites of their eyes and teeth gleaming in the shadows.

I recognized my worker, Noani, being decorated by his father and the look of pride when he was waved in to join the big men. Then they broke out into a spontaneous dress rehearsal on the banks of the river, the sounds of their chanting rang into the clear night air. This is the real Papua New Guinea, I thought.

Darkness was setting in, so we quickly returned to the boats and paddled downriver to the appointed village. We climbed a steep muddy bank as a host of silent canoes floated to the water's edge, rows and rows of them filled with men and boys, women and babies—all in complete solemn silence. Many were smoking, their dark faces lit with a faint red glow.

Canoes maneuvered smoothly into place side by side, then everyone climbed the bank, and we followed respectfully up the carved log "stairs" into the longhouse. Gathering together with their backs toward us, the men began a variety of chants and dances to the shouts of the Tultul [village chief]. First, a shuffle of feet, then a clanging of shells, and then a series of shouts—all to the rhythmic commands of the leader.

The big room was dimly lit and filled with smoke. We chose the side where the lantern hung. My eyes struggled to adjust to the flickering light, then I realized I was sitting beside a woman I had visited after she had her baby, presenting one of Jesse's shirts as a gift. Keymi started talking to me right away but of course I couldn't understand a word, so we just smiled and clasped hands.

As the singsing got underway, the men's voices grew louder. Young boys danced in the center of a ring of men, stomping up and down the length of the whole house over and over carrying decorated spears. The whole house rocked on its stilts with the weight of their procession and the bamboo slats on the floor bounced under their pounding feet.

I swatted a multitude of mosquitoes while a host of questions nagged my mind. Who is this for? What are they hoping to achieve? Are they summoning spirits or appeasing the evil one to fight sickness and prosper their gardens? Is this merely a display of sexual prowess and a celebration of male strength?

The monotonous ritual of waving tobacco, betel pepper and leaves, chanting and whistling, would continue all night long but after a few hours, we stole away with our torches [flashlights]. Picking our way carefully down the muddy slope into the boat, we found it filling with water. Someone apparently pulled the plug— who would do that to us? We had to start bailing fast. Good thing we left when we did or we would have been sunk!

Thank God the motor started.

We rode home on a liquid black road with no lanes, reflectors, or signs, straining our eyes to avoid logs and debris on the surface. We left the sound of drums and chanting behind us, but came away with a challenge to understand Iwam culture.

I subconsciously expected people to adhere to certain "civil behaviors," based on my ingrained ethics. We're supposed to wait in lines, take turns, give preference to women and children, and other "common" courtesies, right? When violated, the hair stands up on the nape of my neck.

We inevitably regard our surroundings in light of our own ideals and contrasts create chaffing discomfort, such as when I realized the Iwam people didn't have a word for 'please' or 'thank you.' It was unsettling to hand someone a gift and watch them take it and walk away; surprisingly difficult to tolerate the absence of "simple" courtesies, even fifteen thousand miles from home.

Of course, they had as much trouble understanding us as we did them, and in our ignorance we blew it on many occasions, like when we visited Aussie friends in a nearby tribe. We only had to navigate a tributary for a few hours. "Be sure to bring a rifle," friends advised. "Wild turkey are real good eating if you see any!" So we packed the gun, the dog, and hopes of getting some wild game on the way.

We were without compass, maps, or radio—just us idiots in the wilds of New Guinea winging it for adventure. Naturally, after a few hours, we were lost. The river twisted and turned so much it was like riding the backs of spaghetti noodles and every bend looked exactly like the last. "How will we ever get out of here?" I moaned.

Ever the fearless leader, Frank said, "Don't worry honey. All we have to do is cut the motor and drift back to the May."

Our little tributary narrowed to about fifteen feet and the water was so black we couldn't see the bottom. Every turn kept us on the edge of our seat because we never knew when we'd hit a logjam and Frank would have to quickly cut the motor and hoist the prop shaft out of the water to avoid shearing pins.

We'd either rev that motor and jump it (an art which the guys learned spending time in the river rat school of hard knocks), or unload everything on the bank and push the boat around. Sometimes, the only way through was to get out a chain saw and start sawing our way through while mosquitoes settled in for a lunch of ankles a la elbow.

Suddenly, Frank cut the motor and stood straight up. "Look!" A flock of fat gray and white birds sat on the water ahead of us. "What the heck are those?" Frank asked.

"Well, I'm just a city girl, but they look like wild turkeys to me!"

That's all Frank needed to hear. "Everyone be still," he shushed, loading the rifle. *Bang! Bang! Bang!* Shotgun shells exploded around our heads, followed by squawking and a flurry of feathers. We bagged a 10kg bird[59] into our boat and Frank hastened the poor guy out of his misery with the butt of his gun.

---

[59] 22 pounds

130

"Don't worry, that's just life in the jungle." He was busting with pride. "We'll be bringing home the bacon tonight!"

Naomi and I tried to ignore the bloody mess at our feet as the poor thing quivered in the waning moments of its life. "How much longer till we get there?" I asked.

Right on cue, we heard voices coming through the dense jungle. Native people appeared chattering excitedly in an unknown language. Women in black grass skirts and children lined up on the riverbank. Voices called through the thick of the trees and we knew we must be near a village. When the men arrived, things grew tense.

"Maybe they've never seen white people before," I said.

"Nah, they just heard the gun and came to see what we shot." Frank assured them in Pidgin, *"Wei! No ken wari. Mi sutim wanpela pisin tasol. Na mipela painim ples bilong Masta Dug."* (Don't worry, I just shot a bird. We're looking for the village of Mr. Doug.)

The people were clearly agitated, pointing at the bird and our smoking gun. *Have these people ever seen a gun before?* Thank God an Aussie appeared on the far riverbank and we realized we had made it to the right place. It was Doug!

"What have you done, you duffers?" he hollered with his hands on his hips.

"We shot a wild turkey for dinner!" Frank said, holding it up proudly.

"No you didn't, mate!" Doug bellowed. "That's Tultul's prize domestic duck!" Now we were horrified. Not only had we killed someone's prize pet, but it was *whose* pet that made it worse. *Tultul* means village chief.

We city slickers didn't know the difference between a wild turkey and a domestic duck! The only ducks we'd ever seen were the scrawny teal mallards in the Boston Gardens or the skinny black ducks at May River. I never knew a duck could stand two feet tall or wear sporty red gobblers under its beak, but we never lived it down.

We brought home the bacon that night alright—for the chief! We had the pleasure of paying for it and he had the pleasure of eating his prize. It was a lesson in swallowing our pride rather than a roast turkey dinner.

17. Babies, Backs and Us

The Iwam newlyweds were scared to death as our plane took off—they didn't have a clue what lay beyond May River. The rivers coiled beneath us and the mountains grew bigger. Then we landed where the air was colder than they ever imagined possible. There were hard black roads, loud trucks, strange creatures called horses, and people of different colors. The deep black skin of the Buka islanders and the lighter red skin tribes intermingled with Papuans, Europeans and Asians. Beaded blue tattoos around people's eyes and bodies, bilums and armbands bore the mark of foreign clans among whom we now walked. Enemy clans!

We had invited Benjamin and Yaku to join us in the Highlands for a working vacation. With their help we could keep plugging away at language study while awaiting the birth of our third child.

In one sense, it was a chance for our informants to 'see the world' and get a break from pounding sago. Here, Yaku cooked rice and fresh market veggies, and enjoyed an 'endless supply' of fish. Yet, this was a world fraught with strange fears.

They wore socks and slept in a bed covered with blankets but the air got so cold even mosquitoes died! And who in their right mind would build houses with stone floors (concrete) that sit on the cold ground anyway? Even worse, why would we use glass windows so the spirits could watch us sleep?

They missed the familiar sway of bamboo floors, the safe height of their "tree houses" in the rainforest, the crackling fire, and the soothing sound of the river. Instead, they were wakened many times through the long night by the frightful roar of diesel trucks rumbling down the highway full of howling strangers!

For Benjamin, the work seemed easy at first. He didn't have to bear the heat of the sun working with Frank. All he had to do was sit at a table and answer questions. Yet, as the weeks wore on, his muscles ached and his mind struggled to stay on task. Combing through Frank's endless stack of index cards with a tape recorder teaching a white man to talk isn't as easy as it looks.

Meanwhile, Yaku helped me with housework and language study. One phrase I should have learned right off the bat is, "Help me! I'm going to die!"

One morning, Yaku carried a basket of laundry outside and started screaming bloody murder. I found her running frantically around the house next door with a longhorn steer stampeding around the yard! She must have thought him a monster spirit trying to devour her. In her frenzy, she couldn't find the front door since these crazy white men's houses don't offer the safety of a proper log stairway. The poor girl ran around in circles looking for something to climb.

"Here, here!" I called, and she bee-lined toward me and scrambled inside, grateful to be inside, but ready to go home. So, my language learning was put on hold awhile, but it was God's timing. Three days later, I went into labor.

Friends stayed with our kids and Frank ran for a rental van for a fast ride to the Highlands *haus sik* [hospital]. It seemed I no sooner showered and put on a gown, when our second son arrived naturally at the stroke of midnight, September 21, 1980.

Frank chose a fitting name, Isaac Daniel. *Yitzak* meaning laughter and *Daniel,* God is my judge. We remembered how I thought this pregnancy was poorly timed, but this child has been a joyful reminder that God knows best.

Our family was now complete and we were overjoyed. We had Naomi our *pleasant faith* in Bible School, Jesse *our beloved gift* in Language School, and now Isaac, *the joy of knowing God knows best* in Papua New Guinea.

We returned to the tribe with a three-week old eager to make up for lost time. Frank was going from sunup to sundown in tropical heat, racing toward the day he could start the "real work" of his dreams.

Progress wasn't going to go unchallenged however. Two weeks later, he was hit with mysterious pains that got so bad he couldn't walk. He flew out for minor surgery on an infected cyst and returned the next day to recuperate. I wish all of life's obstacles were so quickly hurdled.

Isaac was a good baby but I had no safe place to leave a sleeping infant while we worked. The bark slats of the old house floor didn't prevent creepy crawlies from coming in and the new house was a construction site, so I adopted the habit of carrying him in a cloth pouch strapped around my waist. Sleeping and awake, he bounced around with me all day, wringer washing, baking bread, while reaching over his little head.

I hung mosquito nets from the rafters and served fourteen guests with him in tow the day Frank passed his first language check with flying colors. Then I fell into bed exhausted at 8 o'clock.

I awoke in the middle of the night with a pain like vice grips on my lower spine. Oh no, another freak infection? Frank had to tow me to the bathroom with my feet dragging the floor. Medical texts advised bed rest for severe back pain, but "if there is no improvement after two days, evacuate the patient." So we waited.

Becky had to take over with my kids and all the cooking, coming around the clock even in pouring rain to take my baby and give me shots of Demerol. "I can sleep tomorrow," she would say. Or, "What's a few days work for a friend?" God bless her. If only the meds were as effective as her kindness. Even with maximum doses of the most potent meds we had, it barely numbed the pain for an hour before the shooting knives kicked in and I'd start counting the minutes to the next shot.

After two days we called for my med-evac, wondering how we could afford yet another expensive flight. Travel would also be excruciating. "Why don't you take that old army cot?" Mom had said. "It might come in handy someday." That folding cot sailed around the globe in our crates and arrived just in time for my transport. They strapped me into this make-shift gurney and I held on for dear life.

Six inches of rain rendered our downhill trail a muddy slick. I was afraid I'd be tossed headfirst into the muck, but my eyes followed the wide feet of the village elders as they gripped ground without faltering. *"No ken wari misis, mipela holim strong,"* [Don't worry ma'am, we got you] they said. Even Frank, former gymnastic expert, slipped the whole way down, but managed to recover gracefully each time. "Whoa! This is slick!"

135

"Honey! Maybe you should just *slide* to the bottom so you don't drop the baby?" I pleaded nervously, but Isaac loved bouncing with his daddy on a giant slip and slide.

My carriers skillfully navigated every step so well it seemed I practically floated all the way to the river. Who would have guessed these "savage cannibals" could be so gentle? In fact, my 'pallbearers,' Kowi, Philip, Maum, Maikel, and Wankumsipi, rendered the smoothest segment of the entire journey. Tracing every movement from a horizontal angle, I reflected in silent gratitude, *these guys understand pain.*

The rest of the trip was tense and painful: into the boat, up the river, onto a rickety tractor bed, down the trail, and finally "laid to rest" to catch my breath at the airstrip house. For three agonizing hours I begged for injections, but they wanted to save it for the flight. Then, when our Aussie pilot landed, he said a big storm was rolling in from the north. "If we don't get off the ground in two minutes we'll be stuck here."

"What now?" I looked at Frank.

"Don't worry, we're going to make it honey," he said positively. "Let's go for it."

They yanked the seats out of the plane, and I was lifted on the sheets and twisted through the side door. Two-month old Isaac was tucked beside me, but I hurt too much to hold him. Our heroic pilot cranked that engine and deftly spun us around in the mud. "All clear!" Dave hollered, and seconds later we were airborne to outrun the storm.

It was sheer anguish lying on the floor in the turbulence. Every jolt sent shooting pains through my bones. With clenched teeth I cried, *Oh God, I want to die!*

In fact, I never really wanted to die before. Five years earlier I told God I *would* die for him, but it never occurred to me that I might actually *beg him* for it! Three days of pain and a few sleepless nights was all it took. *Take me home now!*

Just then, Dave hollered, "Hang on back there, Karen! There's an ambulance waiting for you!" *An ambulance!* The very thought of professional help gave me a needed surge of hope to get me through the landing.

"Where's that ambulance?" I asked eagerly as they set me on the tarmac with a jolt.

Frank nodded in the opposite direction with furrowed brows. A rather dubious flatbed truck stood nearby and a couple young men struggled with the stretcher.

"One, two, three!" and I was hoisted up, but the second I landed, the whole frame collapsed with me inside. "Ahhhhoooww!" I was sandwiched accordion style! It felt like my spinal column broke in half.

Frank saw the trouble right away. "You have to lock the legs in place," he said, saving me from further horror. As far as professional help was concerned, my hopes were dashed, but we'd heard about an American doctor in Kudjip. At the very least, a professional diagnosis could offer some peace of mind.

Another uncomfortable ride followed as our "ambulance" truck jostled over countless ruts on the mountain road to Kudjip. Frank stood beside me and tried to keep me from toppling over. I was finally carried into a small clinic hoping it would be my last move with pain. I would have rather welcomed the grim reaper with open arms than to be pushed flat against the cold steel of that x-ray table in twelve directions and told to hold still. The only thing that helped me endure was the hope that the *American* doctor could help me.

He knocked me out and manipulated my back while I enjoyed a few moments of sublime rest. The next thing I knew, Frank was calling my name. "Did it work?" But one twitch after regaining consciousness, I knew. The spasms were worse. How I wished I could have stayed in that euphoric state, or woken up in glory! Instead, I was still imprisoned in this miserable aching body. *What are you trying to do, Lord?*

The next day, the doctor tried manipulation again. I counted backwards from 100 to 97, then Frank's voice called me back from a beautiful dream—back to the biting pain where "hope deferred makes the heart sick."[60]

Five days later, the American doctor admitted he couldn't do any more. What a sinking feeling in the pit of my stomach when I heard that!

That's when Frank decided we'd try Goroka Hospital where Isaac was born a few months earlier. After one more grueling ordeal, I lay in yet another hospital bed.

---

[60] Proverbs 13:12

The hardest part of all this was being separated from my toddlers for the first time in their lives. They were in good hands with Becky, but my heart ached for them terribly. The memory of my last sideways view of their tiny worried faces in the tribe replayed in my mind.

When I was being carried out, my two-year-old had dark leathery bands of ulcers all over his little legs and he was flushed with malaria fever. It was awful being pulled away from them. I felt so helpless.

I hated imposing extra work on our partners, too. We came to help, but became an added burden instead. Nothing made sense. Why had everything come to a screeching halt so quickly? *Come on, Lord, five years to get here, for this?*

Every morning I set my mind on the simple objective of getting through the day. At night I focused all my energy on making it through to morning light. Over and over, that became my sole purpose, staring at the cracked ceiling like a heroin addict in cold turkey.

What else can you do when you're flat on your back with no music, TV, or visitors to pass the time? I pounded the pages of my Bible. Resting the book on my chest to read the top half, then holding it over my face to cover the bottom pages until my arms were trembling. But I reviewed Biblical characters all the way back to Genesis, and wrestled with God.

Is this the point Father? Is this a test of endurance like Job or Joseph in prison? Is it a lesson in perseverance like Jacob's wrestling match until his thigh was put out of joint and he limped for the rest of his life? Or, a test of heart, like Daniel in the lion's den? I had never read with a focus on suffering before.

Meanwhile, the nurses went on strike while I lay in this helpless state. Lights and power went out and rats scampered through the hallways.

The most menacing scenario by far was the night I opened my eyes to a big black face hovering close to mine, his eyes and teeth gleaming in the eerie light from the hospital corridor. As my eyes adjusted, I realized he clenched a long knife in his raised fist. Even if I could reach the buzzer, it was broken, and on this rare occasion Frank wasn't there. Contrary to everything I said on that stormy evacuation about wanting to die, I quickly resurrected a will to live. *Jesus, save me!*

Just then, footsteps approached down the hall. Two nurses appeared and my would-be assassin changed his behavior instantly. Dropping his hands meekly to his sides like a helpless child, they took hold of his elbows and escorted him back to the psyche ward, but I never knew when he'd return. After that, Frank never left me.

Even though I had the baby with me, it was practically impossible to nurse him. They lay him beside me but I couldn't hold or comfort him. What kind of a useless mother am I? Again I prayed, *God, I don't care about me anymore, but please sustain my baby!*

The next day, nurse Koropa came to my ward. This wonderful mountain mama fell in love with my baby boy and carried him around the halls to comfort him. I had no idea what she was doing to make him sleep so well, and thought she was smuggling formula.

Finally she confided that she had a newborn at home. Patting engorged breasts she said, "God gave me one side for my baby and the other side for yours!" I squeezed her hand, too desperate to feel anything but gratitude. Years later we laughed about God's provision of a wet nurse with "chocolate milk."

Meanwhile, I read from Jacob to Jeremiah wrestling with frustration and depression. "I am worn out from groaning; all night long I flood my bed with weeping and drench my couch with tears."[61]

Come on, Lord! You have to do something! We didn't come all this way for nothing! Then one striking phrase grabbed my attention. "The beginning of wisdom is the fear of the Lord."[62] Did I genuinely *revere* God and desire wisdom, or was I merely fixated on what I wanted? Wisdom involves accepting Sovereignty.

Finally, a new light dawned. *Okay Lord, if it's YOUR WILL that I... never... walk... again...it's O.K. If you want me to stay on this stinking mattress for the rest of my life, then so be it. I'll be another Joni if that's what you want.*[63]

Every ounce of resistance fled as I waved my white flag to the Almighty. Nothing changed right away, but *I* was different. The wrestling match was over. I confessed needing to "walk in Spirit" more than body, and God began a healing from within.

---

[61] Psalm 6:6

[62] Proverbs 1:7, 9:10 and Psalm 111:10 expresses this same concept.

[63] Joni Eareckson Tada became a paraplegic after a diving accident and serves the Lord from a wheelchair to this day. I read her books prior to going to PNG, amazed at her testimony in facing incredible hardship.

I soon noticed a difference in the verses that sprang to my attention. Now, I discovered promises of newness, restoration, and healing in my bones. I kept talking to God but the attitude of my prayers also changed. Instead of issuing from a place of discontent and frustration, there was a sense of cooperation and yieldedness, trusting God to do what *He* wanted.

"On my bed I remember you; I think of you through the watches of the night. Because you are my help, I sing in the shadow of your wings. My soul clings to you; and your right hand upholds me."[64] But we weren't out of the woods yet.

Frank started having searing pain in his abdomen again. When the doctor came in to check on me, I begged him to look at Frank instead. "He can wait his turn," he said.

"No, seriously, check him first," I pleaded. "I'm not going anywhere!" We expected mercy, but these doctors apparently exhausted their sympathies before reaching us white skins.

Frank's pain got so bad he couldn't talk, but still, no one came, so I told him to take my pain meds in the middle of the night. We both lay in agony wondering why no one would help us. *It's a hospital for crying out loud!* That was the hardest night yet. I was so worried Frank would die of a ruptured appendix or something.

I remembered Peter's admonition. "Think it not strange, my brethren, when you fall into diverse trials…"[65] but it did seem strange. Every couple of weeks we were facing some critical issue or mysterious attack on our bodies. All we could do was cry out to a merciful God. *Oh Lord, you're in control of everything. Please release us from this place of pain!*

In the end, Frank's trouble turned out to be another treatable infection out of the blue. One fire was quenched, but mine kept burning, and no one knew why. We heard tropical parasites and suspected spinal disease or bone cancer, but couldn't get any answers.

The solitary 'treatment' I received was a daily blood draw for a "nonspecific" test to monitor my sedentary blood rate. My numbers were off the charts when we arrived, but after my turning point with God, the numbers started falling dramatically! The doctors couldn't understand it, but I knew God was healing me.

One morning, the lead European doctor showed up with a class of students to examine the freak show in the corner room and try

---

[64] Psalm 41:3 and 63:6-8
[65] I Peter 4:12 KJV

to unlock the medical mystery of my case. Somewhere along the line I heard them say, "sacroiliatis," an inflammation of the sacroiliac joint in the lower back. My case was severe he said, aggravated to the point of an 80-year-old which he had never seen before.

"Here's one for the books," I smiled.

Then one eager med student walked to the foot of my bed and took hold of both my feet and lifted them straight into the air. "Does *this* hurt?"

"*YES!*" I screamed.

Horrified, he dropped my feet while I hollered like a stuck pig. It felt like my back had been slammed with a sledgehammer. So much for helping modern medicine.

As I lay recovering from the best of the brightest in med school, my thoughts turned back to the collapsed gurney, the excruciating ambulance ride, and how I had hoped to be fixed by the American doctor in Kudjip. *Lord, I know it's not doctors, hospitals, or fancy equipment that saves. YOU are my physician and healer and in You alone will I trust.*

Ironically, during these strenuous times, I experienced some of the most powerful times of prayer I ever experienced. A couple times I felt lifted up out of my body for refreshing in the Lord. *If this pain is bringing me closer to you, Lord, it's worth it!*

Then the Lord started bringing visitors to help pass daylight hours, and I shared what God was teaching me about the peace that comes with surrender. I was still stuck in bed and the pain persisted, but now I was rejoicing in the Lord and trusting Him.

After so many weeks on my back I had edema and bedsores, but a mysterious reversal had begun. Encouraged, Frank steered a wheelchair to my bedside one morning. "We're getting you up today!" He got in front and took my hands. Koropa got behind me and leaned.

"Oh, oh, OH!" I nearly passed out when my head left the pillow. I looked longingly at that wheelchair, but my body forgot what to do. "Come on guys, do your stuff!" But my legs trembled like twigs and I barely recognized them without any muscle.

I called the elders from the base and they showed up that night to anoint me with oil. I confessed everything I was learning. "A man may be chastened on a bed of pain with constant distress in his bones… His flesh wastes away to nothing and bones once hidden, now stick out…" Yet, we pray and find favor with the Almighty."[66]

I'm not exaggerating. The very next day, I made it into the wheelchair *without pain.* Three days later, I stood without *any* help and the doctor ordered a walking frame to strengthen my legs. I worked so hard, hoping to see my kids by Christmas.

Every little movement off that slab of foam was a gift, and eventually I could prop my baby on a pillow and hit the hallway on wheels. I'd visit people up and down the halls and "stori" about their families, their villages and sicknesses, enjoying every opportunity to share the Lord. My little world expanded beyond the four cement walls of my room at last.

One afternoon I wheeled out on a veranda and watched people on the streets below. The crippled, blind and elderly, so many dressed in rags and bandages. Slowly, I realized I was seeing the world with different eyes.

It was a vision of humanity, with all our quirks and questions, our multicolored wrappings, wrinkles and woes. I had a new perspective of the disadvantaged. I now understood what it *feels like to be trapped in a body* that doesn't work and a life that doesn't match your dreams. Pain and suffering had changed me.

That day in my vintage wheelchair, the thought hit me like a flood. *How can you minister to hurting people if you've never felt their pain?* It was the soft sweet voice again, giving an 'aha moment' I prayed for. It was a life-changing lesson in compassion.

I immediately wrote a long letter to my mother asking for forgiveness. I had been pitifully unaware and absent in her battle with cancer. I wished I'd been a better daughter. Now I knew what it was like to live from one pain pill to another and to think of little else but, "I wish I could sleep!" or, "I hope I make it to morning."

I called her from my wheelchair that Christmas and she gave me the greatest gift of all, her words as freeing as eagle's wings. "There's nothing to forgive, Karen. I love you and I always will." *Thanks, Mom.*

The first time I stood with the braces I felt like the rusty tin man clanking around on the Wizard of Oz while our witty British doctor ribbed, "You should sign up for the annual race of the snails."

---

[66] Job 33:19-28

Despite trembling limbs, the day I managed to reach the door on my own two feet, I was elated. I had walked about six feet and back and then cried like a baby.

The final line in my journal that year read, "Yesterday I walked to the bathroom two times… no more bedpans!" And oh, the bliss of my first shower and shampoo and returning to a bed of clean cool sheets! After lying on a hot plastic mat for so long, these simple pleasures were huge. I eventually graduated to crutches, then worked for a month to get rid of them.

But on Christmas Eve I was finally discharged to await the greatest joy: our beautiful daughter and sweet little boy were flying up to join us. The only gifts we could afford were a few trade store popguns and candies, but it was the best Christmas ever and that reunion was one of the happiest moments of my entire life.

Sitting outside in my wheelchair with my journal across my lap, I looked out across a span of purple mountains thinking about how much transpired since we arrived in PNG. We'd moved into the tribe, started building a house and learning an unwritten language. I'd given birth to our third child and come through some life-changing experiences, not knowing if I'd ever walk again. I remembered earthquakes, floods, snakes and malaria attacks.

In that first year, I went from barrels to bedpans and from anxiety to awe. Papua New Guinea was aptly named, I thought. They call it, "land of the unexpected."

18. Mama Mia

The awful news crackled across the airwaves of our shortwave in a stifling jungle heat. "Karen, your mother died. Over."

"What? When? Over." Crackle. Crackle.

"Two days ago. Over." Over, just like that.

It happened on February 5, 1981. "Complications due to pneumonia," they said.

We had just returned to the tribe, and it felt like the back side of a desert, a million miles from home. Too late to attend the funeral, too broke to book a flight. I could only afford to cry. So I climbed the trail behind our house and sobbed behind the water tank.

A million miles away, but I still couldn't fathom a world without her.

When I was a girl, I used to think of her as Snow White. Fair and flawless skin offset with jet black hair that curled around her dark brown eyes. She had manners and poise, colorful scarves and matching earrings. I loved her soft hands and long beautiful nails polished candy-apple red.

She loved learning and had an active detail-oriented mind. In her sophomore year she won the New York state spelling bee. Sadly, girls were discouraged from pursuing an education, and she was pulled out of school to put her talents to work in the family business.

I got her bubbly laugh and soprano voice, a love for cheesy Italian foods, and my husband claimed the shapely legs are from her side, too. I acquired a fraction of her management skills and desire for orderliness. Mom was dedicated, disciplined and extremely thorough. Even daily chores revolved around a tidy schedule of ironing or washing sheets at the proper time.

Our linens were stitched with crocheted ladies in pink bonnets and delicate French knots. She crocheted lacy white bedspreads and tablecloths, and tackled yard work and gardening with equal gusto. She lined the sunny west side of the yard with tomatoes, while tiger lilies and bleeding hearts blossomed on the shady side. Everything was pleasant and in order because Mom was the full-time, all-round champion of the household.

I can't remember a time that she *wasn't* there when we got home from school. We'd find her darning socks in the living room or ironing in the den, singing with her favorite Mantovani records on the old hi-fi. And the house was filled with succulent aromas of dinner cooking or chocolate cake—even the bizarre recipe that could absorb leftover sour kraut.

On rainy school days, I'd dread the mile-long walk home, but my eyes would scan the roads and always find her little white Fairlane with the windshield wipers and lights on. She'd roll down the window and wave wearing one of those clear plastic rain hats that folded like an accordion into her purse. "Always be prepared, like the Boy Scouts," was her motto.

Mom was my role model. She maintained a natural grace and level-headedness through every hardship—including her own battle for survival.

Her cancer appeared when I was fourteen. I rode the bus downtown to visit her and started volunteering as a candy striper in response to the helplessness I felt. Working in the candy shop or delivering cartloads of flowers, I'd cheer people up. Funny thing, I was the one that needed cheering.

Over the years, we kids would come home to find her lying on the couch with a scarf on her head. "I just couldn't seem to get moving today," she'd say, trying to downplay the reasons why. "I feel better now." Somehow, she would pull it together to have dinner on the table at 5:30, proof that life would go on as normal in the Judd household. We kids didn't understand what she was going through, and of course she never complained. "Now go do your homework."

After her mastectomies, some years passed in cancer-free living before she casually mentioned a nagging pain in her chest. "Maybe I coughed too hard and cracked a rib," she surmised. "My sister did that once… It's probably nothing."

146

I insisted on taking her straight to the walk-in clinic hoping to be relieved of all our fears, but they told us to go home and collect her things to be admitted that very day. The cancer had returned.

I was standing right beside her when the doctor said, "You'd better think about getting your affairs in order. You have about six months."

She drew a deep breath, looked at me resolutely and said, "At least I have a warning. Most people never get time to get ready." I knew she was thinking of Dad who fell in the middle of the night and never got up again.

How could she see anything to be thankful about at a time like this? But that was Mom. She could immediately snap into a positive frame of mind and find something good to say, accepting each trial with the fortitude of a soldier.

Her eyebrows were raised in classic hopefulness, and she smiled through the tears. "It could always be worse, right?"

I didn't really know. This felt like the worst to me.

Chemo was rough in those days. She would get a dose on Thursday and go to bed for three days to vomit poison and try to sleep it off. Despite these awful bouts she gained weight from the fluids, and after years of counting calories, wearing baggy clothes was demoralizing. "People probably think I'm pregnant," she quipped. "Imagine that!"

When she lost her hair I took her to shop for a wig and we found one that matched her style and color. "Wow, if nothing else, my hair will look perfect everyday now. Why didn't I think of this before?" she winked. "Just think of the money I'll save! I won't need a hair cut for months!" I'm crying as I write this now.

The last time I heard her voice it cost ten dollars per minute for the call. I'd just flown to a hospital in the Highlands of PNG. Mom had been in the hospital too. Despite her ongoing battle, I was encouraged to hear her buoyant voice and drew strength from her cheerfulness.

"Every day is a gift," she said.

"I love you, Mom," across the oceans and continents.

"I love you too, honey," she assured me. She talked about starting a new diet and was anxious to get out of the hospital.

Instead, a few weeks later, she quietly slipped through the celestial curtains and left all her cares behind. She had just celebrated her fifty-fifth birthday. I grieved the memories of all she had been through with shunts and surgeries and chemo treatments.

I remembered offering to postpone New Guinea to stay with her, but she was in remission at the time and resolute that we go. "How would you like it if your daughter stayed with you, *waiting for you to die* so she could do what she needed to do? Nobody knows how much time they have."

"I didn't mean it like *that*, Mom."

"No, you *have to go* when your visas are in," she insisted. "Go, with my blessing."

But why did I listen? It bothered me for years. I left her alone when she needed me most, but I know God didn't leave her alone. For one thing, he sent Christian nurses in. But another proof occurred when my brothers were called to her side in her final days.

Suddenly she said, "I see him!"

"Who do you see?" Steve asked.

"It's *the Lord!*" she answered reverently. They knew she wasn't the type to vie for drama, but she described seeing the silhouette of the Lord, too bright to see his face. It seemed like the sun was illuminating his image and his arms were outstretched. She knew the Lord was waiting for her. God chose that precise moment to reveal himself, for our comfort as well as hers. And very soon afterwards she was united with Him in undiminished brilliance.

Though relieved that her suffering had ended, I was sorry for me. *My mother* was gone. I knew the words were true, but I couldn't accept the fact. Unable to say goodbye in person, or even attend her funeral, I struggled to process such a heavy loss and guilt returned to plague me. *I should have been there! What a terrible daughter!*

I wanted to go home, but that was out of the question after bouncing in and out of the tribe like a couple of pogo sticks. Nevertheless, when I see someone in a similar position, I *always* tell them to go whatever it takes, and many have thanked me for it.

The nightmares lasted for weeks while my psyche attempted to re-write reality, every dream another frustrated attempt to rescue her from death. I'd wake up drenched, clawing in the dirt at her gravesite, or pulling her hands in the casket. *Mom, Mom! Get up! Wake up!* In one bone-chilling episode, her eyes actually opened.

The awful truth seeped in waves. One of the kids would say something comically brilliant and my first reaction would be, I need to write Mom. But the delightful moment of entertainment shattered like a broken mirror. No, there will be no more letters home. *Mom and Dad are gone.* I felt orphaned at twenty-five. *I have no more home!*

I read her final letter over and over. She was proud of me and said she loved me. She had totally and unselfishly given her final blessing to follow the Lord and that was an incredible parting gift— possibly the best gift a mother can give her children.

Before leaving home, I asked for a hymnal from the church and someone suggested having everyone sign it as a going-away gift. Months passed before the book arrived in the tribe and I discovered a small inscription at the top of page 171. I knew she took great pains to find just the right page out of 675 songs to leave a personal message for me, and she knew I'd cherish this final note forever.

The hymn *Jesus Lives, and So Shall I,* overflows with conviction. As we parted for the last time, this is the message she wanted me to hang onto. In a bright blue marker at the top of the page she wrote, *"Till we meet again. Love, Mom."* Here's an excerpt:

Jesus lives and so shall I. Death! Thy sting is gone forever!
He who deigned for me to die, Lives, the bands of death to sever.

He shall raise me with the just: Jesus is my Hope and Trust.
Jesus lives and death is now But my entrance into glory.

Courage, then, my soul, for thou Hast a crown of life before thee;
Thou shalt find thy hopes were just; Jesus is the Christian's Trust.

That same red hymnal still sits on my desk. From scribes of old and the hand of my own mother's pen, these beautiful lyrics still impart courage. *Nothing can separate us from the love of God! Even death is powerless to destroy or rob us who are firmly planted in Christ. It is merely my entrance into glory.*

So, it's never really *over.* We will meet again.

19. Self, Sin, and Circumstances: I Can't Do It!

EYES ON SELF

Five years before we went to New Guinea, two elderly missionary women visited our Bible School chapel from India. They seemed frail as they shuffled to the podium. *How do they do it? How do they manage the rigors of tribal life?* Addressing our roomful of bright-eyed students eager to "reach the unreached" at the ends of the earth, they talked about resting in faith. Then the Holy Spirit seemed to hush the room when they lifted their voices like wobbly little birds and sang a melody I would never forget.

Got any rivers you think are uncrossable?
Got any mountains you can't tunnel through?
God specializes in things thought impossible.
He does the things others cannot do!

Impossibilities? Oh yeah, I found a boat load of opportunities to review this lesson at May River. A home-schooling housewife caring for small children, I felt like a wrung out dish rag by the end of the day. Old men were even calling me to light their cigarettes at the door! I was frazzled.

One steamy afternoon I flopped on the bed in tears wondering how on earth I would *ever* learn an unwritten language and be of any use to a bunch of hard-hearted, nose-pierced devil-worshipping heathen. How could I ever be fruitful here? *Lord, I can't do this! I don't have any love for these people. This is **impossible!***

A parrot flashed by my window, and my gaze fell upon a scrappy Asian fig tree in the yard. Of course this tree had been there every day, but this is the first time I noticed blossoms. As I studied the branches, I was moved to wonder.

Soft plump figs sprung right through the bark, sticking all over the branches like brown cherries super-glued to every limb. *How in the world does fruit spring from the hard wooden bark of a tree? Doesn't fruit usually grow from the buds?* As I sat there puzzling over this odd behaviour, the Lord spoke soft as crickets.

"Karen, if I can do this, I can certainly produce my fruit in you."

I had just been telling God how impossible everything was, and what did he do? He showed me an image of His mysterious power right in my own backyard. He is God of the impossible!

Oh Lord it's true, I've been hard as wooden branches lately. Forgive me, soften me up. Train me to rest in you like a branch in the vine.[67] *YOU are the miracle master, the God who springs figs out of solid wood!*

It doesn't matter where we go on the face of the planet—a high rise in Chicago or a tree house in New Guinea—this fig-popping God of ours is able to reveal himself and do His work. If I just abide in the vine, the branches will yield in due season. But I need to get my eyes off me and onto Him, the master of things thought impossible.

STINKING SIN: EYES ON OTHERS

In addition to the challenge of getting my eyes off of myself, it was also a struggle to get my eyes off others, learning to tolerate differences in day to day relationships.

I'd also noticed a problem with my little kerosene freezer. "I have to clean this thing," I'd mutter to myself. The door wasn't closing properly, but I'd chip at the edges to force it shut another day.

The freezer section of my fridge was only about eighteen inches across and eight precious inches high. In order to clean it properly, I had to let it defrost and forfeit all my ice. A cube of butter would melt and a bag of shrimp (which I collected for weeks) would turn to mush. Afterwards, it would take days to get cold again.

---

[67] John 15:1-8

It was a stinky job, too. Thawing fish, bloody meat, and perspiration—sounds disgusting, doesn't it? All contributing factors to why I kept putting it off.

But that stink! When I couldn't stand it any longer, I went to the kitchen armed with an interesting assortment of spatulas and hacking tools. *Today you're coming clean!*

Regardless of my finest efforts, however, it wasn't going well at all. Solid clumps of all this murky, unusable ice had built up longer than usual. It was exceptionally frustrating as I fought to free the thick corners and coils. I hacked and whacked. Rivers of sweat ran down my forehead and elbows while my last cube of precious butter melted in the sink.

Being such a keen observer of scientific wonders by nature, I puzzled that the things I wanted to keep cold were melting quickly while the only thing I wanted to melt remained so stubbornly frozen. The irony heightened my frustration. It might not have seemed so bad if I had *nothing else* to do, but the kids needed constant help with school, people knocked, and the radio paged.

Beneath the surface of my proverbial iceberg, I harbored hurt feelings from strained relationships with our partners. Even while I hacked at the ice, I'd been rehearsing all the latest offenses in my mind, justifying all my bad attitudes.

Aaaaaaah! Why are you soooo STUBBORN? I felt like swearing loudly. Then I felt a familiar prodding. *I don't like it either. This freezer is just like you.*

Ouch! Wiping my sweaty upper lip with the back of my hand, I took a couple of steps back and leaned on the sink. I was bruised, but knew exactly what He meant.

They warned us about things like this in boot camp. "When you get out there in the tribe, you're apt to think that your partners are your biggest enemies." Now, here we were, fighting over stupid things—so silly, I don't even remember what it was!

To think of the Lord being equally exasperated with my mess of stinking attitudes suddenly put everything in a different light. I was trying to ignore the problem, but the Lord wanted to clean house *in me,* not just my appliances.

He prompted my mind with a laundry list of foul odors that had been building up for too long: pride, obsessing over offenses, and letting mole hills become Alpine slopes. *What a mess I am!*

I felt his tug, then a softening in my heart, and arguments melted to mush like the bags in my sink. *God, forgive me. Thaw out this frozen heart of mine and make my life a sweet fragrance, in Jesus' Name.*

Thank God for helping us clean house.

EYES ON CIRCUMSTANCES = DISCOURAGEMENT

Whether by a fig tree or a stinking freezer, God is never short of ways to convey a message to help us grow in faith. But this one's my all-time favorite.

It had been an especially dark period when teaching meetings were poorly attended, the people were stealing from us, and relationships were strained. Worst of all, the smoldering expressions on men's faces showed that we were hated by the very people we came to reach. We were feeling isolated and discouraged. Would we ever see our prayers for a breakthrough answered? It all seemed hopeless at the time.

In the midst of all this, people came and told us that a woman died in a village downriver. We didn't know her personally, and they were fairly lethargic about our presence. I always imagined people thinking of us the same way the people of Noah's time thought of him—a strange man swinging a hammer on some mountain year after year. A little crazy, but life goes on. They didn't have a clue why we were there.

When this woman died, the people blew the conch and pounded the drums. Relatives and neighbors mudded up and came to mourn. No one had a handwatch to "mark" the time, but it must have been an hour or two before everyone was gathered together.

Then, to their amazement, the woman's eyes opened! Sorrow and grief quickly turned to terror, and cries became whooping.

"What happened to you? Where did you go? How did you come back?"

She described going to a strange and beautiful place but her words were barely adequate to describe it. "There was a river running through the middle of the place, but it didn't move like our water. It was hard and strong enough to walk on," she said.

No one could imagine such a thing. You'd never get your canoe in there or spear a fish. That was unthinkable. How would you eat?

"But it wasn't the color of our river either. It was shining like the sun!"

The minute I heard that, my understanding triggered. This tribal woman had no knowledge of paved streets or anything shining like the sun. She saw heaven's streets of gold!

The great street of the city was of pure gold, like transparent glass... The city does not need the sun or the moon to shine on it, for the glory of God gives it light... Rev 21:21-23

It gets even better. She went on to tell what she heard there.

"You can't stay here now, but I'm sending you back to May River," said the mighty Spirit. "Go and tell your people that they are to listen to *my servants* that *I sent* to May River," and He called us by name!

I knew verses that said, "I have called you by name,"[68] but it's one thing to read or recite, and quite another to hear that God Almighty is actually *talking* about us up there!

Dear reader, whatever it is you're facing right now, please don't lose heart. Whether the battle is sin, self, or circumstances, He is able, He is with us, and He wants us to know Him.

Whether soft as crickets or loud as thunder, He's still God. And, just as chirping crickets and booming thunder are far from each other, so are the diverse, amusing or fearsome workings of our Creator. He's full of surprises and wonder.

He may never do the same thing twice, but His love never changes. His grace knows no limits. He is as near and tender as our bare feet on the grass and as wide and confounding as the heavens.

---

[68] Isaiah 43:1, 45:4

20. Blessings Wearing Costumes

When we went to May River we were saying, "Eight years, tops, and we'll be out of here and onto another tribe!" Our notebooks were full of plans and our heads full of ideas about how the work should progress. Part of it was youthful enthusiasm, but we soon realized that life rarely conforms to our outlines and the people we seek to reach don't care about what's in our notebooks.

By way of example, Frank wrote about his first fish poisoning.

I headed upriver to teach in Aiwanu at 8:00 one morning, telling Karen I'd be back at noon, but on the way home Benjamin asked if we could stop at Wasminap (we called it Crocodile Corner after its known villains) to attend a fish-poisoning. I hoped it wouldn't take too long. My throat was already dry and my stomach growling.

We wound up a narrow stream and I followed him on foot twenty minutes through dense jungle. Just as I was wondering if I could ever retrace my steps, we broke out to a big round pool of water where five long dug-outs filled with men and boys were circling, striking the water with poison vines.

After about an hour, I told Benjamin I needed to get going. I had a "schedule" to keep. But everyone became agitated and started yelling. I couldn't leave, they said, or I'd break the power of the poison. I was stuck.

When the water was sufficiently treated, the men shored to wait for the fish to die. How long would this take, I wondered? I tried asking questions but they hushed me. Apparently, talking wasn't allowed. I started pointing at the dying fish rising up in the pool, and quickly discovered that pointing was another taboo. Oi vey, but how strong can this poison be if everything I do can stop it?

I knew Karen would be worried by now. The men smoked leisurely and chewed happily. Minutes turned to hours while I was

*learning the tribal way of life. You can't force people to your
schedule. In this neck of the woods, you have to stop looking at your
wrist. I only hoped my family wasn't worrying.*

*The signal was finally given and everyone sprang to action.
Some went in their canoes and others wallowed in the muddy banks,
gathering fish by hand and net. I joined them, happy at last to do
more than stand around, and collected a whole basket of bass and
perch. By this time I was so hungry I ate dry sago and mayflies. I was
dying of thirst too, but didn't dare sip the poison water.*

*Another hour ticked by. Meanwhile, Karen sent word by radio
that I was missing, and everyone was praying for my safety. Dave
went out searching by boat, passing up and down the river not
knowing I was 'being held hostage' in the jungle. Just like the fish in
that round water, I was trapped by tribal poison.*

Not only can anything happen when you "leave for work" in
the morning, but what happens to your office schedule when your
assistant is abducted in the middle of the night? Obviously, this
wasn't on Frank's calendar for the week, but that little interruption
forced him out of the office and exposed him to some of the deep
secrets of Iwam ritual as he sat with Tomas in his bush house.

The male initiation was the most gruesome ritual practiced.
The men of the village bound and carried teen-aged boys to a remote
jungle site where no one could hear their screams. They were pinned
down by the clan fathers and their penises were forced to receive the
long shafts of a thorny reed to "bleed out" their mothers' blood.

One anthropologist described it as "a male menstruation, a
purification rite, with overtones of rebirth."[69] Frank compared it to a
tribal bar mitzvah and circumcision-gone-bad, all rolled into one.

Bleeding ensured the passage from little boys who clung to
their mother's legs, to strong masculine protectors in their own right.
They had to sever the ties of a child in order to become a man, but it's
a wonder they didn't sever their ability to become fathers while they
were at it. Unable to walk afterwards, initiates spent weeks
convalescing in isolation while the men provided vast quantities of
food and indoctrinated them with tribal lore.

Initiates are strictly forbidden to tell little boys what's coming
(or something worse may happen), so the mystery is well guarded.

---

[69] *Man as Art*, 1981, Viking Press, New York, Essay by Professor Andrew Strathern, p.
25-26.

We can only imagine the dread of these teens when they are unexpectedly grabbed in their sleep and tied up by their uncles. Many tribes have initiation rites that test strength and endurance in the passage to manhood, but this one has to be among the most severe.

Not only did tribal traditions put a dent in "our plans," but there were times tribal behavior threatened our very lives. One time Frank sat in Tultul's house chatting light-heartedly when the old man was suddenly possessed with violent anger. He grabbed the bone dagger in his armband to stab Frank to death on a whim, but Tomas jumped up and stopped him.

The only reason he gave was that he wasn't in the mood for laughing that day. It reminded me of the uncertainty of sitting at Saul's table in the presence of evil spirits, but all our days are in God's hands.[70]

As a side note to these incidents, nothing was wasted. We systematically filed cultural incidents around universal topics to illustrate spiritual truth and make teaching relevant. For example, imagine how powerfully it impacts an Iwam initiate when he learns about One who went willingly with his captors to bleed in his place. He was pierced for us without resisting because of his great love, all the way to the extent of dying.

I'd come a long way since boot camp. "People before projects," I kept remembering. We hosted a couple of work teams of about 18 college kids, and several went on to full-time missions. I perked to every opportunity to welcome guests—even total strangers who appeared unannounced at the door wormed their way into our fondest memories. I'd start baking bread and hanging mosquito nets, and we'd treat them like family.

I can't think of a time we were ever sorry, with the exception of a winter night in Oregon when we met a homeless man on crutches and took him home. Hard to tell who was more surprised when we caught him stealing in the middle of the night. He dropped the crutches, broke into *a run* and bolted over the back fence, disappearing into the dark!

Believing God to guide and protect us when we opened our home to wanderers, we hosted Austrian, Canadian, Scottish, French, German, Australian, British and even Israeli tourists who found our

---

[70] I Samuel 20:33, Psalm 139:16

door. We even had a team of British scientists researching parasites, and assisted with a riverside clinic in the village.

One day, we heard coworkers talking on *sked* [radio time] about British reporters who passed through. They stayed several days shooting pictures which were later used to smear our organization with audacious lies. In a TV news magazine they blamed missionaries for introducing foreign diseases and exploiting people. Nothing was said of the employment, medical work, clothing, literacy or education being provided at our expense.

Shortly afterwards, a lone traveler appeared at our door in a tan safari suit. He had a hired canoe and driver and villagers brought him to our door in search of "white man's food." Unwilling to become a spectacle in some foreign documentary, there were awkward moments at the door. Frank hobbled down from his office on home-made crutches.

"How are you doing on time, honey?" I asked.

"Well, I could break for about fifteen minutes," he said slowly. Frank was pushing to prepare for a consultant, but we were so suspicious we didn't invite him in.

"Fifteen minutes?" he asked.

"Well, I have a consultant coming in a few days," Frank explained. "Deadlines, you know."

"You've got to be kidding!" our visitor, chuckled. "Aren't you guys missionaries? What are you doing worrying about deadlines? That's exactly what I'm trying to get away from."

Gordon was a world-renowned architect whose wife had just passed away and he came on this trip to get away, perhaps get in touch with the spiritual. Instead, he reached the door of these "humble missionaries" and practically had it slammed in his face!

"I thought missionaries were supposed to *care* about people!"

Ouch, but when we told him our horror story in TV journalism that flew across the radio waves, he softened.

"Just to be safe," Frank smirked, "no pictures." Wise as serpents, gentle as doves.[71]

Afterwards, we corresponded with Gordon for years and postcards drifted in from such faraway places as the Ural Mountains, Antarctica and Tanzania where he climbed Kilimanjaro and got frostbite on his toes. We were humbled and humored to realize that in

---

[71] Reference to a caution from Jesus in Matthew 10:16-17 KJV

his entire trip around the globe his conceptions were altered because of us. He affectionately referred to us as "the crazy missionaries of Papua," and we called him, "the crazy architect from Chicago."

Israelis were our favorite tourists—a savvy, sensitive bunch. The first colorful group arrived when Sepikers told them they should meet the "American Israeli missionary," and the misnomer threw them for a loop. "*Israeli missionary?*" they puzzled. "What on earth is that?" Their curiosity was piqued enough to spend extra days paddling to our village to find out.

Iwam people led them to our house. "*Pren!* Come meet your relatives from the line of Judah!" From a Papuan clan orientation, the blood line of Jesus led straight to my husband, so it was like uniting long-lost brothers in a family reunion. Frank came down from his office and looked in the faces of these handsome bearded men.

"*Shalom!*" they smiled. "Are you the Israeli *missionary?*" Their English was laced with a rich Mid-Eastern accent and their smiles were genuine. Dressed in ragged tee shirts with scarves around their heads, they were sunburned and barefooted.

"*Shalom!*" Frank said, breaking into his equally gorgeous smile. It had been decades since Frank attended Hebrew School, but that single word revived an ancient bond. "Come inside! Let's get you guys something to eat and drink."

I started breaking ice and the kids came running out of the schoolroom to meet our nomadic guests. Iddo, Evi, Zvika, Eran and Daphna—aeronautical engineers, an airforce fighter pilot, and an accomplished dancer from the Israeli Ballet—completed their stint in the armed forces and had been traveling the world together.

They were only going to stay one night, but some of them had pretty bad sores, and I tempted them with some home cooking and recovery time. After all the mud baths they welcomed our bucket shower and wringer washer.

I learned to roll Mid-Eastern chapattis and we talked into the wee hours. "Tell us your stories," we begged. "We've been in isolation too long. Where are you all from? What do you do? What's the most interesting place you've been?" After a few hours of delightful stories about training jet bombers in the Israeli air force, and world class ballet, Zvika asked, "Well? Tell us *your* story. How did you, a Jew, become a missionary, Frank?"

"You don't want to know," he said. They let that ride awhile, but had never seen a Christian (i.e. proselytizer) refuse an opening like that before. Frank, though passionate about his faith, turned the Christian stereotype on its head. I served Turkish coffees while they wondered how to press the matter without offending their hosts.

Eran the elder was nominated. "Are we *children* that we can't handle your story? Tell us what brought you out here to live like this."

"Well, if you really want to know, we have to start at the beginning," Frank began, kicking off daily discussions through Scripture beginning with Moses. By the time they left, we had covered Romans, Galatians, a smattering of Hebrews and the prophets, answering questions with our kids on our laps while we sipped drinks and soaked sores.

After breakfast every morning, we'd invite them to stay another day, which began a daily ritual of convening "Parliament." All five climbed the hill behind our house to make a mutual decision. When they came in to accept our invitation, we were thrilled.

Our excursions provided needed refreshment for us as well. We visited villages along the May, forging local *and* international relations. We even danced the horah arm in arm on the sandbar, and by the time they left we were more refreshed than if we had flown to the coast for a break.

Subsequent letters described their travels through Singapore where they posted word at an Israeli hostel about the highlight of their trip to Papua. "If you can get to May River in the Sepik Province you MUST meet our Jewish brother Frank and his wife Karen for the most unforgettable tribal experience." God used that note to lead subsequent groups our way, becoming one of our favorite perks.

We also recognized divine humor in it. When tribal believers heard that our visitors were from the homeland of Jesus, they would treat them like celebrities.

"God is playing a good trick on us," they'd shake their heads. "In Israel, we didn't even believe in Him, but here all we're doing is telling his stories. He's very clever to make us his ambassadors!"

It was humbling for them to be among "heathen" who believed their Jewish Messiah as Paul described God "arousing my own people to envy through foreign people who obtained what they did not."[72]

---

[72] Romans 11:14, 24 NIV

Who's to say how God should manage your time and ministry, or how many lives can be changed in those unexpected encounters? For all we know, these detours from the schedule accomplished more than an entire term on the mission field.

In 1990, while attending area leadership meetings, I was teaching morning devotions to my kids. We were up to Acts 8 that morning, an interesting story about Philip's side trip to the middle of nowhere. That evangelist must have been confounded by God's leading him into seclusion on a desert road. Yet, the Lord intended his path to cross with an Ethiopian who would carry the gospel to Africa.

I love not only the obvious lesson about God directing every step of this encounter, but Luke's fascinatingly obscure reference at the tail end of the story to the first time-traveler of the first century. After baptizing the Ethiopian, Philip *appeared* twenty miles away to resume his urban ministry—no Hertz rent-a-camel, or anything! [73]

I impressed my kids, "When God speaks, obey, even if it doesn't make sense. He can make up for 'lost' time and get you where you need to be even if he has to snatch you up in a time tunnel to do it. He always knows exactly what He's doing."

Just then we heard, "knock knock!" at the screen door. "Hey Karen, the guys asked if you could join the meeting."

Frank and the men had been hashing out options for needed personnel to help start a school for missionary kids in our Sepik region. "Do you think Karen would be willing to go?" they asked Frank.

"Why don't we call her over here and find out?"

My mouth hung open as they described the sacrifice and "interruption to our work in the tribe." They wanted a year's commitment. Talk about a detour! I listened to everything, then smiled and answered, "Whatever you think, I'm ready to go!"

"Wow," they laughed. "Wish every decision was as easy as that one!" But when the Lord primes you by His Word, decisions come easier.

I'm sure such details preceded Rebekah's leaving home to marry Isaac, Matthew jumping up from his tax desk, or Peter, James and John dropping their nets. Those back stories would no doubt reveal a divine hand of preparation in a stream of directed

---

[73] Acts 8:26-40

circumstances. Take for example, the time a king couldn't sleep and got up to read reports that changed the course of history in Esther, or Peter's prayer time on a rooftop before lunch. It prepared him for a knock at the door that would pave the way for the church age! [74]

Interruptions can be the best thing that ever happened to us; blessings wearing costumes.

So, a few days later, we moved to the coastal town of Wewak to turn an empty building into a home for fourteen kids. Frank's skills and energy were a big plus, and we had a couple college kids visiting to help paint, finish floors and haul appliances. I bought thirty yards of tropical fabrics and ran a marathon of treadle machine miles to cover windows and couch cushions. Amazingly, we were ready in two weeks and the rooms swelled with the unique personalities of school kids from around the globe.

Our own kids loved this interlude in Wewak. They had friends in a *real* neighborhood and a *normal* house with electricity, a driveway, and their own parents living inside. It was a dream job!

Perhaps referring to our household as "normal" is a stretch. We were "Uncle Frank and Aunt Karen" to fourteen kids from five families ranging from second to ninth grade. As staff of our Dolphin Seaside Academy, I also taught fourth and fifth-grade math, seventh and eighth-grade science and social studies, and cared for half the student body, and I loved it.

We sure enjoyed town living after ten years in the bush. Frank and I talked to everyone like a couple of deprived hillbillies. We met Chinese store owners, Indonesian refugees, artists from the interior Chambri Lakes region, and local natives.

Nearly every weekday I walked with my Aussie girlfriend. She was married to the British bank manager in town and lived next door to the Prime Minister. Marilyn introduced me to the upper echelon of Wewak and made sure I was invited to the ladies' teas.

I felt like some comical backwoods character wearing trade store second-hands and local bead necklaces while they modeled the latest styles from Singapore and Paris. Somehow they accepted me when Marilyn oozed about my being a hippie from Boston. "Oh, that explains it," their expressions registered.

The salaries and benefits of *expat* businessmen[75] were mind-boggling. They had hired cooks and guards and sent their kids to

---

[74] Esther 6:1-3, Acts 10:9-35
[75] Expat is short for expatriot, meaning someone from another country

European prep schools. Little gated mansions came with the territory, but beneath a carefully polished veneer, complaints about homesickness, drinking, and cheating were prevalent. I took every opportunity to share the love of God wondering, once again, if this "interruption" was more effective than anything else we did.

Other interruptions were harder to accept. Christmas break rolled around and our dorm kids flew home to their parents. We wanted to fly into the tribe with the Fultons who came all the way from Boston to spend the holidays with us, but rebel forces called OPM from Irian Jaya slipped across our western border and kidnapped missionaries in that region. The men were bound, taken into the jungle under cover of night, and held hostage.

Our Embassy published warnings to evacuate all US citizens near the Indonesian border, identifying our base as a prime target with air and water access, housing, motorboats, a jet barge, and fuel supplies to assist operations in five neighboring tribes.

This meant all our tribal partners were evacuated and we couldn't go home for Christmas. Thankfully, the trouble subsided, the hostages were released unharmed in a month, kids returned to school, and parents flew back to life as "usual" in the tribes.

Life for us in the "big smoke" of civilization was mostly fun and games teaching kids, but anything's possible in a third world country. One day we had to make a fast bread run in the school van between classes, but rounding the corner of the main street, an angry mob rushed toward us waving weapons!

"Roll your window up," Frank said. They swarmed around our van like the bees from a broken nest and we were engulfed in a tangle of angry black skin, some slamming the sides and pounding the hood with fists and clubs. The cloud passed and we were unharmed.

Our laid-back flip flop beach town so quickly turned life-threatening. That mob continued on their rampage, setting fires and doing damage to the town. Fire engulfed the Christian bookstore run by a fellow missionary as well as the local *chemist* [pharmacy] where we got anti-malarials. Black smoke choked the town for days.

This happened in the spring of 1991, the same week we lost our water pump, so we had no water for washing, cooking or filling toilets. The smoke at school and lack of water at home also coincided with the onset of 45 days of bombing in the Gulf War. Since we lived in town, we could watch history in the making on Australian CNN.

Seeing missiles fire on Israel and Kuwaiti oil go up in smoke while our own horizon was black and sooty, stirred the kids' interest. "When's the Lord coming back?" they asked. With all their parents in the Lord's service, these weren't new subjects for them, but live images delivered fresh relevance into our living room, so we started studying end times.

"No one knows exactly when the Lord's coming. That day will take us by surprise like a thief in the night," Frank explained, "but the most important thing is that we're ready. Faith in Jesus is a shield and prayer is our best weapon to protect us no matter what happens."[76] We wanted our kids to know and apply God's Word to their lives, and the Lord gave us even more practice.

A few days later, we heard frantic screaming through the open louvers. I threw open the kitchen door and saw our next door neighbor Roberta wrestling with a man holding an axe over her head! I ran straight toward them yelling, *"STOP!"* Her assailant turned around and saw me coming unarmed, so he let go of her and started coming at me with the axe!

I spun around and rushed toward the house, but half the kids had run out behind me. "Hurry kids! Get back inside!" Not a second too soon, we braced ourselves against the back of that kitchen door as the rascal pushed against us, but 14 kids were a lot of help!

Our Irish freckle-faced third grader was crouching in the corner when she remembered our Bible study. "Should we *pray,* Auntie Karen?" she squeaked.

"Yes, Danielle, start praying!" And so did I. *Jesus, protect us!* The attacker pounded the outside of the door with the axe, then took off running. I ran out to check on Roberta, shaken, but not hurt. "Jesus helped me," she panted. "Thank you!" God does give the strength and surprising courage when we need it.

Another time I was walking around the block and heard a woman screaming. It sounded like she was being cut to pieces and I instinctively ran up the driveway where a drunken man held a broken beer bottle over the woman's head. She was a trembling mess of tears on the ground with her hands up trying to block the blows. "Stop it! Leave her alone!" I don't know what I would have done if he attacked me. "Don't you hurt her!" I yelled.

---

[76] Matthew 24:36, 42-44; Ephesians 6:16-18

The man stopped and looked in my direction. I wish I knew what he saw—maybe mirror images of me from drinking. Or, perhaps he saw an angel with me because he stared, dropped the bottle, and scampered into the trees like a scared rabbit. I remembered the Lord said, "Go in the strength you have... I will be with you."[77]

Speaking of majority powers, we met Australian soldiers in town and invited them up for lunch. Instant heroes, they regaled our little troop with Rambo stories and reciprocated with invitations to the army base for a *barbie*. They were celebrating completion of an obstacle course for PNG army recruits, a course through several kilometers of bush terrain ending with a high dive into the ocean.

I'm afraid of heights, so don't ask how I ended up at the top of that plank with everyone behind me, hollering! "Jump! Jump!" Try as I might, they would not let me climb down the ladder. With my toes clinging to the final inches of solid safety, I stared into the emerald green water hoping a shark sighting would save me from a plunge, but no such luck. It may have been thirty-five feet, but it looked like fifty, or a thousand.

"Don't look down!" they said. "You can do it!" I finally closed my eyes and jumped, screaming the whole way down. Everyone cheered and dubbed me an honorary member of the Australian rangers. It was a big step, but I'm glad I did it.

That crazy leap off a cliff is a perfect illustration of faith. My head may fight against my heart the whole way up, my toes curling around the edges, clinging to familiar ground. In the end, I have to ignore my fears simply because He promised to catch me. Like Philip on the Gaza Road, I may not understand how, but He'll get me where I need to go—by faith.

---

[77] Judges 6:14-16

21. Tea Parties and Hullaballoos

"Are you saying that you're *not* going to support what GOD's done here?" In the field chairman's eyes, we were ingrates. "These buildings are the result of years of blood, sweat and tears! We even poured the cement blocks by hand!"

"I'm not against the mission school, but I can teach my kids," I said meekly. "I've already been teaching them at home and they're doing fine." (Truth is, Naomi was reading like a fifth grader by the age of five and Jesse was already reading at three.) "Why don't parents have the prerogative to choose the right time for each child to go to school? Our kids are entrusted to parents, not to organizations."

In 1982, confronting mission school policy was not popular. We were rebels from Boston—the city made famous for challenging the status quo and staging tea parties. Like most administrators, the chairman wanted everyone to march to one rhythm and send their kids to school for first grade. Naomi was only five, but if we were allowed to sidestep rules, others would follow and what if kids fell behind?

He finally threw his hands up in the air. "If I knew you were going to be so headstrong about this, you wouldn't have come to this field!" They did allow me to keep Naomi home for first grade, but leadership was leery.[78]

Meanwhile, my lively daughter began feeling she was missing all the glamour and excitement at school. The thrill of jumping in a muddy river with her little brothers had long lost its appeal, and she'd often break out in hives when she played outside. Other kids gushed

---

[78] Happily, field policies changed after this and it was no longer mandatory for every child to be sent to school "on demand" for first grade. My sons were subsequently allowed to home school through 3rd grade.

on the radio about sleepovers, skate nights, and parties in the dorm, and that's where she wanted to be.

"Dear God, I can only do this if I know it's your will and timing—not policy driven or pressured by people who think it's a good idea. Please speak to me, Lord."

Months later, I was nursing the baby when the Lord spoke. *"Next September, I want you to send her."*

After such a long battle, the walls crashed down like Jericho as the peaceable voice of Jesus settled in my soul. It was the same "small still voice" I had grown to trust. [79] Reminded of Hannah leaving her weaned child at the temple, I wholeheartedly committed her to the One who is able to keep what we entrust to Him.

I was glad for the months we had to prepare for the day Naomi buckled into that little plane to join the "big kids" in second grade. Another unexpected benefit, my own partner Becky was her first dorm-mom and loved her like a daughter. What a God-send!

Regardless of how good and loving dorm parents are however, little ones often get lost in the shuffle. Eighteen children under one roof forces quiet kids into the background while louder personalities demand attention.

You can line up the troops in clean clothes and march them out the door on time. You can get rows of little tin soldiers to the table, but who's there when they cry themselves to sleep? Who notices when they wander around feeling picked on or lost? Oh my heart, it happens all too often, right under our noses.

In November of 1983, we flew back to Goroka in the Highlands for Naomi's seventh birthday. Her little bedroom was nicely decorated and she was surrounded with lots of other bubbly little girls. She showed us around happily and it seemed she was thriving, but the next morning we all got up to walk her to school as a family and Naomi bolted out the door in a panic.

"Naomi, wait! Let me help you fix your hair," I called, but she burst into tears. "I'm going to be late! I'll get a *hullaballoo!*"

"Honey, you have fifteen minutes before school starts."

"Nooo! I have to go now or I'll be late!"

"Naomi, what's wrong? What in the world is a hullaballoo?" For the first time, I saw the stress she carried. She was overwhelmed and no one noticed. Not even me. Naomi's a strong kid with a good

---

[79] I Kings 19:12

head on her shoulders, too. What happens to the shy or introverted kids? That experience helped immensely when we were asked to serve as dorm parents.

Family style dorms were generally happy places and most parents had their hearts in the right place, but there were inescapable concerns and some abuses. Many MK's came out of that experience with life-long scars.

Issues of discipline and fairness challenge every parent, but managing other peoples' children gets complicated. How do you govern so many lives with healthy rules and discipline while relaxing enough to let kids *be kids*? How do you keep the tribal kids from feeling like second-rate citizens?

From the kids' perspective, dorm food is rarely what you're used to, and rules are harder when "we get to do this at home." One dorm makes you eat peas and another can't mix milk powder so it's not "lumpy and gross."

Some parents tell you you're not sick when you are, but dote on their own pampered kids who stay up late and go in the fridge whenever they want. My boys complained of being hungry in one dorm because they couldn't eat as fast as the big kids, then they'd get in trouble for *stealing* bread at night!—the bread *we* paid for!

Staying informed had challenges of its own. Some kids were more expressive and some hardly remembered what they wanted to say in our weekly five-minute radio conversation. My youngest couldn't even remember the revolving *sked* times in the middle of the afternoon.

Through all the years that our kids lived in dorms, it was largely positive, yet, they were forced to live with a host of revolving parents, roommates, and rules. Our three made life-long bonds with dorm brothers and sisters, but we also experienced some regrettable upsets and boundary issues over the course of time.

One time our little whipper-snapper bullied another boy behind the gym after school. Even though it happened after hours, three adult males grilled him for *three hours* in the principal's office! His dorm parents were right down the road but they weren't called until afterwards.

In this mother's ears that was akin to Medieval torture. My complaint wasn't against the need to deal with conflict, but in an age-appropriate manner that doesn't cause more harm than good. Another

171

time, our daughter was called for private counseling in the home of a high school coach. I was furious about over-stepping bounds.

At times, we missionaries acted like wild cowboys running free on the ranges with pistols blazing, but thank God for increased awareness in mission organizations today.[80] These are our kids for goodness sake, and the abuses and resulting hurts and resentment can hinder a child's faith for life. May God heal the brokenhearted.

"Old school" missionaries simply ordered their kids to obey the rules without complaining. If failure caused their parents to be pulled out of their tribal ministries, they'd face God's wrath for obstructing their calling to the Great Commission. I was strictly warned by one of these elder missionaries in orientation, "Karen, don't *ever* let your kids think that when they get into trouble they can just call you to bail them out." Wrong!

We made it a point to tell the kids to call if they ever needed us or wanted to come home. We weren't retiring as their parents, and they didn't *have to* go to boarding school. As far as "interrupting" our ministry, God would understand because they're just as important to Him, and they're the most important people in the world *to us*.

You can sacrifice a lot of things in life and be fine. You can live on slimy greens and buggy flour, or go without phones or TV or even Christmas presents. You can endure isolation, malaria, snakes and bugs—but all those trials rolled together were nothing compared to the pain of sending our kids away.

God knows, that was the hardest thing the Lord asked of me on the mission field, like laying down on an altar to die. Is it any wonder He tested Abraham by asking him to give up his son? Or, that He demonstrated the full extent of His love by sacrificing His Son on the cross in the same place? There is no greater love than this.

In 1989, we returned to the field and dropped all three kids off at their new dorm. They had new sneakers and school clothes and they were excited to be with old friends. But after a wonderful furlough year, I was suddenly bereft of all three kids in a day, in a full-blown case of empty-nest syndrome that felt like death.

After climbing into the five-seat Cessna and taking off, I opened my Bible but I couldn't read. My eyes clouded with tears as

---

[80] See Pres.of Compassion Int'l, Wess Stafford's A Candle in the Darkness, Christianity Today, May 2010.

we pulled away from the ground, leaving all three kids behind for the first time.

Frank called above the roar of the engine. "How ya' doing, honey?"

"Okay." I lied. It felt like a knife in my heart.

Oh God! How can I do this? I wanna go back! I looked out at the expanse of virgin land spread like a shaggy carpet as far as the eye could see. *You sent us here to reach the lost, but right now, I don't care about any of them as much as my own three kids! I want to do your will, but this is too much for me.*

Fumbling at the pages of my Bible on my lap, I desperately wanted to hear from God. *Oh God, my heart's in a shredder! Give me strength!* I poured out my grief against the little window pane.

When I opened my eyes I saw a perfect round rainbow shimmering underneath us like a ruby gem. In ten years of bush flying, I hadn't seen anything like it. Then I realized the center of its colorful orb held the shadow of our plane in perfect silhouette. *That looks like an eye! And our plane is in the middle of it!*

Immediately I heard, "My eye is upon you, Karen. You are the apple of my eye."

I recalled Hagar saying, "You are the God who sees me!"[81]

Then, as we moved over a low blanket of white cloud the rainbow jumped up onto its surface and grew bigger. Within seconds we passed over another layer of cloud, again and again, magnifying its image. *Boom, boom, boom!* That rainbow "eye" leapt closer and closer on cloud steps until it was right underneath me! The perfect shadow of our plane remained in its center, almost life-sized now.

"Karen, I am with you," the Lord whispered.[82]

I was overwhelmed with the sense of his nearness in that moment. Yes, the Lord loves all the tribes down there and desires to reach the lost across the global expanse, but He cares about *me* just as much! He is right here listening to my heart and wrapping his arms around me as only he can do.

The Lord may ask you to walk through fire, but the amazing thing is that He stands right there with you so you will not be burned.[83]

---

[81] Genesis 16:13
[82] Matthew 28:20 this promise is included in the Great Commission
[83] Reference to Daniel 3:24-25, the divine presence in the fire

22.   Prince of Power

"Father, we need wisdom if this work is to continue. Masio is still spreading lies and inciting people against us over land issues. How can we appease our enemies?"

"Yes Lord, how can we show the people we want peace?" another missionary prayed. "Maybe we should have a sing-sing for the people—"

Of course! It was one of those why-didn't-we-ever-think-of-that-before moments. By the time we finished praying, we knew it was a golden solution. The sing-sing is the traditional demonstration of sincerity and seeking favor.

On the appointed day, Frank and a few area missionaries mudded up at the river's edge and sat in somber silence at the meeting house. At first taken back by the sight, the people hushed respectfully just like we would act with a row of black veils and a hearse.

Our "big man," the field chairman flew down to address the people. "We have heavy hearts today over the fighting here. Why did Frank and Karen take their children away from their clans to live at May River? What compelled them to leave their mothers and fathers and work all these years to learn your talk? It isn't for this ground, for money, buildings or pigs. It is for the God who sent us to you. We came to give you His talk."

Everything was done with appropriate cultural sensitivity and the people were deeply moved. It made perfect sense when they heard our views presented in native terms and they were genuinely humbled. Then we surprised the big men with a monetary gift from our own pockets to "buy the worry" in true New Guinea tradition.

The following week they responded with a sing-sing for us and the Tultul made his "big man" speech in return, offering to settle our peace. The "whiteman *singsing*" bought time for us to move ahead with translation and teaching and left a lasting impression on us about the inspiration that comes from prayer. God is able to sustain us despite such powerful enemies.

The prince of power of the air still enslaves people through fear with a deeply entrenched system of rituals for productive gardens and fishnets, for health and safety. Tribal life revolves around bondage to these things.

Of course, the devil could care less about a peaceful life or eternal blessing but merely tantalizes with temporal delusions. He's an illusionist who appears as ancestral spirits or takes the form of loved ones who died and holds powerful sway over darkened hearts with such cheap tricks.

A prominent figure in Iwam life is the shaman and our informant's father Wili was greatly revered for his spirit powers. This jovial man was an enigma to me, sitting on our front step having coffee and biscuits one day and summoning evil spirits against us the next.

"Big papa" of the land, he resembled a town mayor swaggering around with his potbelly laughter and endless streams of tobacco. We often invited him to our weekly gatherings in the village, but Wili always found an excuse to be somewhere else.

"Maybe someday," he'd smile with the vague look of a man who had no intention of obliging. We knew why, too. He served another master, and people paid well for his spiritual incantations praying over the sick or calling spirits into their puny dogs so they could kill wild boars. How could he give up such a lucrative livelihood?

We prayed often for this kingpin of the spirit world. If such a key figure were to surrender to the Lord, surely many would follow. Then when Wili showed up at *lotu* one day and humbly asked to speak, we thought our prayers were answered. He shocked everyone when he said he was finally ready to denounce his spirits and make a genuine change for God.

"What happened?" everyone begged.

Wili stood up in the middle of our village clearing and began pacing back and forth.

I dreamed I got into the canoe of a trusted friend and sat behind him. My friend was in front of me and another man stood behind me steering.

"Where are we going?" I asked.

They didn't answer, but instead they paddled faster. We headed out across the May River in high water. When we reached the deep water, the man in front of me suddenly changed in appearance. His back grew scales like the skin of a crocodile and when he turned around to look at me his eyes were glowing red like Satan's.

"Where are we going?" I asked again. "Where are you taking me?" He kept laughing and I realized I was his prisoner.

By this time, we were too far out for me to escape and swim back. I was in a state of panic but there was nothing I could do.

When we shored on the opposite bank, the village looked like nothing I have ever seen. The houses and trees had burned up and all the ground was scorched. It was a desolate place filled with black smoke and smelled like death.

I noticed the faces of my ancestors cowering in the darkness. They saw me and beckoned, "Come join us!"

Then a hot wind blew and the flames grew higher. My ancestors were engulfed in the smoke and fire.

"No, no!" I screamed and ran back to the canoe. That's how I woke up, frantically trying to escape and paddle back across the river to the land of the living.

Now I've seen the land of the dead and I don't ever want to go back. God showed me what lies ahead for those who don't accept His Word. They will follow Nanto (Satan) to this desolate place because he's deceiving us and taking us away from the Lord.

Wili's vision presented a perfect Iwam illustration with the river representing life and a canoe depicting a man's chosen direction. The phrase, "to sit in Jesus' canoe," was adapted for a commitment to Christ, and depicts the essential trust in the One who steers.

Wili had chosen Satan's canoe, though he isn't the benevolent spirit he seemed. His deceptive nature came across loud and clear when he transformed into a scaly crocodile—that merciless killer lurking in familiar waters. Wili was heading for a tragic ending.

The dream should have convinced him that the devil's taking him for a ride, ultimately planning to abandon him at death's door, but Wili reverted to old ways and forgot about denouncing his spirits.

As Jesus said, "it's easier for a camel to go through the eye of a needle... but with God all things are possible." [84]

We continued to have flare-ups of opposition for years and struggled to navigate the log jams obstructing the breakthrough we so desired. For a glimpse inside the Iwam mind, my partner Becky wrote Wankumsipi's story.

It is good to sit here in the doorway of my house and let the sun warm my aching bones. I can see my wives pounding sago and all my grandchildren playing in the river. The white skin man is talking in the village square again.

They call him yenkam [human], but I'm sure that my first impressions of him were right. I always said he was a wankam [spirit]. Just look at the unnatural color of his skin! And where did he get his powers to make things? No man could make all those radios and motors and that magic needle that heals the tropical sickness and pulls babies back from death's door. He came from downriver and we all know the spirits live downriver.

I was young and strong when we heard the thunder and saw the big fighting birds in the sky. Sometimes we found them in our jungles and we would kill them easily, but we were afraid to eat them because of their skin.

Years later the white skins floated past our villages in a big canoe. We young warriors conspired to kill them and chased them in our canoes firing arrows at them until they shot a firestick at Nuwais's canoe and it broke like a piece of dry firewood.

Then there was the Yellow River Massacre. That was a good one (chuckle). We invited the Yellow River people to a sing-sing and right in the middle of it we killed them all, sending the remains of their bodies downriver in canoes! We really tricked them! But other white skins arrived with firesticks from Aussie. The first man that tried to fight was killed on the spot and the others were taken away to a place called kalabus [jail] where they were fenced like pigs!

Many high water seasons came and went and our children grew taller. Then Masta Bob came to live with us.[85] He had just begun to learn our talk when my old crony, Neno, worked poison on him and he got real sick. A big loud bird came in to get him and he never came

---

[84] Matthew 19:24-26 and Mark 10:25-27
[85] Bob and Joanne Conrad, Wycliffe missionaries, arrived in 1964 to do linguistic analysis, living in a houseboat for six months.. This is a tribal perspective of their story.

back! Yeah that's right, (smiling to savor the victory), our poison is powerful!

Many seasons later when my sons were young men, a giant bird came out of the sky and landed like a water spider on the river in front of our village. The spirit boys got out and said they came to give us some important talk, but they had to learn our talk first.[86]

The young men wanted them to live here, but not me. Too many changes have been coming into our world and it's upsetting the spirits I've spent years learning to appease. Despite my apprehensions, when they were about to enter the big bird's stomach, I asked them to bring me gifts from the spirit world. (I didn't want to miss out on anything.)

They eventually came back and built an odd dwelling on the hill. They got their food from the water bird. Then they brought their long-haired women and golden-haired children and gave our babies medicine. Some of the young men ate their medicine, but I didn't. How do we know if they're trying to poison us like we tricked those fools from Yellow River?

A lot of my people befriended them, brought them food, and helped them build their houses, but I've kept my distance. They have no respect for our spirits and break ancient taboos all the time, so I'm watching to see how long they last, these spirit boys with pale skin. We old men speculate on why they've come—to steal our wives, our land, or our spiritual powers?

After they started using our talk, the spirits became very unpredictable indeed. They seem angry with us, and it's getting harder to summon them. They won't even come into our little dogs to kill pigs any more. What next?

As I sit here on my front porch, I can hear snatches of the talk of those spirit boys. Sometimes I am strangely drawn to it, but let the young men chase these new ideas. I've done just fine following the ways of my father all my life. I don't need to rock the boat now.

---

[86] In 1973, Don Meyer and Steve Bram arrived in a small seaplane to begin the Iwam work. The Brams stayed three years, but left suddenly due to their son's critical health. We arrived in 1980 as their replacements.

Wankumsipi was one of many brooding over our presence. Accustomed to following familiar spirits, they rightly sensed that we followed a different spirit.

Others, like Masio, angled for political power and physical property, while unseen powers conspired against us. Dark expressions and black eyes leered at us when we shored in the village. There was agitation, sickness, and even death.

Yet, we serve the Almighty Spirit warrior who doesn't cower or bow to ancestral incantations. Jesus promised, "All power is given unto me in heaven and in earth. Go ye therefore, and teach all nations…and lo, I am with you always, even unto the end of the world."[87]

He swore his presence to go with us even to the ends of the earth, and we were banking on it.

---

[87] Matthew 28:18-20 in KJV, known as the Great Commission

23. The God of Heaven Thunders

This brings me back to where I started, in the airstrip house in 1986. We sat on the floor holding hands in a small circle of area missionaries while the tribesmen surrounded us with spears and arrows flying into the thatch.

Frank's prayer distinctly mentioned the Lamb of God, bringing us back to the reasons we came to PNG in the first place. Isaiah's words lifted off the pages of my memory. "He was led like a lamb to the slaughter, and as a sheep before her shearers is silent, so he did not open his mouth."[88] That image took hold in my heart, a surprising peace in the eye of the storm with the madness stampeding around us. We asked for courage to follow in His footsteps.

Then, a letting go. Anger melted like giant raindrops that fall on the river and float away. We might have been minutes from a cannibal shiskabob, but the words of our mouths were unreal, even to me. Maybe this is what it feels like when you're about to slip into eternity's skin. Time stops. All is calm.

"We look to you, Lord. Accomplish your purposes here today, Father."

Someone outside asked, "Hey, what are they doing in there?"

Another peeked in the slats. "They're sitting in a circle on the floor! They're calling their spirits!" Not something to be taken lightly in a tribe of sorcerers, a reverent hush fell over everyone, the kind of silence that makes your ears throb.

---

[88] Isaiah 53:7

181

Then, another buzz of voices as tempers and tensions mounted. Frank translated as many comments as he could decipher, like an audible game of pick-up sticks.

"They want to roll all the fuel drums onto the airstrip! They want to throw everything in the river and destroy our boats!" Suddenly, they rallied and charged up the front steps to get us.

"Here they come!" Frank yelled. I tucked my head down and closed my eyes wincing, *Lord Jesus!*

The house shook as they stormed up to the front door. Jemis, handsome prince and eldest son of the Tultul, ripped a slat off the screen door and turned to face the onslaught. Holding the stick above his head, he cried, "No! *Ka papa tet!*" [Stop, don't do it!] The men were bunched up against him, pressing his back against the door.

A solitary voice with the broken slat of a moldy door, he stood against the angry mob. Why would Jemis do this, siding with foreigners against his own people? But his shout fell like a wet blanket on a smoldering fire and quenched the chaos.

Hot minutes passed with us still seated in positions of prayer. Then, just as mysteriously as the whole episode started, it ended. Our fearless warriors disbanded and relief mingled with dazed exhaustion. Without any exchange of words between us, our front door never opened, no shots were fired, no one was harmed. That human snake simply slithered away, sulking into the shadowy places from which it came.

Eventually we let the kids downstairs, but not knowing if we were still in danger for a second act of the whole production, we hunkered down inside. The day's events certainly proved that anything is possible, and cries of intended destruction still rung in our ears.

Afterwards I echoed prayers of David, "Come and see what God has done… He has preserved our lives… They surrounded me on every side… They swarmed around me like bees, but they died out as quickly as burning thorns… the Lord helped me… he has not given me over to death."[89]

---

[89] Psalm 66; 118:10-18

Yet, looming questions poked my innards the way prickly heat chafes our skin or a bee sting brings an angry swelling. Will we ever feel safe again among such volatile people? I know we should be glad to be alive, but what now? Like earlier disciples on the road to Emmaus,[90] I wondered how such a powerful God could let everything go *so wrong.*

Overwhelmed by a sense of betrayal from people we counted as friends, the whole episode replayed like a loop tape of language drills in my mind. Our own neighbors stormed to the forefront with weapons! Not only did they join the attack, but they sipped coffee on our stoop while they planned it! Why didn't they ever "out their worries," face to face? If our best friends bait us like a pack of wild pigs, how much more would they do?

Mechanically, I baked bread, taught the kids, and washed the clothes on my trusty old wringer. One morning as my worn clothes and ragged emotions were wringing through the rollers, I realized that I trust my fifty-year-old washing machine more than the Iwam people!

Like a raw wound I kept bumping, questions bled out and the pain went deeper. *I thought we were friends!* Why did they turn on us like this? And the one I kept trying not to think about, what would they have done if Jemis didn't stop them?

The people kept their distance too, enforcing the awful vacuum we felt. It's a typical response. Despite fierce outward images as warriors, the Iwam are wimps when it comes to verbal confrontation. None of our workers showed up and I was getting jumpy.

I carried a load of clothes to the lines outside where a host of katydids mimicked a thousand violin strings buzzing with suspense. Where is everyone? Are black eyes peering at me from the darkness?

In the film *Never Cry Wolf,* a lone scientist named Tyler is heading for the Arctic on a mission to discover how wolves survive the long, harsh winters. Surveying the frozen wilderness from a little chartered plane, he is suddenly stricken with fear. "I can't do this! How on earth did I get this job? What if somebody just spilled coffee on their desk, shuffled some papers around and made a bad typo. *Maybe this is all a big mistake!"*

---

[90] The Road to Emmaus story is recorded in Luke 24:13-25

Similar thoughts plagued me like annoying reruns in my brain. Haven't we earned trust after living here so many years? We've nursed their sick, fed their hungry, and clothed their naked bodies. We've been warmed by their fires, seated in their canoes, and even dipped together out of the same soup pots.

Where did we go wrong? Maybe we never should have brought our children to such a God-forsaken wilderness. What made them turn on us like this, and why would God allow it?

Three black hornbills called *mok* burst from the trees overhead and scared the daylights out of me. The birds in New Guinea are *really* big, with a four or five-foot wingspan. *Mok* resemble ancient pterodactyls, slow and clumsy with big hammer heads and loud flapping wings that sound like shaking a rubber mat. Their honking cries echoed loudly across the humid expanse.

Aaaaarrkkkk! Aaaaarrrrrrk! They mocked me, looking down on my head and I imagined them snickering, "What are you doing here city girl? Go back where you came from or I'll poop on your laundry!"

Iwam shamans would hear spirit messages in their cries, but I only heard another reminder that we were aliens in an unpredictable world.

Five agonizing days passed. Most business takes more time in third-world affairs, but that week was painfully slow. Provincial offices on the coast kept saying they intended to fly out, but there were no planes available. That worked for a day or so, then they needed fuel. Finally, they said, *"Sori, no gat pilot."* [Sorry, we need a pilot.]

We finally pulled out the citizenship card and said, "We have citizens from America, the U.K. and Australia living out here. We have no choice but to report your inability to send assistance to our embassies in Port Moresby. Maybe they can help us."

Minutes passed with radio static. Then the speaker crackled back to life and the officer announced that a plane had just been located and would take off within the hour! We never knew the actual reasons, but as in most Asian cultures, shame is a powerful motivator.

Word traveled quickly that a government plane was on the way to hear their "talk." This time however, the people were armed only with placards demanding *ERSTRIP KOMPENSATON* [*airstrip compensation*] in large, running letters.

It seemed almost comical, like a tribal version of a Charlie Brown cartoon. Funny, how my mind reverts to this sort of thing at a time like this, as though I had no other mental drawer in which to file this bizarre scenario. It seemed like a crazy dream where a clown shows up at a funeral.

By this time, villagers had been drumming up enormous figures, nursing wild ideas about the value of their land. They thought they were going to win the jackpot, assuming the government would guarantee *expat* safety by forking out drums of money. Who fueled such inflated expectations?

After all the suspense, a sleek twin prop aircraft finally touched down on our earthen strip. We greeted officials who were poised and diplomatically dressed in light khaki suits, offered drinks, answered a few quick questions, then retired to a respectful distance. The suits marched out to confront the people and at last, the dark underbelly of the beast was exposed.

The whole plot was the work of our zealous local leader, Masio. Good-looking, tall and well-educated by tribal standards, he was elected Area Minister for the Sepik Provincial government. Due to rank, he became accustomed to uncommon luxuries such as flying to Wewak at government expense to attend provincial meetings where he fueled up on alcohol at the international hotel and made a spectacle of smashing glasses and starting drunken brawls. He was well-known by district police on the coast who held a thick file in his name we discovered.

Where we lived along the muddy banks of the May River, Masio was greatly feared. In the minds of the people we were the dispensable outsiders, but he represented national power. We often prayed like the villagers in a Jewish musical for the Rabbi's blessing for the Czar. "May God bless and keep him… *far away* from us."[91]

He may have been the director of our hostile demonstration, but Masio was nowhere to be seen on either of these dress-up occasions. While coordinating everything behind the scenes, he secretly nursed hopes of ousting us *expats* and taking over the airstrip. Then he'd fly in all the booze he wanted and set up residence in our houses as area kingpin.

---

[91] From Fiddler on the Roof

We also learned about similar uprisings erupting in Wewak and other coastal regions, where ground disputes over hospitals and provincial buildings ended in huge settlements as high as K90,000 kina.[92] Masio wanted to get his hands on that pot, and persuaded our villagers to follow his schemes—right up to a call to arms.

Government officials patiently explained their stance concerning May River. Funds were unavailable to meet their demands, and that proud band of warriors was told that they put precious little value on this remote strip of swampland in the rain forest. Instead, the amount they were offered was a meager three-digit settlement.

"*Poa hantret kina,*" they announced in Pidgin, the equivalent of about eight hundred U.S. dollars. Unfortunately, split between all the participants families, that's a meager booty of a few kina each—enough to buy a bag of rice and a couple tins of fish.

We listened from the sidelines, watching as expectant expressions turned to crestfallen sighs. With the sun beating down on their glistening bodies and such pitiful words assailing their ears, we could see their spirits melting by degrees. Not only were monetary figures coming up short, but the worst was yet to come.

Officials then announced that everyone who took part in the demonstration broke the law by bearing arms against private and peaceful parties. Remembering local history of the bloated bodies of *expats* floated downriver filled with spears, they were taking a strong stance now. They were all going to be charged, courted, and incarcerated.

In the wake of this news, we experienced the full gamut of emotions. On one hand, it was a relief to see the strength and competency of the government agents (once they arrived), but internal conflict can be worse than facing bows and arrows!

---

[92] The PNG dollar, pronounced kee'-nah, was roughly equivalent to US$200,000 at the time.

With dashed expectations of any good we hoped to accomplish, guilt then reared its ugly head. Granted, we purposed to take a back seat in proceedings and officials determined the sentences, but we felt like miserable failures. What sort of missionaries were we? I recall something about "setting captives free" in Scripture, but we were about to see half our tribe locked up!

Then fear led us to wonder what would be remembered from this awful week? Did they betray us or *did we betray them?* Suppose things get twisted in the collective village storytelling, and they blame us? After being imprisoned, these men could return embittered, and retaliation could put an end to us. Would we ever be able to live peacefully at May River?

The people's response in all this was also bewildering. Not one of them even tried to run away. They could have vanished into uncharted jungle territory when they were sent home to pack their things, but every single one reported to the airstrip dutifully packed, with their few earthly possessions in little string bags. Were they proud of this? Excited even?

Then I pitied them. Fifty-six of the strongest men found responsible for the riotous affair were sentenced to six months in prison. (Many were excluded for age and health reasons.) Those convicted would be forced to leave their families and gardens to face *kalabus,* incarceration in a foreign world.

Women wailed in mud, and naked children with runny noses wandered around in confusion arousing my compassion. They cast hurt and angry glances in our direction, but mostly grief and fear.

Why God? Why did you allow all this to happen, knowing that the whole future of the work here is at stake? Relationships are shot and after all we've done here, *they hate us!* They lined up to trade us for a few silver kina! Our lives and our kids were threatened for a small cash profit over a tiny strip of mud that's worth nothing in light of eternity. What's the use? This is a complete disaster and a total waste of time!

Nagging doubts, hurt, and anxiety have such long teeth, twisting like underwater crocs. We wondered if we should just start packing—at least find people who want us.

A couple of geckos scrambled across the rafters and my eyes fell on a needlepoint picture on my living room wall. Flipping a frame over in my hand I gasped at the cobwebs on the back of the fabric.

What a mess! Beneath layers of dust and bug droppings I noticed the workmanship, so full of abrupt changes and far too many knots and tangles. It didn't make sense, but especially when it came to the finest details. Wherever I attempted the most ornate flower petals or delicate butterflies, things got downright ugly on the "working side" of the fabric—just like the landscape of my life.

Why are you focusing on the underside of the fabric? I'm not finished yet.

I had no problem seeing it in the colorful maze of threads in my hand. I'm fixated on every knot of conflict, the long trailing delays of 'unanswered' prayer, and all the cobwebs of confusion, but on this journey of faith the Lord wants to demonstrate an elevated viewpoint.

Not until each loom is silent and the shuttles cease to fly
Will God unroll the pattern and explain the reason why.

The dark threads are as needful in the master's skillful hand
As the threads of gold and silver in the pattern He has planned.[93]

The attack of '86 was one of a long string of events in which Masio initiated attempts to undo our ministry and incite people against us over the years. Though we weren't even aware of what was going on in many cases, God manifested His strength on our behalf.

My favorite account happened at a secret meeting in Mani at the base of our airstrip. This is Tultul's village, the revered landowner of the ground and the focal point of the conflict.

The men and leaders gathered in the village clearing as they had done for years whenever there was a battle to be fought or a dispute to be settled. All the local heavyweights were present, gathered around the ancient *quila* tree.[94] This particular landmark anchored the prestigious village, flanked by Tultul's long house and the only airstrip in Iwam territory.

The sun was high in a bright blue sky when they started rolling tobacco in banana leaves, smoking, and passing *buai* [betel

---

[93] Streams in the Desert, Madame Guyon
[94] *Quila* (kwee'la) is "ironwood," known for its strength and durable red wood

pepper] to their *wantoks* [friends]. Then, they began discussing the missionary problem. Going around the circle, Masio pointed out the advantages they'd enjoy if they regained controlling authority over all our leased property.

Someone suggested holding a mock court against us. If they could prove that we had been operating in our own interests and harming theirs, they could succeed in an airstrip coup this time. "Operation extinguish missionary" was now underway. One by one, the leaders assigned lies to various members of the group.

"You, say that the mission stole your money from the store account and you say they withheld your payments for the airstrip work. You, make a charge against them for taking your trees without compensation." And on it went. One trumped up accusation after another, until the Lord Himself couldn't stand it. That's when it happened.

A loud *CRACK* ripped the skies and a bolt of white lightning struck the ancient *quila*. It came out of nowhere and split the sky right above their heads.

"We scattered like cock roaches," Tomas told us. "The hair stood up on my arms and I could feel the power of that bolt in my chest. The trunk of the old tree was scorched from the top down and it was still smoking as we sat shivering in our hiding places."

"What was *that?*" a tremulous voice whispered.

Then, one old man broke the silence. "It was *their God*. He heard us... and *He* didn't like it." The smell of charred wood filled their nostrils and the sound of thunder still rung in their ears. One by one, the men who had been assigned to testify realized what this signified. If our great Spirit would throw a lightning bolt while they merely *talked* about this plan, what would He do if they followed through with their plans?

"You know what?... I'm not going to say what you told me to say," one said slowly.

"Neither am I," said another, and another, until there were no willing witnesses remaining for the mock trial. It was court adjourned at that point.

Frank's informant Tomas Wili (don't ask me why he was there unless pressured by his father Wili) told us, "The strangest part was that there wasn't a cloud in the sky."

They recognized it as a response from above, a hurled dagger from the Almighty. Enemies grudgingly admitted that our Spirit was fighting for us. God demonstrated his power in a way they could understand, precisely when they were conspiring to do us harm.

Nevertheless, during the six months our tribal "storm troopers," were incarcerated on the coast, we started receiving eviction notices from Masio. He would pick a date and advise us to start packing. He even threatened to throw us and our kids in the river if that date arrived and we were still in the village!

We continually took the matter to God, asked people to pray, and believing we should hold our ground. Yet, in the back of my mind, I wondered, dear God, *what if?* The whole situation resembled Haman's plot.[95] Masio erected his gallows and eagerly rubbed his hands together for the day of our demise.

Instead, after years of harassment and conflict, the Lord turned the people against him. When our men were released from jail, we were the ones who helped them get home. And when they came back, they threw Masio in the river!

Despite the fact that Frank was known to have walked right over the back of snakes and sorcery and witchcraft failed on us, there were repeated attempts to hinder our work over the years—but in every situation, God was greater.

He is an excellent marksman!

---

[95] The book of Esther tells the story of Haman's fury and how he was hung on the gallows he built for his enemy. See Esther 3:5-6, 7:9

24.   Faith Comes By Hearing

"Faith comes by hearing the Word of God..." Rom 10:17

For the first six years, it seems we did little but battle the elements and put out fires, and we wondered if our presence would ever truly make a difference to the Iwam people.

I remembered Moses complaining that God hadn't delivered the people at all—in fact, conditions were much worse after he arrived on the scene. God answered him, *"Wait and see what I'm going to do. **I am** the Lord!"*[96]

A year into our second term, Frank had compiled enough lessons to begin a new program of systematic teaching we nick-named "the Chron." We'd teach God's Word chronologically, amplifying key lessons from Adam to Jesus, teaching twice a day, five days a week, for sixteen weeks in two locations.

Untimely obstacles peppered the days leading up to commencement. Aiwanu's village Tultul was nearly killed in a local skirmish—a bold attempt to wipe out our most avid supporter. We flew him to Wewak hospital and heard it would take six weeks for his broken bones to heal. Miraculously, he only missed the first two days of teaching.

The first night of teaching in our village, Frank was battling malarial symptoms and his voice was weak as he started. I sat praying for his strength as he taught about God and his angels. Gradually, he grew stronger and louder as God's presence took over. Even Wili the sorcerer's head was bowed.

---

[96] Exodus 6:1 paraphrased in my own words

As Frank taught about Creation, we watched storm clouds turn away and winds die down so that everyone could stay through the entire session. God even provided his own class visuals!

During the first week we took a daring move and taught on Lucifer, the origin and work of Satan. Frank employed cultural imagery of the savvy hunter's pig blind. The people loved his reenactment of baiting the prey and fattening the kill to heighten his final success. Then he filled the fattened pigs with his arrows and prepared to feast in victory.

After the drama, he addressed them plainly. "This is exactly how Satan has been treating you! He eyes you the way you watch a family of pigs in the bush. I'm telling you the truth, Satan is the hunter and you are his prey! He set up his blind right around your villages and has been baiting you with lies for generations. When he responds to your witchcraft, it's only because he wants you to be comfortable eating out of his hand while he waits to destroy you and take you to the place of fire."

The men were incensed and upset, squirming uncomfortably. The women clucked their tongues in disdain. "Did Frank just call us a bunch of stupid pigs?"

Frank's eyes filled with tears and his voice cracked.

"Look! He's crying," they said.

"*Wei! Hani waikai!* [Hey, listen to me!] Satan doesn't care about you any more than you care about your prey when you go into the jungle to hunt. Don't sit here in ignorance and let the devil destroy you!" he pleaded. Then he prayed, asking God to open their eyes.

Tomas was walking through the village afterwards and felt a hot blast of air on the chest. He found Samuel and told him, and he had felt the same thing. So they started discussing the *lotu* message and Tomas began to cry. He said he cried all the way downriver, realizing that God's Word is true. Jemis told his wives, "We've been tricked like pigs!" He ordered everyone to rehearse these lessons in their houses at night.

The young men put messages to music and sang in their string band. The old men said, "We've never heard like this before," and started confessing sin.

Though conscious of our inadequacies, the Lord encouraged us daily as we read His promises. "I AM the Lord your God; open your mouth wide and I will fill it."[97] He was moving in hearts as they heard His Word.

In a neighboring tribe, coworkers were also teaching "the chron," and as they neared the gospel presentation, catastrophe struck. A flood crashed through the village in the night, wiping 20' off the end of their airstrip, demolishing houses and sweeping two lives away. The people fled to the mountains in fear and we knew it was another attempt of the enemy to keep them from hearing what Jesus accomplished on the cross.

We were also mindful of the spiritual battle. As evil spirits were losing their grip in the advent of God's Word, they acted like a jealous girlfriend. For example, Wili said his spirits weren't responding to his summons since they were listening to our teaching.

When we dramatized Abraham on Mt. Moriah, our daughter played Isaac. Frank raised a knife in the air and God called to Him from behind and Naomi said her line sweetly, *"Apu, sipsip pari?"* [Father, where is the lamb?] People were deeply moved.

One perceptive old man asked, "What are we doing about our debt to God? We come to hear God's talk, but our sin debt is still standing. We don't have a lamb!"

Frank answered much like Abraham to his son Isaac when he asked why they had wood for a fire but no lamb for the sacrifice. "You'll see. God has made a road for you," he explained. "He will provide Himself a sacrifice."[98]

Since there are no sheep in the jungle, it fell upon us to introduce a new animal for the Passover. Nothing in their natural world—crocodiles, snakes, fruit bats or tree kangaroos for example—even comes close to depicting the nature of our Lord as he was led to the slaughter.

We used a stuffed lamb from the kid's toy box to teach them about the paschal lamb. We killed the lamb, painted our doorpost and ate our meal while the angel of destruction passed by. There were over 100 in attendance at that session.

The pace was difficult and both of us fought an onslaught of physical challenges. By the middle of the program I already had my fourth hit of malaria. But it wasn't about our strength or talents or personalities or any other thing—it was God's own greatness and

---

[97] Psalm 81:10
[98] Genesis 22:8 KJV

mercy that was beginning to change lives. "Not by might nor by power, but by my Spirit, says the Lord Almighty."[99]

The brass serpent story[100] was acted out with zeal by the teens and young men in Aumi. Tossing coiled vines all over the village clearing, they reenacted an infestation of death adders. Our male actors should have won Oscars for dying with such flourish.

Little by little, people began receiving the Word of God. Some sought Frank privately or rapped on the door of our house at night with a spiritual question nagging at them.

Phillip came after a sleepless night of wrestling with where he was going to spend eternity. He had begun to "turn his thinking" like a canoe heading down an unknown river. Since he was heavily involved with evil spirits they were nearly driving him mad. After two hours on the porch he understood. If he wanted to find peace with the Creator God, he had to change canoes and turn away from the "things of the ground." *Kowa ni Yenkam Purik*, "the Great One Above," could not commingle with his ancestral spirits.

Moses was shaping his canoe paddle in the village when the Word of God found its mark. He suddenly realized his neediness and asked God to make him clean. Dropping his tools on the ground, this macho warrior came to share the news and pray in tears.

After four months of steady teaching morning and night, we announced the "BIG TALK," and anticipation mounted steadily. The gospel presentation would give people an opportunity to fully understand the message of the cross at last, and prayer went up around the world for this event.

The men produced props including a life-size cross and a whip and crown of thorns. They dug the hole to stand the cross in our "Golgotha" and prepared places for the trials and burial. The women helped organize costumes and prepare our actors. Roman soldiers were outfitted with aluminum foil helmets and swords, apostles needed mantles, and chief priests got robes and turbans.

Our informant Tomas Wili was chosen to emcee the event. We rigged up speakers and a microphone to the airstrip tractor battery and he felt like a national celebrity. Frank looked authentic as a bearded Jewish Jesus, the young men from Aumi were a perfect band of Roman fighting soldiers, and our gentle Aiwanu men were apostles.

---

[99] Zechariah 4:6
[100] Numbers 21:4-9

The soft-spoken Daniel was well suited to play the disciple Jesus loved with his big brown eyes. Nakom was perfectly suited to play Judas, having a reputation of a thief, shifty-eyed and greedy for gain. When he saw that he would get to wear a bright flowery shirt he begged for the part! Everyone snickered as he stole away to betray Jesus, knowing it was just the sort of thing he would do in real life.

I felt like a school teacher the day of the Christmas pageant, nervous that some of our 27 actors might forget their parts in the final production. During the rehearsal there was so much clowning, I thought some might blow it or clam up at the crucial moment.

People turned out in droves on the appointed day, several hundred from all the surrounding villages. Despite our somewhat comical appearances and the muddled impressions from those who had never seen a performance, there was a prevailing sense of God's presence. It felt like Jesus Himself was standing with us. Then, as everyone did their parts and Tomas's voice boomed out with the living and powerful Words, the Holy Spirit, our true director, did what He does best.

Frank was arrested by our band of Roman guards and hauled before the priests and governors to be sentenced at court. This is pretty close to the Iwam norm for handling tribal upsets. It is generally immediate and loud, and weapons are flashed on the spot. People were clearly emotional as Jesus was pushed before magistrates, tied to a post and whipped.

They followed every detail of Jesus blindfolded and beaten, jeered and mocked. "Tell us who's hitting you now! Prove yourself!" These are people accustomed to fighting. Whole clans could rise to an uproar in minutes over some perceived insult and take sides to protect the family name. The betrayal, arrest and trials made perfect sense, but it was quite another matter to understand why all the disciples abandoned him at a time like this since clan loyalties run so deep.

Even harder to understand is why Jesus did NOTHING when He was taken captive. Why wouldn't Jesus the "powerful spirit man" defend himself like a man? Isn't He the same one who raised the dead and healed people? Why would He turn out to be such a wimp at a time like this? There was a ripple of murmuring as these parts of the drama unfolded.

Then they nailed him to the cross, pounding the spikes between his fingers while Frank prayed they wouldn't miss with the heavy mallet. They raised the cross and some of the women started wailing when they saw tomato-red blood spilling down his side. When our Roman guard speared him and Frank yelled in excruciating pain, some of them thought he was actually stabbed.

"If you really are the Christ, save yourself and us too!" the others jeered. Then they gambled for his robe beneath his bleeding feet. "Father, forgive them! They don't know what they're doing!" Then, he said, "It is finished," and he bowed his head and gave up his spirit.

Despite our simplistic reenactment of the greatest story ever told, we were witnessing the power of salvation, displayed for all to see. No matter how many times I read or hear it, the impact never wanes. Who is this God who loves us so much that He would send Himself in the form of human flesh to be subjected to such a cruel death on our behalf?

Then, the greatest part of the story comes after Jesus was taken down from the cross. Village women were still crying in our audience, but it only made it feel more real as disciples wrapped up the body in a sheet and carried him to the tomb, sealing it with a bamboo mat. Guards were posted and Tomas explained that three days passed with Jesus in the grave.

Our disciples went home and mourned, another extremely powerful part of Iwam life. Until we moved into the village, I never experienced mourning the way they do. All of life ceases and the entire family gathers to wail for weeks on end. All through the night you can hear the crying.

It's nothing like the way we observe death in America, where your own neighbors rarely know what's happened down the street. We wear black at the funeral and follow a hearse to the cemetery, but the civilized world mourns stoically.

In our drama, the disciples gathered together after Jesus was buried. Bewildered and sorrowful, they mourned Iwam style and wailed, "How could he leave us? What do we do now?" This is a typical Iwam response in mourning.

I've watched people dance and anguish around a body strung up to the center post of a house. Shockingly, I've seen them aim spears into the face of the corpse yelling, "WHY did you leave us? Who's going to take care of our fish traps and our sago gardens? What are we going to do without you?"

Then it was Sunday morning. Everyone gasped when Jesus stood up and came back from his grave. Frank left his white sheet in the tomb, and walked away while Tomas explained that Jesus came back to life. Death could not hold Him captive. "He is stronger than the grave!" Tomas hollered.

We women went to the tomb looking for His body. The angels asked, "Why are you looking for the living among the dead? He is not here. He has risen!"

Then Jesus appeared to the disciples gathered in their house and showed them the scars in His hands and side.

To tribal people accustomed to talking to spirits and seeing spirit manifestations of their dead relatives, that wasn't hard to believe. But Jesus broke bread and ate with them. He was in fact a resurrected body, not an apparition.

They were amazed at his spirit powers, especially when he offered, "Thomas, come and put your finger in this hole and see that it is I. Put your hand in my side." No wonder Thomas fell to his knees! "Blessed are those who believe without seeing."

I watched the people's faces as the whole gospel story was fleshed out in living Iwam color for the first time. We ended with Jesus returning to heaven saying, "Go and tell the whole world this good news..." And that's why we came. At last, they understood, God sent missionaries so they could understand what He did for them.

Afterwards, Jemis our prince stood up and said, "We have seen and heard what Jesus did. From now on, we have no excuse." I imagined angels recording that statement in heavenly places.

For many days, we reviewed the heart of the gospel message with people face to face. "Jesus died in your place so that you don't have to. He demonstrated power over the grave. We can also be raised to life if we believe His Word. Sit in his canoe and let him take the oars and steer you to eternal life where you will never die."

As far as we could tell, more than 400 took a seat in His canoe, and their names were added to the lamb's book of life!

25. Sleeping with the Skull

Now that the Iwam church was born, teaching and translation continued to be our main focus for ten more years. We shared the load with our single partners, Hope and Linda, and a few years after Meyers left to do full-time field leadership, we were joined by John and Debbie. A gifted teacher, John learned the language quickly and began sharing the teaching. Frank focused on Bible translation, and Hope, Linda and I taught literacy.

Of course church growth wasn't immediate or steady. Interest rose and fell from time to time and problems arose. There was jealousy, territorial fighting, and some even preached for the ulterior purpose of getting the attention of women.

Frank once shored to find everyone in an uproar over five adulterous women, whose husbands were punching their faces and kicking their stomachs in the middle of the village! Thank God they stopped when he arrived. Obviously, the lesson plan was scrapped that day, but they were amazed when he taught them about Jesus and the woman caught in adultery. Mercy trumped Mosaic law.[101]

In one good week Frank could cover as much as four chapters of the New Testament. Though he was a natural translator with a good grasp of "discourse analysis," everything ground to a halt when informants didn't show.

Tomas was the best we had in the early years, but he had so many outside interests we eventually lost him to his own developing businesses. We made it a matter of prayer until the Lord raised up another faithful man. Frank needed guys that could grasp concepts

---

[101] John 8:1-11 Legalists and religious leaders wanted to stone the woman but Jesus convicted them of their own sinfulness and freed the woman.

quickly and continue for long hours in the office. That was hard to come by—until we found Mark Maum.

Mark was smaller than all his brothers. He didn't grow as tall or as broad as the others. When it came to felling trees, carving canoes or building houses, Mark never excelled. So when Frank decided to give him a shot, he jumped at the chance to work in the office. He was only about fifteen when he hired him, but lo and behold, this wiry young man had a sharp mind. In fact, he developed quickly to the point that he could practically anticipate what Frank was driving at before the words were out of his mouth. What a gift!

Every morning, rain or shine, Mark showed up early and ready to go. I'd serve a pot of coffee and some biscuits or fruit and then they were off. They started every session with prayer for wisdom in "turning God's talk" and Mark's enthusiasm equaled Frank's.

I'd hear them laughing in the office at the back end of our house, or see them out taking breaks while I was in the schoolhouse. Whether walking out to the river to bail the boat or take a dip to cool off, they were usually talking a hundred miles an hour. Mark was becoming a carbon copy of Frank in many ways.

One morning, Frank pulled out his log book to track the hours for wages, and Mark surprised him. "I can write my name in English, wanna see?"

Frank gave him a pencil and he proceeded to write his name perfectly, in the same style as Frank's hand, except for one thing. It was backwards and upside down!

"Where did you learn that?" Frank asked, staring at the paper.

"I've been watching you," he said, beaming.

Mark was also soaking up the Word of God in huge doses every day. One day, he asked, "Frank, do you want to know my number one [favorite] story?"

"Sure," he said. This would be great feedback since they had covered a lot of the Old Testament lessons together and Frank was always interested to hear which ones hit home.

"Baby Moses in the basket."

"Really?" Frank thought he'd pick one of the "great" miracle stories such as the Red Sea opening up or Noah and the flood. "Why is that your number one?"

"That story showed me that God was watching over me when I was born, and He has a plan for my life."

His curiosity piqued, Frank asked him to tell him about it, and we never forgot the story of Mark's birth.

"My mother was overwhelmed when I was born. She was sorry she had me. So she asked her clan sister to take me out to the jungle and leave me there."

It may have been a bad case of post-partum blues combined with the tough realities of survival, but Mark was abandoned to the elements as a helpless infant.

By an act of mercy, the old woman who put him there couldn't sleep. It was our little gardener, Nonut, who kept imagining that she could hear him crying. She tossed and turned and finally returned to retrieve the baby. To her relief, no wild animals had found him and nothing had harmed him. From that night on, she raised him.

Mark summed it up. "I was left in a little *bilum* [net bag] in the bush, but God rescued me just like Moses. Even though I could have died, God had a plan that was greater. When I heard this story, I thought, God must have saved me for a reason just like Moses. This must be why you asked me to do this work and why He has given me the head for it. God is using me to help deliver His talk to my people."

Frank sat astonished. That little story explained Mark's avid dedication. God had set apart a man from birth whose heart would follow him and fill this all-important role. To this day, he remains involved and faithful in the work.

Together with such key language helpers, Frank unearthed fascinating tidbits from the tribal culture to enrich teaching and translation. Intrinsic beliefs and customs provided effective illustrations to illuminate spiritual truth in a powerful way, like the Apostle Paul proclaiming the unknown God to a city that worshipped a host of deities.[102] These built-in illustrations are most valuable tools for redemptive analogies.

A good example is the significance of blood and bloodlines, of which the Iwam are ever-mindful. When twins came into the world, the second-born was traditionally sacrificed because it was believed to be evil. Though we would never condone such an act and we taught that life is sacred, that cultural belief helps teach that we are born

---

[102] Paul addressed the people of Athens, a city full of idols, even citing their poets w/great cultural awareness, in Acts 17:16-31.

under a curse. We are all under Adam's curse from birth, but God can redeem us from its penalty by his mercy.[103]

Earlier I described the blood-letting of the male initiation to cleanse the mother's blood from a young man's body. More commonly, blood-letting was practiced in the form of releasing pain, even the pain of a headache. People nicked their foreheads with razor blades to let out the sickness and "bad blood." The ghastly sight was reminiscent of a ghoulish Halloween costume when people appeared at the door with the telltale trails of dried blood running down their faces.

In tribal thinking, shedding blood can be viewed as a solution to a variety of life's problems. Whether for the elimination of evil, cleansing or healing, blood is powerful. God's Word teaches that the life is in the blood. More importantly, without the shedding of blood there is no remission of sins.

Redemptive analogies are rich and powerful where there is no prior foundation of Judeo-Christian roots. We were excited every time we discovered another cultural analogy, such as the ritual performed by a widow who wanted to remarry.

Before she could be united to another man, a widow would wade out into the river to the waist, wearing her old grass skirt. Untying it underwater, she would release it and let it sink to the bottom, representing the end of her "old life" and relationship with the deceased. Coming up out of the water, she'd tie on a new skirt freshly made for the occasion to symbolize the beginning of a new life with her new husband.

Putting on a new skirt is a fitting metaphor for putting on Christ. It also relates to baptism, illustrating how a believer dies to the old man and is raised up to a new life. We adapted cultural examples like these to bridge to Biblical truth whenever possible.

The people were growing to appreciate the power in the name of Jesus. Some of their testimonies amazed us, as the Lord demonstrated his glory in his church. The old Tultul spoke at one of our *lotu* services about the day he was given the cloth teaching books.

"When the books were given to me I promised to take good care of them, but as I was paddling upriver a huge storm rolled in. I prayed, 'Lord, hold your hand over my head like a banana leaf so the

---

[103] Romans 5:12-21 teaches that one man brought sin upon all mankind, but another man, Jesus, brought salvation.

books don't get ruined.' Sure enough, the rain came down on my left and right, pounding into the river, but not a drop landed in my canoe! When I shored in the village both my skin and the books were bone dry. 'How did you stay dry in that storm?' everyone asked me. And I told them, 'Jesus put his hand over me.'"

A young mother cut her work short in order to attend *lotu* and was going home empty-handed and hungry. Yet, like the woman in the story she had heard, she had faith. Looking up to heaven as she walked down the trail, she asked Jesus for food to feed her family, and a large hawk swooped over and dropped a large fresh fish right in front of her!

To underscore the miraculous, this meaty fish was a bottom feeder not found near the surface that time of day. She praised the God who multiplied the bread and fish heard her prayer. "He is able to provide all our needs," she said. "Jesus can do anything!"

Power in the Name of Jesus was evident, yet many straddled between the old ways and the new just as first century Christians struggled to integrate Jesus with Judaism. What's wrong with using *all* the spirits in time of need, hoping someone would respond with favor? When their children got sick, young believers prayed to God, then they were pressured by family members to visit shamans to work their magic as well.

We can relate to the fear and anxiety you feel when your baby is sick, but we urged them not to go back to "the old ways of the ground." How would God be glorified if you're still calling on ancestral spirits? He is a jealous God and won't share his glory with another. Believers spoke candidly with God, even begging pardon as they tried to incorporate Jesus with their old ways.

One day Whuni stood up in the middle of the village clearing when a fight broke out. He put his hand up in the air dramatically and called, "God, wait right there! I'm going to go fight like a man now because I'm angry, but I'll come back later and tell you how sorry I am."

"That's not a good custom," Frank explained. "God doesn't want to be treated like an old shirt to be cast aside and then called on when you get into trouble. 'Talk-sorry' [repentance] is good, but he doesn't want you to beat people up when you're angry. He wants you to learn new ways to live and make peace."

Sometimes, semantics caused confusion as we integrated new terms into the teaching. One night there was a knock at the door and Whuni came in agitated. "I can't sleep and I can't wait until morning for an answer. Why does God call us his shrimp?"

That sounds hysterical in English, but Frank knew why the old man was confused. That afternoon he borrowed the Pidgin term for "kingdom," which sounds like the Iwam word for shrimp, *kindam*. The poor man couldn't rest with the image of the church groveling around in the mud—though that may be a more accurate picture than we'd care to admit. We had a great teaching moment.

The people created some of their own expressions too. "Skin Christian" fit believers who put on their best shirt for *lotu* and then lived like unbelievers the rest of the week. Their faith was only as deep as their outer wear, and their heart was far from Jesus.

When we introduced baptism, everyone gathered along the widest sandbar to witness the big event and we could tell there was some agitation. "What's the matter?" Frank asked.

Some who were new to "the talk" [new to faith] came forward. "Pren, what will happen to the people who live downriver?"

"What do you mean?" Frank asked.

"All these Christians are washing their sins away and the river's going to carry their evil [or sin] onto the people who live downriver and drink this water [as a curse]."

"Oh no, we're not literally washing sin into the water. It's *tok piksa,* an illustration of what it means to die to our old ways and rise up like a new man."

As new believers waded out into the current to be baptized, the solemnity of the moment was shattered by the voices of the women. "Hey! What are you doing out there in front of everyone? I know what you did last week!" Another called, "Yeah! And you were just fighting last night, you hypocrite! I heard you!"

We Americans might *think* of such things, but who would disrupt a church service to bellow accusations in front of everyone? In the tribal community, people know your lifestyle and hold you accountable.

Frank waded out of the water and patiently reiterated the significance of baptism as our identification with the Lord. It doesn't make you perfect, nor is it a claim to perfection. While it's important to live a godly life, no one is without sin or ever will be. We must choose to follow Him every day.

Another social challenge involved our key leaders being tempted into polygamous marriages, disqualifying them for church leadership roles. The Patriarchs and kings aside, the Word of God stipulates that a church leader needs to be a one-woman type of man, but very few were left. We couldn't actively enforce the issue or there would be a sudden glut of unwed mothers and fatherless children in the village.

Social patterns so deeply ingrained in culture take years to change as believers learn God's ways are higher. Not only would they experience greater harmony in their households, but there would be more available women for the young men to marry.

We did teach it, dissuading young men from a discipleship standpoint, but even our closest friends lied about multiple marriages. We knew their families applied great pressure to ensure there would be many children to carry on. It was the law of survival. In some cases the wife's younger sister, determined to get a strong husband and ensure her own security, would climb into a man's net at night or follow him to the gardens to seduce him repeatedly.

In fact, young girls were urged to do so by their parents in the same way Naomi urged Ruth to go to Boaz. Even Mark eventually buckled to such advances. Consequently, we couldn't appoint him to church leadership,[104] but he continued to work on translation.

I remembered a Bible school class challenging us to be most guarded against things deemed socially acceptable. Divorce is widely practiced and growing in acceptance in the church today, and teens don't even need parental permission to "eliminate the problem" of an unwanted pregnancy. We may admit these things aren't ideal, but many succumb as society pushes quick-fix solutions down our throats.

In the tribe, we took the approach to polygamy that Paul used with slavery. Namely, whatever state you find yourselves in when you are saved, serve the Lord.[105] We taught new believers that one wife is the best way, but we didn't meddle with existing marriages.

Another example revolves around the pressure to perform sorcery and witchcraft. Resisting the role of the white know-it-all missionary, we stepped aside to let the Lord take his rightful place in the church as we sought his help *together*.

---

[104] I Timothy 3:12 stipulates that a church leader must be the husband of one wife.
[105] I Cor 7:26-27 Concerning marriage, Paul's advice was to stay as you are.

One night, our friend Nonai came in for Bible study. I used to call him *omweis aiti*, egret legs, because he was so tall and thin, but on this particular night, he was hunched over like a fretful chicken with the worries of the world on his shoulders.

"What's the matter?" Frank asked.

"I'm in trouble and I don't know what to do. Jesus is going to be so mad at me."

"*Tumusik? Papa ti yo?* Why? What's going on?"

"My uncles are making me sleep with the skull tonight in the bush. They said if I don't do it they're going to put me out of the house. What should I do?"

Hmmm, this was a tough one. We didn't want to directly oppose village leaders. How do you tell a teenager that he should oppose his entire family and risk eviction from his household? Sometimes, a question is the wisest answer.

"What do you think God wants you to do?"

"If I sleep with the skull and pray to the Lord, maybe God will forgive me." Nonai suggested. "But if my uncles know that I'm praying to God it's going to interfere with their spirit powers. They'll be mad at me either way!"

Sleeping with the skull was an act of sorcery that fed into the never-ending system of pay-backs. As mentioned earlier, death is perceived to be the work of an enemy's poison rather than "natural causes." It was the duty of survivors to determine who was at fault and retaliate by taking another life from the offending party.

One method involved digging up and beheading the corpse in the middle of the night. Then they'd call his spirit back to reveal who was responsible for his death. They'd put his skull in their canoe and paddle up and downriver at night until it rocked like the hand piece on a Ouija board to pinpoint where the culprit slept.

Other times, family members would sleep with their heads against the skull, asking him to reveal himself by vision or voice so they could seek the appropriate retribution. After divining the cause, they'd remove facial hair, tie it into a bundle, say their incantations over it and place it in the mouth of a black ant colony. When the closure was completely sealed by the ants, the guilty party would die in an endless cycle of death and paybacks.

In this case, we encouraged Nonai to trust God's protection and guidance. Together, we asked the Lord to undertake and the problem was solved overnight. His uncles decided that Nonai would obstruct their spirits and they actually *told him* not to come! However, they also decided that he wasn't welcome in their home any longer, so he wandered from house to house for some time.

There was a cost for choosing Christ, but the Lord protected him from harm. Nonai could walk tall again simply because he learned a great lesson. Jesus, not the missionary, is able to keep you from falling.

26. Becoming Big Fish

During our third furlough after 15 years on the field, Fultons challenged us to consider returning to the States for a "window of time" so the kids could acclimate to our home country and move into their college years.

Fultons had grown into the role of parents after mine passed away, unofficially adopting me as their fifth daughter. Yet, in all the years we'd known them I can't recall a decision they impressed on us as much as that one. Having served on a number of mission boards over the years, they had seen MK's "fall through the cracks" before. We couldn't dismiss their counsel lightly and began praying about this "window" with concerted effort.

At first I was appalled by the thought. How could we leave the mission field? How could we abandon the believers and the work God had given us at May River? "Hand to the plow" was an expression we'd used for commitment in the Lord's service.[106] But is God's will limited to a one-time chosen location forever? On closer inspection, the little command to "follow me" preceded the Lord's statement about the plow.

Then again, how could we send our own kids to a "foreign" country to fend for themselves at such a critical time in their lives? Naomi was already a senior at the boarding school. Would we send her home alone at the end of the year? We prayed continually about this decision, asking God for His perfect timing.

Just as we had done with the weighty decisions about when to send the kids to school the first time around, we were wrestling with similar issues about sending them to America. The issue is the same. What is God's specific plan and timing for our lives and our kids?

---

[106] Luke 9:62

Dear God, you spoke so plainly the first time we faced this. Please show us clearly.

We returned to New Guinea for that sixteenth year, unsure of what to do. We dropped the kids off in Goroka, and flew back to the tribe eager to unpack and get back to work. We were especially anxious to meet with the believers and hear how they fared in our absence.

Upon reentry, we were pleasantly surprised to find the young men standing taller, more assured and a little wiser. A core group of leaders reported that they had hosted an area conference on their own. They proudly emphasized having implemented the event without us, even inviting believers and former enemies from neighboring tribes. Century-old barriers crumbled as believers were beginning to embrace one another as brothers.

I taught school every day and Frank translated, stockpiling Scripture and teaching in the villages. We started hinting that our time might be short, encouraging them to take the Word to heart and make it their own. God "planted" a church in their midst and now it would be up to them to follow Him.

By the end of six months we knew God was leading us on. We weren't taking our hand from the plow. The "crops" were growing, and other fields awaited.

Before making it official, we flew to regional meetings on the coast. We had served with area leadership for ten years and had developed a wonderful trust and love for each other. The purpose of the meeting was to reach a consensus about this decision.

They reminisced about appointing us to Wewak to establish the new school, and witnessed God's blessing firsthand. They knew how we thrived in the "big smoke," and praised our contributions. Some teased that they were amazed that free-spirited Frank stayed at May River as long as he did.

The committee admitted they could see why the Lord would call us to another "corner" of the field. They were sorry, but said we'd be a blessing wherever we went. In the end, it was unanimous and everyone felt peace. Deeply touched by their support and affirmation, we knew it was still going to be hard to say goodbye.

Not everyone shared their sentiments, however. One couple made hard accusations. They said we weren't committed. We were out of God's will. That hurt to hear, and I fumed at Frank, "I have a hard enough time trying to understand God's will for my life, let alone telling someone else what to do!"

Frank was unruffled. "It's okay. 'Let every man be convinced in his own mind.'"[107]

Looking back on so many relationships with partners over the years, we know that God not only saved us from our own folly and protected us through perilous circumstances, but He was also refining us together. There will always be personality clashes, differences of opinion, and control issues when you're "living in each other's back pockets," but God used an assortment of partners like a tumbler for polishing rocks. He grated and polished some of our rough edges a little bit smoother each time.

One area leader gave me occasion to grow in grace. He was talented and respected, but this particular cowboy felt it was his mission to rope me in. He felt that we city kids were in too much of a rush and we thought him too rigid, unwilling to change. I found him legalistic and unyielding, and he thought me a little too wild and verbal, can you imagine?

In one of many attempts to hammer out our differences, he decided to set guidelines, even to the extent of how much time I could spend in language study every day. Frank didn't agree. "She's not your wife," he argued. "I want her to be involved in ministry."

Then I shocked everyone, including me, when I stood up and yelled, "I need GRACE to live by!" That was a turning point.

The healthy off-shoot of all this head-banging was a determination to seek and study grace. We were tired of suffocating and would instead seek to set each other free. Frank means "free man" after all, and much like the tenderhearted David, we needed to grow in grace and extend that to others. God could handle the rest.

And He sure did! The Lord was working in all of us and winds of change were blowing against an authoritarian emphasis on submission. God wanted a servant leadership and began to shake things up from the top down. Grace became our target and the glue that bound us more tightly than our titles.

In every situation the Lord worked through our differences to teach us how we ought to love and complement one another

---

[107] Romans 14:5

rather than wrestling for control. It's funny. We went out there thinking we were going to SAVE the world, but God was just working on shaping his tools most of the time.

If you still have a missionary bubble after all these pages, let me pop it now. You name it: divorce, adultery, and children in emotional havoc, we are all so devastatingly human and flawed.

Perhaps the most devastating news came when a coworker took his own life on furlough. Unwanted by his parents as a little boy, he was deposited on the doorstep of a grandmother who unmercifully slammed the door in his face as he stood holding his baby sister.

This dear brother had a heart of gold and worked circles around all of us, but he still felt unwanted. He decided to end it all with a suicide note, leaving his forlorn wife with three small kids while on furlough in Australia.

Truth is, God worked in spite of us. We are nothing but a bunch of broken people being sent to reach some more broken people with a message of grace. That's the story of missions in a nutshell.

So, after those final regional meetings, we returned to the tribe and started telling the believers we had six months left. Immediately, attendance picked up at all our meetings and people spent more time "hanging out" with us. These may have been our most effective months of all our years in the tribe!

I'd look at their faces, remembering how we'd seen them grow into adulthood. Danet, for example, practically grew up in our house coming every day to do chores for food and pay. I used to call him Cozbi because he reminded me of Bill Cosby both in features and sense of humor.

As a little boy, he had to stand on a stool to reach the sink. Now, he stood about six feet tall and his voice had thickened to the voice of a man. I watched him sharing a testimony in *lotu,* and fought back tears seeing the upright leader he had become.

Jackson, my right hand man in teaching literacy, was another who had faithfully labored with us for years. I would miss his smile. There was the bright young Nasak who excelled in school, and went on to train others. Gabriel, Joseph, Pita, Silas, and a host of others who had become an integral part of our lives.

Many of our "kids" were now married and bearing children of their own. Would they remain faithful or would they drift away? At every gathering my eyes would drift around at all the faces and I'd pray under my breath. *Lord, keep them close to you. Let them never forget your Word and your love.*

For extended periods Frank and I managed the airstrip alone including the community store, and teaching. Since all three kids attended boarding school during these final years, cooking and laundry required less energy so we practically worked around the clock. At times it was overwhelming, borderline crazy.

One day, we noticed an empty water tank that had lifted up in a current of rising water near the sawmill and started floating away! We raced to the nearest boat and paddled frantically down the back baret trying to retrieve it without capsizing.

How awkward, how ridiculously comical our predicament seemed, like two mice attempting to maneuver an elephant upstream. Around and around we paddled in circles, both of us struggling to tug it back against the current and anchor it to the ground until the water receded. Then we got hysterical. "People at home would *never* believe this!" I roared.

I loved our little schoolhouse on the side of the airstrip best. In low water, it was just a walk across the yard but in high-water season, I'd paddle out in a dug-out canoe, eventually mastering the art of keeping all my papers dry and tiptoeing up the notched log ladder.

Our simple facility had bark floors, bamboo walls and a thatch roof. Big chalkboards at the front of the class were Frank's plywood painted with glossy paint. I improvised work sheets and printed materials when our generator was running in the evening hours. Our daily routine included Bible study, prayer and singing, then literacy until noon each day. It was a blast!

The older men who attended school were most challenging. It required incredible effort and a surplus of patience for them to learn how to even hold a pencil. These were men who could hunt with great prowess and identify a single tree in the middle of the jungle, but ask them to detect the difference between an "a" and an "e" on paper and they were frustrated to the max. Part of it was their inability to spend long hours in school when they had work and gardens to tend to.

For the quick-minded teens and young men, literacy progressed speedily. Nothing was more rewarding than connecting with eager students, but even the best and brightest faced an uphill battle due to distractions. If a plane came in we had to recess and help unload cargo or perhaps roll fuel drums into the shed.

One time after a flood only a thin patch of grass was visible on the crown of the airstrip while the posts of our schoolhouse still stood in about two feet of water and felt like a houseboat. Water lapped the sides of our canoes tied to the ladder like so many horses around the hitching post of an old saloon. How they noticed I'll never know, but right in the middle of drills my students jumped up, tossing books and pencils to the floor.

I stood dumbfounded at the board as my students produced spears out of the thatch roof and started jumping out the windows into the water! *I guess school's out,* I thought dejectedly, and started gathering discarded materials. They reached the ripples of the receding waters where a couple of emperor fish were trapped in the thick grasses.

In a crescendo of whooping glee, they surrounded and speared their prizes which would provide a generous feast for their families. Some freshwater varieties of red snapper can grow up to three feet in length and weigh 80 pounds feeding on algae and shrimp. These were about two feet long and would certainly fill a lot of empty stomachs. It's no wonder they were beaming when they returned to school, stashed their weapons, and sat back down dripping wet. "Okay!" they said smiling. "Where were we?"

I'm really going to miss this place, I thought smiling at my now attentive class.

Our days were tinged with sadness as we watched the calendar months count down but I assuaged the sorrow with a dream that these students would become the teachers and leaders of tomorrow, and many of them have.

As people came to say goodbye, I presented gift packages. We had a houseful of usable stuff, though much of it would find new uses. I once saw a toilet seat cover being worn as an old man's fuzzy headdress! Kitchen curtains would become wrap-around skirts, and towels would wrap babies. We hoped books and paper wouldn't be shredded for rolling tobacco. One could always hope.

Watching our house being emptied for the last time I knew a huge part of our lives was coming to an end. I wondered if even the floor boards would one day be pulled up for firewood. What would remain of all our years in the tribe? *Oh Lord, hopefully there will be souls prepared for your kingdom when you return!*

I made vats of coffee, fish and rice and as people came we would visit together. Contrary to American chatter to smother pain,

214

our closest friends were the most silent. They'd sit beside me and just say sigh, "Oh, sorry!" They couldn't fathom how far away we were going. Some said they were not coming back to my house again because it would only make them cry.

Impossible not to feel heavy-hearted in those final weeks. The older men came solemnly wagging their heads and looking at the ground. "We know we will see you again because we're going to meet in God's place on top," they assured. "We didn't know the road [the way to heaven] before you came but now we know and we'll be there together someday."

We sat down on the grass with the men from Aiwanu the day before our plane was due. The men were smoking, not saying much. Old Tultul started rubbing Frank's thigh in a sign of true friendship, and his eyes were streaming unashamedly.

"Oh Pren, when you came here to live with us your face was white and your body was thin. You were just a boy. You didn't know our talk and you didn't know our food. You didn't know anything, like the little fish that swim close to the surface, nibbling at mayflies.

Now you have become a big fish. You have become like the big fish that settles down on the bottom of the river and knows his place. When you fish them out of the water, there is no one to fill that place again. They have left their mark on the ground."

The American equivalent might be "big dog" or maybe a "big cheese," but in the tribe when someone has grown significant they have become, what else, but a big fish! Tultul wagged his head and held Frank in a rare expression of Iwam affection. The old chief was saying Frank made a mark in their lives and would be greatly missed. Hearing this, Frank cried with him.

The airstrip remained open for other area missionaries for years and phase-out was gradual. The Iwam Bible was printed and dedicated in 2008, nearly 30 years after we first became river rats. The finish work was completed by Hope after she relocated to Wewak on the coast where God gifted her with the detail orientation to cross every "t" and dot every "i" in the manuscript's checking—a marvelous and heroic effort on her part! And now she assists other teams with literacy and continues adding to the Iwam library.

Periodically, she hires our old informants and hears news from May River, but not all of it has been good. After we left, the alcohol moved in and when money ran out, moon-shining became the all-consuming passion. Sadly, our old friend Jemis fell victim to it, too.

He got drunk, fell into the river, and drowned. His empty canoe was found floating downriver and three days later, his body surfaced.

However, others have been standing strong in faith though sorely tested. My "son" Danet hiked out to send this letter:

"This is your brother Danet writing to let you know about the heavy burden I am carrying. My wife died on July 23rd and we buried her on the 24th. This is weighing heavy on me but it will not cause me to lose faith. Why? I can thank God who holds life and death in his hand. God gave me my wife and he called her back to Him.

In His Word he instructed us that we must trust him always, even in hard times. I Peter 5:7 urges us to give our worries and anxieties to Him. I am relying on his strength and He will make a way for me. Thank you for your prayers. God bless you and me. Danet"

Another positive note came in 2010, when Hope wrote to say the Iwam were stockpiling fish to host another national believers' conference for nine area tribes. Church leaders are dealing with their issues, trying to function as a body, and Frank's old informant Mark is reading an Iwam Bible to his eight-year-old son!

What a privilege it's been to bring the sweet message of the cross to people who never knew it. Frank translated the Word of God and taught it to "the ends of the earth," just as he had seen in his dream. He stood by that river surrounded by a sea of black faces and preached his heart out in a foreign tongue, and yes, they understood it! God's perfect will had come to pass in the fullness of time.

Were our methods always on target and our faith perfect? Of course not, but we stepped off a cliff and God caught us on wings of mercy. He revealed his eye in the rainbow, his protective fury in a flaming bolt of lightning, and He turned a tide of warriors through a tribal prince. His never-ending compassion continually wooed us to worship and through every trial, he showed Himself greater.

No, it isn't pride that fills my heart, but reverent awe and gratitude. God has done great things—not because of our goodness, but because of his redeeming love for every tribe, tongue, and nation.

I should know by now to persevere in faith, for, *"He will keep you strong to the end... [since] God, who has called you into fellowship with His Son Jesus Christ our Lord, is faithful."*[108]

---

[108] I Corinthians 1:8-9

27. The Real Thing

When we left America the first time, we had two toddlers and one on the way. When we returned, we had a daughter looking for college and two in high school. Landing at Logan Airport with a pile of suitcases, I wondered where we would live and what we would do. Both my parents had died and my brothers had moved away. We were coming back to our home country, but we had no home.

Fultons took us in for the first few weeks and even loaned us a car. Before long, Naomi was on her way to college, and the boys found jobs. We found a little ranch in our home town, a mile from where we grew up. Every need was answered as God made a place for us and the kids thrilled to experience "normal."

Frank started a carpentry business working with gifted hands. Bostonian Jews would comment, "I've never heard of a Jewish carpenter before," to which Frank would reply, "Let me tell you about another one," introducing Jesus. Some weren't interested and a door or two was slammed in his face, but his disarming friendliness and love for people opened more doors than closed. While kitchens were remodeled and homes renovated, curiosity was piqued and lives were touched. He even worked for a Holocaust survivor who gave him the keys to her house and treated him like family.

Real estate kept me moving. I sold two million dollars' worth of property in six months, then migrated through a string of corporate offices while taking classes. First, I was the assistant to the dean of a prestigious Boston business college where I loved working with international students. For two years I assisted the president of a fiber optic company, and finally moved on to work for the CEO of a high tech company for a few more years.

The best part about these roles was the exposure to people from all over the world and a wide variety of backgrounds. I traveled to Europe and the Caribbean, and helped orchestrate worldwide sales

217

meetings at a five star resort with a 2001 theme of achieving things thought impossible. As our main stage filled with smoke, Captain Lovell of Apollo 13 fame walked out to address the crowd with an inspirational message. *Yes, Lord, help me believe you for great things in my life. Expand my horizons to serve you!*

The pastor of one of our donor churches in Oregon asked if we wanted to join his group on a trip to Israel and we jumped at the chance to fulfill a dream. For two exhilarating weeks we traveled all four corners of the Holy Land, sharing freely over Turkish coffees and on the streets. Frank was invited to preach to the group on the Sea of Galilee and in the Garden of Gethsemane.

What an unforgettable journey pairing our knowledge of Scripture with the incredible geography around us. Every tree flourishes with meaning, every rock and pebble holds a breath-taking memory in that land.

We rode a cable car to the top of Masada as Israeli jets soared overhead defending Israel's borders like the eagles of heaven, our Jewish guide said. We floated in the Dead Sea and walked the winding streets and marketplaces of Jerusalem, the City of David. We rode a camel, toured ancient Roman ruins and toured ancient villages where Jesus walked. We even stood at the valley of Megiddo where the end will come and blood will flow to the height of horses' bridles. Finally, we entered the empty tomb and saw the place of the skull, Golgotha, worshipping the One who died for us there.

Above all, the highlight for me was the Wailing Wall, remembering Solomon's dedication of the temple for those who come from distant lands to pray to the God of heaven. Hundreds of years ago He promised, "My eyes will be open and my ears attentive to the prayers offered in this place... I have consecrated this temple so that my Name may be there *forever. My eyes and my heart will always be there.*"[109]

I stood listening to the voices of a multitude—the shrill calls of Mid-eastern languages, Russian Jews, the Orthodox, even African voices—all blending together in a press of seeking humanity. Petitioners rocked and chanted earnestly before the ancient edifice. Stepping closer, reverently, I surveyed countless folds of paper where supplicants left their requests for the Almighty between the giant

---

[109] 2 Chronicles 6:32-33,40; 7:15-16

rocks. I was drawn to it. Enormous stones towered a hundred feet above me as I pondered the many layers buried beneath my feet.[110] For centuries these stones have been standing as as a silent tribute to the God.

I crept closer and closer, weaving among a rainbow of colors and prayer shawls, and watching flocks of tiny sparrows flitting in and out between the rocks. Finally, I pressed the palms of my hands flat against the stone and the Lord spoke to me about living stones and the eternal kingdom He is building.

He confirmed his personal promise to provide a place for me and be with me forever. Blessed be the Name of the Lord who said, "I will be your God throughout your lifetime! Until your hair is white with age. I made you and I will care for you. I will carry you and save you."[111]

My fluttering bird heart would hearken back to those words in time to come, and those awe-inspiring moments in His presence made the entire trip worthwhile. The Lord sees me and knows me no matter where I go. He is with me forever!

Back home in Massachusetts, Frank became an elder at our church and we were involved in various studies and groups, but we kept wondering where the Lord would send us next. We toyed with ideas of Mongolia, Israel, and we were asked to consider serving as mission reps or going to South America to run a guest house. Strangely, my free-spirited adventurer husband felt God was keeping us right where we were.

"How big is this window of time, Lord?" we prayed. "Is it a picture window or a porthole?"

Being employed in the Boston burbs, my job benefits included tuition reimbursement so I studied for my masters in Cambridge while my kids pursued their undergrads. I worked full-time and attended classes nights and weekends while Frank did custom woodworking.

One weekend in the spring of 2003, I drove into the city for my 9-5 class, but I wasn't feeling well. *Nothing serious*, I thought popping aspirin, but by mid-afternoon I left Cambridge with a persistent but unfamiliar chest pain. *Gee whiz, Dad had two or three heart attacks by this age! What if this is an early sign of heart trouble?* I reached the doctor on-call on my way home.

---

[110] I think there are as many as seventeen layers beneath the ground.
[111] Isaiah 46:4 in the New Living Translation

"Hi, I'm a patient of this office and wonder if you could tell me the women's symptoms for heart attack." Academic that I am, I wanted a text book list of symptoms, but even as the words came from my lips I had a sneaky suspicion I wasn't going to get one.

There was barely a pause before a doctor came on the line asking, "Where are you right now, mam?"

"I'm heading west on the Mass Pike, on my way home."

"Do not pass go," he said quickly. "I want you to come directly to the ER and I will meet you there."

"Oh, you don't understand. I feel fine. I don't have sweaty palms, my eyes aren't dilated and I'm not even nauseous… I just have this *one little finger of pain* in the middle of my chest." Okay, now I knew he wouldn't answer me.

"Ma'am, I repeat. Do not pass go. Meet me in the ER and I'll answer all your questions when you get there."

Next thing I knew I was wearing a white gown, hooked up to tubes and wires. It so happens I was in the middle of a new book called, *Girl Meets God* by Lauren Winner, and I had it with me that day. It was God's good humor that I was holding that particular title in the waiting room.

Everyone that saw the cover inquired about it and got quite an earful! From distraught patients to the doctors and nurses who checked on me, everywhere I was moved over that long weekend, that book paved the way for great discussions about what it takes to start a relationship with the living God. *Thank you for bringing me here today, Lord! (Thank you for such a great title, Lauren!)*

Frank came from work straightaway and my daughter rushed in with her baby in a stroller looking as worried as I did when visiting my dad and mom. We were all sequestered in a side room while doctors and nurses were being paged this way and that. I kept assuring everyone I felt fine, really, but Frank stopped me in my tracks when he posed one of his life-changing questions.

"Honey, if this was the real thing, would you have any regrets?"

Hoo boy, what a great question! I leaned my head against the pillow, then blurted, "I haven't written the book yet!" For years, when people asked what I did, I'd say I work in this or that office, "but I really want to write someday." School and work were so busy I didn't have time to pursue such a dream.

My weekend in the ER turned out to be nothing but a bad case of reflux, probably due to an extra busy week and too much coffee. I called it the $2000 burp, but I was grateful for all the people I met wheeling up and down the hallway meeting my roomies, just like old times in the Goroka hospital. I even had great conversations with the overnight janitors and food servers. It was like a night out on the town for this little chatterbox!

Afterwards, I resumed work and finished my masters and then my company began a series of layoffs. As our staff dwindled, I was asked to assist a few more VP's and even fill in for the company receptionist. One day I was signing for some packages out in the lobby when it hit me. *My workload has increased and my pay decreased! What the heck am I doing with my life? I feel like I'm eighteen again punching a clock for the phone company!*

Frank's question in the ER came back to me and once again an epiphany brought me to a fork in the road. If *not* writing is the one thing I'd regret at the end of my life, what on earth am I waiting for? I soon gave my notice and went home to start writing. Though it was a step of faith to drop all the "cush benefits" of my office job, we believed it was time.

One day in the summer of 2004, we had all the kids and their spouses over for a barbecue on the deck and the conversation turned to life goals. When it came to me, I said, "I'm thrilled to be writing finally. I may not have a lot of years left."

My kids laughed. "Why do you say things like that? You're still young and healthy... you shouldn't talk like that."

"Not really," I cautioned. "My memory's going, my eyes are straining, and look at my family genes. I'm almost the same age as my parents when they died! None of us knows how much time we have left on this earth."

Before we knew it, summer ended and the air got crisp. Frank and I took our two-year-old grandson Judah to the top of a mountain. Judah means "praise" in Hebrew, so that seems to carry a beautiful message as I'm reflecting on it now. We scooped cold water from a rippling brook and played hide and seek among the birch trees.

Sitting on a ski lift snapping pictures from the top, we marveled at this new stage of life we were beginning together as *grandparents.* "Can you believe it? We're Papa and Nana now!" Who knew that we'd be getting new titles at this stage of life? So much to share, new horizons to explore, and there's nothing quite like the joy of grandkids to reignite hope for the future. It was one of those memorable days that seemed like a dream.

"I'm so glad we can share this together." I said, savoring every moment. "I've loved living life with you!" Like all mountaintop experiences, the day ended too quickly.

On October 9th Frank started complaining about headaches. We knew pollen counts were high and the oak dust was especially thick so he started taking sinus meds, but the headaches didn't quit. I'd find him soaking in the tub after work and when he'd wake up early the headaches were still there (which we later learned was a tell-tale sign). It wasn't like him to take off work, but he couldn't function. We graduated to extra-strength over-the-counter meds, but nothing touched the pain.

Blood work ruled out malaria, meningitis, and the flu. The following week we got in to see a neurologist who prescribed migraine meds and sent us home. Migraines at the age of 52? This specialist cost over $200 for half an hour and looking at all the degrees on the wall, we figured he must know what he was doing. Oddly, he asked Frank to stick out his tongue and he shined a light in his eyes. "I don't see anything," he said at the end of the exam. *Really?* But he thought the medicine would eventually knock it out. "Just give it time," he advised.

By the second day he was still so bad I doubled his dosage. I started calling the neurologist and a chemist, and I was hunting online when Naomi stopped by. We were alarmed when Frank was unable to stand.

"Honey, put your feet on the floor," I urged, trying to pull him up.

"I'm trying," he said weakly, but his speech was garbled like he was drunk.

Was the sluggishness a side-effect of the meds? When we saw that his feet were turning sideways, we decided to head straight to the ER and I called the boys on the way. Jesse was living in California at the time.

We waited about six hours in the ER while various tests and scans were taken. I wondered if the disk in his neck had deteriorated putting pressure on his brain. Maybe he would need surgery, and how would we afford that now? I hated thinking about finances at a time like that, but it had been five months since I stopped working. We had no insurance and our savings had dwindled. I kept praying for courage and peace but my mind was numb.

Meanwhile, poor Frank was in intense pain. After eleven days of headaches he was now cycling in and out of consciousness. A few times when he was alert and feeling good my go-getter would say, "Okay, enough of this waiting around. Where are my pants? Let's get out of here and go home and watch the game!" I finally hid his pants.

During our stay in the ER, the Red Sox were playing the Yankees in the Championship series. Relieved to have the diversion, everyone relayed reports of the last great play up and down the hallways and cheered them on. We shared a sense of patriotic camaraderie—or maybe it was a sense of hopefulness that we could all leave this hallway of desperation for a few minutes and return to better times.

When the doctors left the room we held hands and prayed, asking God to surround us with his peace and use this for his glory, which became our constant prayer.

At about 11 p.m. we were still sitting in the darkened room when they finally returned with the results of the MRI. The minute I saw our doctor's face I knew it would be dreadful.

"We found the cause of the headaches," she started. "You have two masses on the brain."

"Cancer?" we asked in unison.

"Yes," and her eyes got glassy. "I'm so sorry," she said kindly.

Frank and I looked at each other in stunned silence, then Frank said, "I'm in God's hands."

After thirty years of knowing him we would trust him still. I cupped my hands together and added, "He's got us right in his hands."

"Why is it these things happen to such good people?" The nurse was fighting back tears as we said good-bye.

28. A Class in Fruit

Everything kicked into high gear after that. We needed to move to a Boston facility and an ambulance was already ordered. Brain surgery was requested urgently and there was no time to lose.

The kids came back in and we repeated everything together. It seemed unbelievable.

Frank was squinting his eyes in pain so we decided to slip out and let him rest in the darkened room. We walked outside, huddled together on the sidewalk, and cried in the cold night air.

It was time to start making calls. Jesse and his wife were preparing to board a plane from LA right away. My cell battery died, so Isaac ran to get his car so I could charge it and finish making calls with his heater running. I saw when he hunched over the steering wheel sobbing, and it tore my heart.

At midnight we finally climbed into the ambulance for the forty mile ride to the heart of Boston's medical center. Frank was sedated and strapped to a stretcher with a paramedic named Scott attending him, but the morphine didn't slow his conversation at all.

I was up front with Paul, the driver who immediately opened up about his Catholic upbringing and we talked the whole way about the grace of God and a personal relationship with Jesus. By the time we arrived, Scott was asking, "So Frank, what's the name of that book by Lewis again, *Mere Christianity*? I have to get that."

These two escorted us into the ER and stayed with us like old friends until we were officially turned over to the Boston staff. They didn't have to do that, but parted with such a tenderness of affection we knew God was already using this whole ordeal. No circumstance is wasted in God's economy, not even an ambulance ride.

Frank's humor was delightful, even in some of the hardest moments. While being prepped and questioned with the standard neurological exam before surgery, his mind was on one thing only. He hadn't eaten in a couple of days and he was dying of thirst. So when the doctor started hitting him with a barrage of questions, Frank answered, "I'll tell you for an ice cube."

He chuckled politely and tried again, but Frank quipped, "How about a *picture* of an ice cube?" The doctor laughed so hard he broke down and called for a cup of ice.

Jesse and Brianne landed first thing in the morning and brought a surge of emotional strength. All my kids were there propping me up, keeping me strong. While Frank was in surgery we waited in a lounge area, jackets and water bottles strewn around the furniture. "I guess I'll have to put the house up for sale," I said as surgical fees danced in my head.

My daughter's generous-hearted husband Nate said, "Don't worry. We'll sell the farm if we have to, but we'll make it." They were a God-send to me but I hated thinking I would become a liability to my kids.

There were long sleepless nights, shifting from bed to bed and sofa to cot as I tried staying by Frank's side like a zombie. There were long lines and delays, paperwork and prescriptions at pharmacy. I had to navigate parking garages, a complex of tunnels, elevators and corridors despite the mental fog I was living in.

Emotionally too, it was a maze. We were up. We were down. Two masses became three when we got to Boston, but the surgery was deemed "successful." They removed the lemon and the golf ball so then we were down to a pea, but that's when we started hearing the words "incurable" and "malignant." At the same time we were latching hopefully to every ounce of encouragement. The biopsies wouldn't be back for about ten days. TEN days!

"Don't jump to conclusions," the doctor advised with a tender smile. "It *could* just be an infection from New Guinea."

He walked out of the room and I rushed to the kids. "Did you hear that? It could only be an infection!" We held onto each other and cried in the middle of the lobby. I think nobody else even noticed. Everyone there was in the same boat—waiting, hoping, and worrying like yo-yos.

We were moved from room to room and ward to ward. I was numb with exhaustion but by God's grace, surrounded with people and opportunities to share our living hope along the way. We had even prayed around Frank's bed with the neurosurgeon before they wheeled him in for surgery that first morning.

These dire circumstances paved the way for heart-to-heart conversations. In one waiting room I had curled up to sleep a few minutes but noticed a Brazilian woman sitting across from me. We talked and prayed together before the doctor came to meet her. She broke down when she heard the bad report, but hugged me fiercely—two weak and weary women clinging to the Savior. There were a lot of precious souls on this journey with us.

Another time I stepped into an elevator outside the ER and saw a woman about my age with a terrified look on her face. When our eyes met we recognized the look of the grieved wife. She asked me, "Which floor do I need?" Her husband had just been taken in for emergency heart surgery. My heart went out to her in this moment of terror, so I asked if she knew the Lord.

Thankfully she did, so we clasped hands in that elevator for a brief but oh so powerful moment of prayer to regenerate strength. "Dear God, lift our spirits and help us rise above these awful circumstances. Help us to remember your promises and to find strength in your presence today." We not only rose from the physical dungeon of gas fumes and hellish sounds in the parking garage, but we rose in a spiritual sense as well. God is with us!

Hard to believe we only crossed path for a minute, but by the time we walked out of that elevator, we both felt stronger. Hugging and wishing each other well, we parted outside the same doors where Frank had laid on a stretcher, was it just a few days before?—it already felt like months had passed.

The fellowship of the saints is a precious gift along the path of sorrow. Like a couple of characters in *Pilgrim's Progress*,[112] we brushed shoulders in an elevator to lift each other up, just a little, out of the slough of despond.

Another day our primary radiation nurse Rachel came in to see us and closed the door behind her. "What is your faith?" she wanted to know.

Frank asked, "What's your last name?" and her answer confirmed she was a daughter of Abraham.

She said, "Frank, I just have to know..." and we had a wonderful private discussion about the gospel of grace available to everyone through our Messiah, Jesus.

---

[112] Pilgrims Progress, 1678, a classic allegory written in an English prison by John Bunyan

Our social worker Genevieve did the same thing. "Tell me what it means to be a Christian," she asked the minute we were alone, like waving a red flag to a bull.

"Well, it *doesn't* mean that you'll be exempt from all of life's trials as you can see," we began. "But you don't have to go through them alone. The Lord promised his presence to be with us forever." We shared happily what Christ means to us on a daily basis and she asked a lot of questions.

"I'm learning a lot," she said taking copious notes of passages we mentioned to read.

"So are we," I smiled.

Almost overnight, I had become full-time care-taker and administering nurse of a dozen drugs, and in my spare time I researched clinical trials and alternative treatments. To my surprise, I found more than 500 studies for glioblastoma on government Web sites.[113]

I also discovered effective natural herbs without side effects and became an avid proponent of Ruta 6, discovered by a family of physicians in India. Determined to fight this thing by his side with everything I could muster, but I never stopped praying for healing.

After the initial hospital admission of six days, we were released to go home. *Is that it? Now what? You just can't expect me to return to life as usual. My whole world has been set on its head.* I was exhausted and overwhelmed.

A major concern was loss of balance and the consequent risk of falling, so I tried to be at his side wherever he went with the devotion of a service dog. We felt like 80-year-olds all of a sudden, walking slower, leaning on each other. He wrestled with frustration and a loss of independence.

In those early days there was a sweetness knowing that we do, at least, still have each other. "We're best friends," he told the nurses as they smiled at us. Later on, I cherished that thought, logging in my journal, "We're soul mates, like the geese that stay together even when they can't fly. We'll get through this together somehow."

These weeks were punctuated with shock and horror, but those eleven days passed like molasses waiting for the results of the biopsies.

---

[113] One such site I researched is: **www.clinicaltrials.gov**

On the first of November we drove back to Boston to meet the doctor and hear the results. Frank seemed so calm, but I was on pins and needles the whole way. Even so, the Lord held us in the palm of his hand.

That night I wrote in my journal, "They removed the stitches and reviewed the MRI scans with us, showing how the two biggest tumors (now gone) had actually been pressing his brain to one side-- it's no wonder he was in such pain! Then the doctor gave his report on the pathology. Malignant. Not what we were hoping, but we were ready at the same time--a mysterious capacity we can only attribute to God's dear presence."

"We are now being referred to Dana-Farber Cancer Institute and the Center for NeuroOncology. We will be walked through the next steps i.e. radiation and chemo, with a very highly reputable professor of neurology at Harvard Med School.

Despite all the fancy names and elevated titles, we are convinced that our lives remain in God's own hands, something we never questioned for the last 30 years. We are his! We can still rejoice even when the road looks dark or dreary. God never changes."

"OUR PRESENT SUFFERINGS ARE NOT WORTH COMPARING WITH THE GLORY THAT WILL BE REVEALED IN US... AND WE KNOW THAT IN ALL THINGS GOD WORKS FOR THE GOOD... I AM CONVINCED THAT NEITHER DEATH NOR LIFE..., NEITHER THE PRESENT NOR THE FUTURE... NOR [BRAIN TUMORS] OR ANYTHING ELSE IN ALL CREATION, WILL BE ABLE TO SEPARATE US FROM THE LOVE OF GOD THAT IS IN CHRIST JESUS OUR LORD."[114]

We were back and forth to the hospital constantly, living in a haze, but on November 11, 2004, the doctor looked him in the eye and put it all into a time-frame for the first time. Some inescapable phrases we heard that day included, "incurable," "most aggressive type," and, "GBM. Stage IV." Out of 260 different forms of cancer, this was the worst kind.

They gave him nine months to live.

After hearing all this, Frank looked at me and seeing the pain in my eyes, he said, "Don't worry honey. Everything's going to be all right." Imagine that. He was trying to make me feel better!

---

[114] Romans 8:18, 38-39

Our lives revolved around new routines, driving to Boston every day for radiation and meds, blood tests and exams. He suffered shooting pains in his eyes, nausea and debilitating headaches. He had some adverse reactions to treatment and then one morning he "went missing." I ran frantically up and down stairways and elevators, and finally found that he had collapsed on the lobby floor. It was crazy.

Despite all our efforts, the MRIs showed increased activity as the pea-size tumor grew to an egg and then it spread like sand throughout his brain.

I heard a comedian asking why we don't just have "a class in fruit" instead of trying to learn the metric system in school. No one knows what a 6cm or 10cm mass really means, but tell me a grape or lemon and I'm with you! Still, thoughts of all these things growing in my husband's skull were horrifying. How much time do we have left?

Somehow, word traveled around the globe and emails, cards and phone calls started trickling in. Frank was amazed to see how many old friends and acquaintances were praying for him. Even in the tribe, Iwam believers had heard and were praying!

In those early days Frank would cry a lot. They said it was a common reaction to surgery, but these are the things that moved him most. When he was sharing his faith in Christ and whenever someone said that he touched their lives, the tears would flow.

Frank was never overly "impressed with himself" and he couldn't get over the fact that people sincerely cared about him. Like George Bailey in the film, *It's a Wonderful Life,* he may never have realized how much his life was valued if it wasn't for this little scenic route through the valley of brain cancer.

I tried probing beneath the surface, but he was tired of round-the-clock inspections and the endless query, "On a scale of 1 to 10, how are you feeling now?"

"No more questions," he would say, wincing in pain.

Finally, in a quiet and peaceful moment, I had the chance to ask him, "Honey, how are you really doing with all this?"

His blue eyes reminded me of still waters. "It's all about surrender," he said. Through all the pain and suffering Frank never asked, "Why me?" or shook his fist at God.

Honestly, I fought harder. It was my wifely duty! He was disabled, off-balance, and weakened by pain. While he grew more childlike, I was forced into the role of vigilant protector. I took notes at every meeting, tracked meds and documented his biological life.

Our medical staff encouraged me but Frank started resenting it. He would even downplay his physical symptoms in the doctor's office, so they'd look at me and ask if I was seeing anything different. Yeah, I was trying to save his life while he was losing it!

He was losing it by degrees right before my eyes, beginning with industry and independence. No longer allowed to drive, I became his chauffeur. When his license was revoked, he accused me of reporting him to the police. Of course, that was a hospital function since seizures are a huge safety risk, but I became a scapegoat for all his frustrations.

A simple drive to the doctor's office or pharmacy was the only reason he had to get dressed anymore. One morning, I brought him breakfast and asked if he wanted to come with me to do some errands, but he looked at me sadly and said, "I have nothing to look forward to anymore." I'd never seen him so deflated in all our 30 years together.

Then there was the pain of watching my champion decline. My agile gymnast lost muscle in his legs to the point where even the stairs became too risky. We moved the bed downstairs. Then he couldn't climb in and out of the bathtub anymore. Handrails, walkers and props appeared everywhere as constant visual reminders of his weakness.

Inevitable sadness infiltrated every area, but especially when he could no longer work. I drove his truck to remodeling jobs at first, then watched as he struggled with ladders, materials, and most of all, the measurements. He wanted to do it so badly but I had to keep toeing the line between supporting wife and managing nurse.

"I can do it!" he insisted, but his mind was clouded and I could see the confusion. I called the boys to take over and he was forced into early retirement from a job he loved.

He would still get up and put on his work clothes and go out to the shop, but I'd find him sitting in front of the wood stove with our sweet golden retriever. Frank loved the shop, the smell of the wood and being surrounded with all his tools, but he was too tired to do any more than stoke the fire. His industrious and creative life slowed to a standstill.

More than just being sick or recovering from brain surgery, the tumors were growing in the frontal lobes of his brain that affected his personality. My free-spirited sweet-natured husband became short-tempered and he took out all his frustrations on me. The nurses kept insisting, "Don't take it personally, this is the tumor talking," but that didn't erase the hurt. In fact, it hurt so much I started trying to stay out of his way except for giving him medicine and necessary care, just like hospital staff.

Oh Lord, please don't let this cancer destroy our marriage. Bring peace to our home and keep us close! It was bad enough knowing his days were numbered, but far more heart-rending to be losing him before that day came.

One day I came in with groceries and found a big pool of blood on the doorway soaking into the carpet. Frank had fallen into the doorjamb and cracked his head. He didn't know how long he was on the floor before pulling himself back to the couch where he lay with a blood-soaked towel around his head. The seizure left him confused and weak, and me, guilt-ridden for not being there to help him up.

I got involved in several online brain tumor communities and shared the journey with others. Support from people on the same "BT Journey" was invaluable, and I also found ways to share eternal hope with those who were seeking God. Shared information was usually a boost but sometimes, an awful drain—especially when various members said their farewells or announced, "David got his wings this morning at 6 a.m. May he rest in peace." Oh no! I'd grieve for every one, send little notes of condolence and then think, *who's next?*

I found natural supplements to fortify his body (and mine) for the onslaught. While chemical treatments and "antees" (antibiotics, anti-seizures, and anti-inflammatories) robbed his body through a host of damaging side-effects, glyco-nutrients and herbal supplements showed tremendous benefits. Naomi and I decided that if anything like this ever our way, we wouldn't do chemo.

One day I was rushing home from the grocery store, my mind a whirl of medicines and doctor appointments. I was driving too fast in the final miles home when a car pulled out in right front of me without even looking. I stomped on the brakes and narrowly missed her. My nerves were tense, and I dreaded reaching the house. What would I find this time? *Oh God, how can I go on like this?*

I flipped the radio channels until the captivating voice of a rising country star filled the airwaves. "Jesus, take the wheel! Take it from my hands 'cuz I can't do this on my own!"[115] That song broke over me like Niagara Falls. I pulled over, killed the engine, and cried

---

[115] In June 2005 Carrie Underwood's *Jesus Take the Wheel*, by Arista Records, topped the charts

over my steering wheel as Carrie Underwood's voice transcribed my soul. "Save me from this road I'm on! Oh! Jesus, take the wheel!"

When our daughter announced she was expecting again, it was exciting news. After a couple miscarriages, the family soaked up the welcome moments of shared joy. Then it dawned on me—we would be counting down the months of her pregnancy simultaneously with Frank's life expectancy! The very same months would measure the awaited grandchild and Frank's final days on earth. Nine months to life and death simultaneously! How could I do this?

An acute awareness of the passage of time became inescapable. Whenever I opened a new bottle of shampoo, I found myself wondering morbidly where we would be before it runs out. I bought gifts he wouldn't use and clothes that would outlast his failing body. The stark reality was a constant weight as "normal" slipped further away.

My journals filled with the struggles as I anguished over fear and loneliness. I was losing my leader, my bread-winner and my best friend. My prayers generally consisted of a divine exchange: my weakness and brokenness for His strength.[116] *Oh Lord, catch me! I can't do this! Please give me the strength to match these days.*

I poured over the Word of God finding solace in the lives of giants in the faith who have gone before me. Joseph in his prison years, David in his wilderness years, and Abraham's years of waiting and walking across hot sands of sacrifice resonated with me deeply. None of these men understood what was happening when they endured such lengthy and intense periods of testing.

I'm sure they questioned God often in soul-searching anguish. Yet, as a result of all their trials we've gained great insight and encouragement. God will continue to work out his plan in his time, they tell us. Wait patiently for the Lord, my soul!

I especially bound my heart to the painful steps of Abraham as he walked up Mt. Moriah with his son, knowing that when he reached the summit he would be sacrificing his beloved. Why would God require it of the one he promised to bless? Every pounding, blistering step must have been agony, but he bravely continued, speaking only what he hoped. "We will worship and we will come back again."[117]

---

[116] Deuteronomy 33:25-27

[117] Genesis 22 tells the story of God testing Abraham's faith, telling him to sacrifice his only son.

He could only do this because by faith he figured God was able to raise him from the dead if that's what it takes. No wonder Abraham fills such a notable place in God's Hall of Faith.[118]

One time in particular, I slipped into dark despair. It happened the day my daughter-in-law miscarried at twelve weeks. This was my *fourth* grandchild in heaven now due to miscarriage, and I sat outside on the swinging chair in our yard sobbing where Frank couldn't hear.

"LORD! Where are you, Father? Isn't it enough that we're watching my husband in the throes of death? Now this? The loss of another innocent infant, too? Have you forsaken us? Oh Lord!... am I... *condemned?*"

I could feel myself slipping into hopelessness like a deep dark pit, before coming to my senses and remembering his promises. *"There is **no condemnation** for those who are in Christ..."*[119] "Lord, I cannot deny you! Help me, Father!"

A brisk wind started, but I couldn't go back inside. I sat on that swing looking up at the deep blue clouds sweeping above my house. I was depleted, forlorn and afraid. I watched a formation like eagles' wings spread out across the horizon above me. *Oh, that reminds me of a great angel.*

Then, between the vast wings a face suddenly came into sharp focus, like a mighty warrior or the captain of the Lord's army. Fierce and strong and as detailed as a Michelangelo, it took my breath away. There was no mistaking it. The fierce eyes of that champion looked straight toward my house, toward the spot where Frank lay!

I've never seen anything even remotely as beautiful as that warrior in the sky, and what a great time to see it!

"Oh Lord, thank you! You are definitely watching over me and my household! Thank you Father!" I sobbed at this vision of His mighty presence, and determined once again to cling to his promises no matter what.

I am not alone.

---

[118] Hebrews 11 focuses defining and providing examples of faith heroes
[119] Romans 8:1

29. Through the Valley

The days weren't long enough to process pain and sorrow, so it spilled over into my dreams...

I was standing in the rising river surveying the encroaching danger. The scene resembled the muddy yard around our old house on the airstrip and a flood was coming up fast. Standing in two feet of water, I frantically called for my little boy Isaac. Afraid he might have slipped underwater, I called out to people to help me find him, but no one would help. Everyone looked the other way.

I was holding a phone in the middle of the jungle trying to call for help, but there were problems with the lines. Being transferred to a technician to repair the connection, I recognized the voice on the end of the line. Dave Schrag, a former coworker with his wife Barb and four strapping sons managed the May River airstrip years ago. He was a competent manager and his wife a wonderful nurse, but even they were unable to help.

I was supposed to wait while they tested the lines, but how could I stand still when the tide was rising and the one I love could be drowning? Why couldn't anyone help me?

My subconscious mind often blends the tribal world with this modern world. I go back there in my dreams with an odd assortment of characters and circumstances that mingle the rawest human emotions with the frustrations of this high-tech world. Drowning was a recurring theme in those days.

Maybe the sound of rain running off the eaves triggered memories of the jungle, but that dream was so vivid I woke up feeling like I was still standing at the river's edge helplessly holding the phone. I woke up groaning, torn by the outrageous madness of it all. I'm watching the water rise in this senseless situation while even the experts are unable to save the one I love.

I pulled on some wool socks and my fluffy robe and tiptoed to the kitchen to make hot tea at 5 am. I needed to dig into the Word of God to chase away such anxious thoughts, and turned to Romans 8 like an old friend.

"We know that the whole creation has been groaning as in the pains of childbirth right up to the present time. Not only so, but we ourselves... groan inwardly as we wait eagerly for... redemption... We do not know what we ought to pray for, but the Spirit himself intercedes for us with groans that words cannot express... the Spirit intercedes for the saints in accordance with God's will."[120]

That morning I found the Comforter more satisfying than woolens and fleece. I wrapped myself in the royal robe of my acceptance in the Beloved and quenched my thirst with something more soothing than tea. What indescribable peace can be found in life's darkest hours. Jesus is still on the throne.

September 6th brought a wonderful celebration. A birthday! Though weak and wobbly, Frank held Eliana Joy in the hospital when she was two hours old—life and death, joy and pain colliding like waves of the ocean on a granite wall. I was done with the nine months of counting. Now, every calendar page that turned felt like a victory.

In the beautiful month of October, I decided to get Frank out of the house and take him to Wellfleet, his favorite ocean spot. I found a little cottage to rent at a great off-season rate (they were very kind) where he could see the harbor and walk to the water without having to climb steep dunes. The kids also came down and we ate at his favorite places. It was a sweet time, but he wasn't quite himself.

As we started our drive home, we had a carton of blueberries and Beach Boys in the CD player. After a few minutes of driving, I glanced over and blueberries were flying all over the car and his hand was in spasm. His head was turned past me and his mouth was open but no sound was coming out. Even worse, there was blood in his mouth and the expression on his face looked like he was trying to call me but couldn't. He was having a horrible seizure.

I pulled directly into the corner gas station with my hand on the horn and yelled, "Please! CALL 911! CALL 911!" I jumped out of the car and ran to his side, pulling him up. "Frank! Frank!" I thought he was dying right before my eyes.

---

[120] Romans 8:22-27

An ambulance arrived in what seemed like ten seconds. I spouted the list of medications he'd had in the last 24 hours while they loaded him onto a gurney. Police arrived and stood between me and him, detaining me as they started pulling away.

"I have to go with him," I protested. The hospital was half an hour away and I was on the verge of panic. What happens if I get there and he's gone? *Oh God, don't take him now! Not like this!*

He pulled through it, but was severely weakened, and the next day I called hospice to ask for nursing care. We got a hospital bed in the living room and our world shrunk to a pillow and a light, a glass of water and a bookshelf lined with meds. His wakeful hours also began to dwindle.

This is a time when I fell in love with Psalm 23, prayer-walking and meditating on every solitary word of those lovely lyrics. I noticed that David changed tenses in verse 4, talking directly to God rather than about him and discovering the Lord to be present in the valley of the shadow of death. It also occurred to me that a fleeting shadow can't hurt you. Neither can death harm a child of God, but merely ushers us into His presence where we will walk on streets of gold in his presence forever.

If nothing else, cancer makes us focus on heaven where, "He will wipe away every tear from our eyes and there will be no more death or mourning or crying or pain…"[121] I studied passages about our living hope and that golden city and shared them with Frank.

Incredibly, we made it to the New Year of 2006, a full fifteen months since we first heard the horrifying words, *glioblastoma multiforma*. Each month past the predicted doomsday felt like a victory. We were beyond the doctors' predictions and thankful to God for every holiday and milestone reached, but nothing could quell the rising tide of questions. *How much longer, Lord?*

The kids and I grieved to see Frank decline. Memory, energy levels, focus and strength dissipated steadily. Then his appetite, conversation, and vision faded.

Dear God, all you have to do is say the word and he will live, but am I praying selfishly? Are you going to heal Frank or is it your will to take him home? I need to know.

---

[121] Revelation 21:4

On January 6th I decided to fast for forty days. Moses did it. Jesus did it. *Dear God, I'm going to fast until I hear you speak.*

I marched to the kitchen calendar to pencil a little "F" for fasting, then counted off forty days and put an "X" near the middle of February. *Either I will hear from you by then Lord, or I'll probably die myself.*

Noticing a line of fine print at the bottom of the calendar box, I reached for glasses to decipher the words, "Day of Epiphany." *Isn't this when the Magi arrived?* An online dictionary expanded the definition across my screen: "Day of divine manifestation."

Wow, what a great day to start a fast to hear your voice! Manifest yourself Father!

I went about the day, tending to my husband, massaging his feet and changing sheets. *Oh Lord, how much longer do we have together? What are you going to do here? Please speak to me.*

At 2 p.m. I heard him clearly. "Karen, go to the store."

Really, Lord? The store?

"Go to the store, now," he said firmly.

You have to understand how ridiculous that seemed. My poor husband couldn't eat and I was starting to fast. What on earth could I need at the store? Nevertheless, feeling so compelled, I grabbed my coat and keys and dashed out thinking maybe somebody needs help. I took a shopping cart out of sheer habit and hurried in out of the cold. *Lord, what am I here for?* I started walking slowly, looking around.

First I noticed a big brown table inside the doors, filled with leftover poinsettias from the holidays. They were wilting and faded, but a large sign still showed full price. *Fifteen dollars? What a rip off! They should throw those out.*

Just beyond the poinsettias stood another table. Instead of dying decor, this table held only one thing: a solitary yellow pot of daffodil bulbs. Beautiful bright green shoots stood about two-inches above the dark soil. *At least those show some promise!* I smiled approvingly.

Then the Lord spoke again. "Karen, get those. Those are for you."

Oh right, like I'd buy a fur coat or a Cadillac for myself at a time like this, I mused. But this wasn't about my slim wallet. The Lord said it again, even more deliberately, "Karen, get those. Those are *for you.*"

Mystified, I reached down to twist the pot around, looking for a price tag. (Oh, how does he put up with me?) Why would I do that after the Lord had just spoken two times? I was happy to see it was only five dollars, and I think I had about ten. *Well, that's good!* I picked it up, beaming. It felt like the muscles in my face cracked from sheer lack of use. It also felt like I'd just received a personal gift from God. *Thank you Lord! I love flowers!*

At the checkout stand, the clerk asked if I wanted him to bag the flower pot. "Yes please," I said. "It's freezing out there." But then on the way home, I turned the corners a little too fast thinking of Frank lying alone in the empty house. I heard the bag rolling around in the back of my Pathfinder. Good thing there were no blooms to be broken and good thing the clerk tied that bag!

I rushed into the house and set my treasure on the granite island talking to Frank in a blue streak. "Honey, I'm home! You'll never guess what happened! The Lord told me to buy these daffodil bulbs—wait till you see them, honey—I didn't even know what I was going to the store for but the Lord was telling me to—hang on, honey, I'll show you!"

All the while I had been scooping up the loose soil from the bag and packing it around the bulbs. I was rushing to clean up the mess so I could show Frank. But that's when the Lord spoke again.

"Karen, stop." I froze with my fingertips in the soil. *"Do you see what you're doing here?"* he asked gently. It was the same tone my father would have used, wanting to teach me some important lesson. *"You're rushing around, tending to the bulbs and fussing with the soil...* (I felt somewhat ashamed of my Martha-like behavior, but he didn't berate me for it. He simply continued.) *"Look at the dirt... This isn't why you wanted these daffodils, is it?"*

No, Lord.

"Look at the bulbs. That's not what you wanted either. They're just the dying shells. No, you wanted these because of the promise, the hope of the glory to come."

I remembered when I first laid eyes on this pot—"At least those show some promise!" I thought.

"Remember I Corinthians 15?"

Yes, Lord, I love that chapter.

"It is about the transformation of life to glory. This is the work of making something new through resurrection." I stood motionless, as that passage washed over me in timeless beauty. *"We are sown a*

perishable seed and raised imperishable... sown in weakness and raised in power... sown in mortality, and raised in immortality..."

Then the Lord said, *"Karen, don't focus on the dying shells. Focus on the hope of the glory to come! This is my specialty! This is what I do best--"*

I glanced across the room at Frank just as the Lord said, "and *this is what I'm doing with Frank."*

Bam! There it was.

Looking across the room I searched Frank's expression, wondering if he had heard it too, but he was unmoved. Silent, but looking in my direction.

I stood stunned by the words of God, overwhelmed at the way he appeared to speak to me so personally, and answer my questions so clearly. Here, I was going to fast for forty days, but I looked at the clock and realized, *I only missed lunch!* The pure and peaceable Word had come, and I accepted it.

Rushing to my desk, I read I Corinthians 15, brimming with eternal hope in God's transforming power. I soaked up the words hungrily again and went back to the little yellow pot with a black marker. I wrote on the pot, "God's Miracle, I COR 15." The phrases, 'raised in glory,' 'clothed with immortality,' and 'raised in power,' were deeply *implanted* on my mind.

I also revisited Abraham's steps up Mt. Moriah. What was it like as he neared the place where he would have to turn to his beloved and lay him on that altar? Isaac asked where the sacrifice was as he carried the wood and fire, but his father only answered, "God will provide *Himself* a sacrifice."[122] And they marched on, trusting God.

Up to this point I always identified with Abraham in the journey, the one who had to give up the one he loved. Now, I turned to Isaac, the one who had to lay his own body down. What was it like for *him?* Did he wrestle against his father? Certainly a young man could have put up a fight with a man in his hundreds, but Isaac layed down willingly, a foreshadowing of Christ. He had learned the path of surrender from his father's example.

I looked at Frank and saw the same attitude, a sweet fragrance to God.

Here I am, Lord. Do as you please.

---

[122] Genesis 22:8 in KJV, literally and prophetically speaking, God DID provide HIMSELF for our sacrifice.

30. Miracle of the Daffodils

Every time I rushed past the counter that weekend, I noticed those fresh green daffodil shoots, stretching up at a remarkable speed. I'd put three fingers beside the shoots to measure their astounding growth. Even in the jungles of New Guinea, I had never seen anything like it.

The miracle of the daffodils unfolded over many days. As I'd notice the purposeful grace of these budding shoots, the Lord kept whispering reminders in my heart. *"Karen, remember, it's the hope of the glory to come!"*

Another time I heard, *"This is my specialty."* Again as I was weeping he said, *"Remember Karen, don't focus on the dying shell."* As I was nursing Frank's dying body, the Lord kept reminding me that Frank was going to live forever, through the glory of his resurrection power.

Everyone who came—hospice nurses, neighbors and friends—heard the story of the amazing daffodil bulbs. One nurse commented, "I've never seen anything like it."

I boasted about my heavenly Father. "These have been supercharged!" I said. "God spoke to me through these daffodils." It was my burning bush, defying nature itself.[123]

Standing in the middle of the kitchen one day, I gave the run-down on meds and our hospice nurse Lois asked, "How are *you* holding up Karen?"

I paused, then looked her in the eye and said, "The day I come down here and realize that I'm alone in the house and he's gone, I'm going to hit the deck and I don't know if I'll ever be able to get up!" Tears spilled out with those bleak thoughts. "Oh, I know I'll see him

---

[123] The burning bush was not consumed, against all natural laws. It brought attention to a holy God whose love knows no limits. Exodus 3:2-4

again, but I just can't conceive of life without him. I always thought I'd be the first to go." Very few relatives on my side ever made it past 55, but on Frank's side, 80 and 90 was common. Yet, those words would come back to me later on.

Monday morning I woke with a bang before sunrise. I heard Frank's outburst from a dead sleep and rushed to his side as he fought to clear his throat. The nurse had given me morphine for such a time as this. "It's not just for pain, Karen, but to help him breathe," she'd said. So I gave it to him with trembling hands, and he slept the rest of the night. *Oh Father, I don't want to keep him breathing with morphine, but I can't stand to see him struggle. Please give him rest.*

At three o'clock on Monday afternoon, three days after starting the fast, I was praying at my desk when the Lord urged me out of the blue, "Karen, it's time to call the funeral home."

"Lord, where do I start? Please, just give me one name and number. I can't handle an executive search on cremations right now."

I immediately remembered an email buried in a mailing list from months before, but I hoped I'd never need it. Surprisingly, I found it quickly and even more surprisingly, the director asked, "Where are you calling from?"

"I'm in Franklin."

"Oh, that's forty miles from here," he noted.

"How did you know that exactly?"

"I used to live in Franklin," he said. "Here, let me do you a favor. Why don't you call my buddy Joe," and he rattled off the number for a funeral home in the center of town that would handle everything. *Thank you Lord!*

I still had no idea how precious little time we had left. Doctors and nurses warned Frank would slip into a coma for four to six weeks, so I assumed we still had a lot of time. But God knew and pointed me to Joe on Monday afternoon, telling me what to do "when the time comes." He would take care of everything.

Meanwhile, our house was full of a surreal peace. And the daffodils had grown to a height of 24 inches with full buds formed—an incredible seven inches *per day!* It was a spectacular visual reminder of God's transforming glory.

Naomi had asked if they should go away that weekend and I urged her, "You have to make time to make your own family memories." So they went to northern New Hampshire for Nate's birthday. Yet, remembering how hard it was to lose my parents without saying goodbye, I begged God repeatedly to give my kids closure, and kept running to Him with all my anxious thoughts.

Lord, please don't let Frank go into a coma. Please let us all be together, and please wake me up if it's the middle of the night. I know, Lord, you're going to do it perfectly, but please let all the kids be here when the time comes.

That same Monday, Naomi called to say they came back from their trip early since the baby was sick, and oh, by the way, she wanted to come over with my sons that night. We never got together on Monday nights!

But we spent that evening together…a meaningful and tender time, relaxed, reminiscing, and thanking him for being such a wonderful husband and father. We gave Frank's wedding ring to our elder son. We held hands, listened to hymns and said all the things we wanted to say. Best of all, he heard everything. No coma!

Then I slept deep and hard for three hours.

January 10, 2006, at 2:45 a.m. I felt someone touch my shoulders and whisper, *"Karen, it's time to get up."* I heard the soft sweet voice and opened my eyes with heart-pounding wonder. The voice sounded like my mother waking me for school as a child!

Who was that? And why am I awake? Then I realized I could hear Frank's breathing from the next room, panting like he was running a marathon. Was he trying to call me? I tore off the covers and ran to his side just as his eyes were going up in his head.

"Honey, I'm here!" Isaac had stayed the night for the first time in months, and he flew down the stairs the minute I called. I grabbed my cell and speed dialed the other kids. Since they both lived within two miles, we were all together within fifteen minutes.

We gathered around the bed and held hands. Frank never did slip into a coma but was "with us" the entire time, hearing every precious word. I didn't feel fear, but a certain heightened awareness. *This is it.* After a lifetime of saying dreaded good-byes, I felt the weight of forever on this one.

"Honey, I think you're going to be seeing the angels any minute now." And sure enough, they came. It was obvious when he started seeing glory.

"Oh! Oh! Oh!" he said over and over as though the door of a great party swung open and he was recognizing faces in the crowd.

He was filled with what I could only describe as joyful wonder, like a child at Christmas discovering great gifts under the tree.

I was right beside his head squeezing his hand. "I wish I could climb into your eyes and see what you're seeing! I want to go with you!" I cried.

He couldn't speak, but he came back and lingered, not ready to go. "I think you're trying to tell us not to be sad. If we could see what you just saw we'd be happy… but we're going to miss you, honey."

"Look! He's crying!" Naomi said beside me. His final sweet farewell came in the form of five precious tears that rolled down his cheek.

"Don't worry about me, honey." I said. "I'll be coming right behind you, and you have to show me around when I get there!" I have every confidence that he will, too. "Honey, it's time. Go now, and enjoy your reward."

With that, he breathed one last long sigh, and went with the angels.

Jesse waved up at the ceiling, "Goodbye Dad!"

Surely, Frank was rising right above our heads. I met a man whose dogs stopped abruptly on the driveway and looked up as though they saw someone above them. He waved instinctively at the spot, and when he went inside he was told that his mother had just died. Her body was still warm. "I know," he said. "I just waved goodbye outside." Yes, I thought, we should always look up and wave.

Frank saw heaven's doors opened on Tuesday morning at 6:30, the same time he used to head out the door to begin a new day. And a new day had certainly begun!

Within the hour, the house began to fill with friends and family. We had an initial gathering of about twenty of us, seated in the room where angels had just met Frank. There was a lingering sense of God's presence. There was also laughter as we imagined Frank looking down and saying. "Okay, enough of this. Everybody get to work now."

I called the funeral home down the road at noon. "Frank left us this morning, Joe. He's gone home to be with the Lord." He was surprised. I had just told him the day before that we were probably looking at six weeks, but not even 24 hours had passed.

Joe arrived, a staid and solemn professional. He zipped up the red body bag. I felt so strangely distanced, yet at peace. I knew in my heart that what remained was just the "dying shell." I had no desire to hang on. No, I will wait and see him again, *alive.*

"Are you ready for this, Joe?"

"For what? The funeral?"

"No, for *dying.*" It caught him completely off guard but I was surprised someone in his profession wouldn't have thought about it.

"What can you possibly do to prepare for it?" he asked, and we talked for forty five minutes about the answer to that question.

About an hour later, the hospice company came for the bed. "Yeah, Frank doesn't need these things anymore *where he is!*" and I had another good hour to share the hope that lies within me. Both these men were surprised to learn that I was "the wife of the deceased," but I was filled with a joyful expectation that God would use Frank ***even in death***.

Looking at the empty living room, the spot that had consumed my every waking moment for months, his absence felt horrendous, but I kept saying, "What is he doing *now?* What is he *seeing?* Can you imagine? He must be loving LIFE again after all this time lying flat on his back!"

The next morning I came downstairs and froze in the middle of the kitchen. It dawned on me that this is the moment I dreaded. I stood in the very spot where I confided my deepest fears to the nurse.

I gazed at rows of medicine bottles on the counter, along with mixing cups, spoons, syringes, and doctor's numbers… all the collected paraphenalia of our battle. With a long sad sigh I thought, *It's the end of an era. There's no one to check on or take care of. It's over. Oh Lord!*

Tears started filling my eyes and I turned my head away. My eyes landed on the daffodil pot on the island just as a golden streak of sunlight streamed in the dining room window and hit the first big daffodil. It snapped opened right before my eyes!

"Karen! I'm still here!" came the familiar whisper.

Oh Lord! You are a God of life, not death! Help me remember this moment forever! Even as I write this, my eyes are filling up at the thought of God's mind-boggling intimacy. Truly, He is with us in the valley of the shadow.

Wherever you are, and whatever you're going through as you read this, He is alive and present, just a breath away from you!

Surprisingly, the miracle of the daffodils continued to unveil. We set the date for the memorial service for January 20th and every day filled to the brim. I was even interviewed by the newspaper reporter who recognized our names from an article that was published when we left for New Guinea years earlier! I shared God stories for two hours and they published a lovely tribute.

I never set visiting hours, but told friends to let the Lord orchestrate it. "I'm here," I said. "Let people come when they want." That resulted in a pleasant flow of personal conversations with people. God was in control, so why should I interfere?

High on my personal agenda was finding just the right flowers for the memorial service. As soon as I could, I headed right back to the store for more daffodils. I wanted to fill the church with blooming bulbs, but to my surprise, the clerks answered, "Oh no, we don't get daffodils until late in February. It will be about six more weeks."

I looked at them like they had three heads and determinedly drove from store to store asking all the florists in town. At every stop, I got the same answer. "I'm sorry, it's too early in the year for daffodils. Try back in a month or so."

I remembered that brown table with the single yellow pot of bulbs. How did it get there? Then the words flooded back to my mind. The Lord specifically said, "Karen, buy those. Those are *for you*," and I now realized how deliberately he urged me, *go to the store, now!*

My supercharged daffodils were divinely orchestrated! Not only did He speak to me through those beauties, but apparently He gave me the only daffodils in Massachusetts on January 6th!

I still have that little yellow pot and the bulbs bloomed for three more years, their ongoing life reminding me of God's presence in the valley. With resurrection power He transforms the ordinary things like a handful of bulbs into the extraordinary—dozens of two-foot daffodils in golden splendor. He is a God who shows up in a handful of dirt and in all our messes to speak to us in love. He is God of divine surprises.

In the days leading up to the service we prayed that lives would be touched for God's glory as we remembered Frank's life together. Emails circled the globe asking friends and missionaries to pray for God's presence to fill the service, and we heard many proofs of God's answers.

I didn't plan the service. Our pastor Bruce came over and provided a strong shoulder to lean on. He must have done the lion's share of it, but we were amazed. People appeared like a rainbow after the storm, with all their blended colors and hues of trade and talent. They volunteered services, food, a classical pianist, even the ushers were men whose lives Frank touched or mentored.

We were blessed by a Hebrew prayer of mourning read by Chad Meyer who grew up with our family in the tribe and the May River Band flew from San Diego to lead music. "We would have walked if we had to," Seth said. The Robinsons grew up with our kids in PNG.

New Guinea coworkers and family members shared heart-warming testimonies and Isaac's friend Jonathon came in full Highlands dress to offer a moving tribute of *Amazing Grace* on bagpipes. I have never heard it again without the most heart-stopping tenderness.

During these weeks of raw emotions, music filled a deep void and soothed my spirit in a way nothing else could. It is a sacred balm to the broken hearted. In light of God's working to see me through those final days, I fell in love with a beautiful old hymn and asked the May River Band to play it.

The lyrics highlight the unfathomable wisdom of the Creator God who makes his presence known, even in a blooming pot of daffodils. I worship the Sovereign ruler of the universe despite the pain, and wanted everyone in that service to know He is still good. He is still present, *no matter what.*

*"**I Sing the Mighty Power of God** that made the mountains rise!... Lord how thy wonders are displayed where'er I turn my eye, if I survey the ground I tread or gaze upon the sky. There's not a plant or flower below but makes His glory known, and clouds arise and tempests blow by order from his throne. While all that borrows life from thee is ever in thy care, and everywhere that man can be, thou, God, art present there!"[124]*

---

[124] Song lyrics by Isaac Watts, 1674-1748.

I also wrote a tribute to Frank's life. It came to me unexpectedly on my birthday while tugging at the covers to make my bed. My toes kicked something on the floor, and reaching down, I discovered Frank's work shoes, now forgotten and collecting dust. I hugged them to my chest in tears, then sat down to write this poem in one sitting. When it was done, I was surprised to see that it resembled a footprint on the page.

Frank's Shoes

Solid, earthy, sturdy brown,
These are the shoes that he wore around.

These are the shoes that a craftsman chose;
Yes, these were much more than a place for his toes.

Rich dark leather and sturdy thread,
What are you doing now under the bed?

When you were formed in a shoe shop quaint,
Did you ever think you'd be worn by a saint?

The distance you've traveled can never be measured,
But now you've become a thing to be treasured.

Why can't you journey longer here,
In the shop and the house and this world, my dear?

I look at the insoles remembering your ways,
And the imprints you made on us all of your days.

You walked with God, lived strong and free,
And loved the Lord and your family.

These shoes will stay long after you're gone,
And teach me to follow till my days are done.

Softened leather so strongly soled,
Apt in all weather your purpose to hold.

Bruised and worn, so gently broken,
Forever let this tale be spoken.

Inspire me to choose steps as well;
Let me serve others and His story tell.

Christ Jesus, a craftsman, just like you,
Worked in a woodshop until he was through.

Then to his heavenly home he returned
But he left us his Spirit and Word to be learned.

He must have some projects in mind for you there,
To get everything done till we meet in the air!

And now there's an empty pair of shoes
To remind me of the life I choose.

A gentle spirit, a zeal and drive,
A privilege just to be alive.

I, too, am empty, but ready to fill;
Teach me, my Father,
to do your will.

Dec 29, 2005

My son Jesse, musician and film maker, wrote a song called
Legacy, [125] and bravely sang it as a solo. It brought fresh tears when he
sang what he had been carrying in his heart for months, ***Don't go!***
Not before, I let you know, You're my light in the storm, my hero!

Another incredible gift came in the form of a slide show Jesse
edited and set to music. This beautiful remembrance honored a life
well-lived. One song by Keith Green was an old favorite of Frank's,
and reiterates his life passion.

---

[125] *Legacy,* lyrics and music by Jesse Low

"I Make my Life a Prayer to You"

I wanna tell the world out there
you're not some fable or fairy tale
That I've made up inside my head—
you're God the Son,
you've risen from the dead![126]

We glimpsed a lifetime of travels and gatherings brightened by Frank's exuberant smiles and free spirit. There were wedding shots, birthdays, graduations, and jungle adventures dating all the way back to the bearded surfer I had fallen in love with at sixteen.

Thirty-one years seemed far too brief. I was numb.
How would I live without him?

---

[126] Make my Life a Prayer to You by Keith Green, Sparrow Label Group

31.　Spring Step to Heaven

Three weeks after the memorial service, friends at church offered their time share on the Cape. "Why don't you go down for the week and spend some time writing? All expenses paid!"

Even though it was the middle of February, the ocean is my favorite place for rejuvenating, so I gladly accepted and headed to Falmouth. Checking into a condo across the street from the beach, I threw open the curtains and soaked up the glorious panorama.

I played music, prayed, studied, and wrote around the clock while the moon floated across the blue horizon. I studied through a book called, *Experiencing God* by Henry Blackaby. I'd read it years before, but as I was leaving home I felt the urge to take some time with it now. In between, I wandered into Falmouth's tea shops and bookstores on streets lined with snow and walked the beach admiring windswept seascapes, just me and the gulls.

Late in the day, I'd walk about a mile down the beach to a little British pub for fresh clam chowder. One night with a clipping northeast wind blowing, I changed my mind. *I should drive into town tonight. If Frank were here, we'd find something new and different every day of the week!* Frank was always the one to choose our path. He'd make the plans and I'd follow happily. "Let's go in here," or, "do you want to try this place?" Everything seemed so simple then.

I drove up and down the dark street, finally finding an empty spot that seemed big enough for an SUV. *Frank always made this look easy,* but parallel parking took half a dozen attempts, crunching over frozen ruts. I finally clamored over a mound of snow to the doorway of an enchanting restaurant adorned with strands of twinkling lights.

Thinking the hard part was behind me, I pulled open a handsome oak door and stepped out of the crisp night air to stand

251

beside a "please wait to be seated" sign in the entryway. I glanced beautiful tablecloths and fresh flowers on the tables.

Ahh, this is nice! Such a warm inviting atmosphere, but standing there alone stirred up fresh pain as I imagined my husband beside me. How many times in 31 years had we celebrated special occasions at such a place? Now, I wondered if I'd ever celebrate again...

Just then a perky waitress emerged from the back and rushed up to me. "Oh, are you *alone?*" she asked a little too loudly. Then, clearing her throat in an attempt to correct herself, "Is it *just one* tonight?"

My face blanched and for a few seconds I imagined answering with a line from an old comedy, "Why don't you get a megaphone and shout it toward Moscow?" Instead, I managed a weak, "Yes, thank you," but walking to my little table my eyes were stinging. *Yes, I am A-L-O-N-E!* The words sank deep as a hot knife through a slab of butter.

Thankfully, she left me with a menu and disappeared. Then, glancing around the room I realized my predicament. Everyone around me was dressed for romance with pearl necklaces and frilly blouses, diamond rings and elegant heels. It's Valentine's Day! I was the only single, dressed for a late night supper in an old pair of jeans and boots.

I'm usually relaxed at meals, but that night I sloshed through my seafood chowder in solitude and slid out the door. Back to the comfort of a dark night and howling winds. This was one of many such discoveries in the journey of widowhood to be filed under the heading, "Situations to Avoid From Now On."

The next day I walked the beach for an hour in freezing cold. Hands deep in my pockets and a scarf covering my face, I huffed along the frigid sands hashing it all out with the Lord. My eyes stung with tears as I poured out the pain of my newfound reality.

"A widow! Lord, I hate the word. Am I going to be defined by death from now on? Oh God, I miss Frank so much! Why did you do this, Lord? You took the wrong one! Didn't you know I needed him more than he needed me? He would have been fine without me, but I'm so lost without him!" I fussed and fumed and kicked the sand.

"I can't even figure out where to park the car or get a cup of coffee!" Looking down at my frozen legs I yelled, "I'm so off-balance and handicapped, I feel like you've cut off my left leg!"

At that moment, a couple of white gulls swooped right in front of me and darted into the air. Surprised, I lifted my eyes to the brilliance of a red-orange sky shimmering over the harbor. I lost my breath for a second. It was beautiful, like a princess dressed for a glorious ball, draped with a golden radiance I hadn't even noticed.

"And where is that left leg now, Karen?"

"Well... I guess it's in heaven with you, Lord."

"Then you're half-way home. You're in the *spring-step to heaven.*"

I stopped in my tracks and felt his smile as the poetic beauty of those words settled on me.

"Wow, Lord. That's an incredible thought."

With my eyes on that glorious sky aflame with brilliance over the sparkling sea, my whole outlook brightened. Talk about *experiencing* God!

That little chat on the chilly beach of Falmouth turned my head around, and quite frankly, it still blows my mind that He would speak so tenderly in the middle of all my ranting accusations.

Spring step to heaven? What a delightful expression! I was focused on my loss and consumed with sorrow, but Jesus gave me exactly what I needed. He lifted my eyes to a golden panorama and expanded a myopic view heavenward. *I'm on my way to Heaven!*

Lord knows, this is the hardest thing I've ever faced, but not a tear drips from my eyes that he doesn't notice.[127]

I rehearsed this whole conversation walking back to the condo and realized that God never disagreed with my feelings. He simply raised the bar.

I need not be defined by death, but *hope!* "Since then, you have been raised with Christ, set your hearts on things above, where Christ is seated at the right hand of God."[128]

Now, I can picture my husband doing handstands, running around enjoying oceans and music, and exploring new horizons. Frank, my free man, has been set free indeed!

Heaven offers hope, and helps me focus on accomplishing what He's left me here to do. Whether teaching in prisons or in the everyday encounter with people on the street, the Lord put the spring in my spring-step to heaven!

---

[127] Matthew 10:29-31
[128] Colossians 3:1

The Master transforms my pain into glory. He picks up all the pieces and makes something beautiful out of them.

On one of the first sunny days in spring, I drove to Newport for some fresh ocean breezes with my friend Troy. He was still recovering from a near-fatal motorcycle accident and had come to Christ, but his body was wrecked and he felt his life was in ruins.

Standing on the shoreline, I noticed an old man coming toward us with a walking stick and I called out a friendly hello and asked if he lived nearby. He lifted his cane and pointed out to the opposite finger of land. "I was born on that point 83 years ago."

Looking at his weathered face and determined stance, I said, "Wow. You've had a good long life! After 83 years of walking this beach, what wisdom do you have for me?"

He gazed out to sea while I imagined what memories must have sparked to life. Hoping he would muster some rich nugget of truth, I was stunned when he finally turned to me and answered, "To mind my own business!"

Troy laughed as he headed down the beach, but I pleaded, "Come on, Joe! Surely you've got something better than that! Come back!"

He ventured down shore awhile, eventually returning with a grin. Reaching into his deep coat pocket he gathered a handful of sea glass and said, "I picked these for you."

"For me? First you walk away and now you're bringing me gifts? What next?" I teased.

To my surprise, Joe began telling me about each piece and where it came from, teaching me like a grandfather. Afterwards, I asked if I could share something precious that we found and we talked about the lasting treasure we found in Christ.

As I thought about it afterwards, I realized Joe had certainly given me a pocketful of wisdom in those broken remnants and to this day they remind me to persevere in the storms of life. It sounds terribly cliché but it's absolutely true. God isn't finished yet.

We may start out in life like a beautiful glass vase, colorful, curvaceous and useful, but one way or another, our fragile lives fragment. We crash into the rocks, sea-tossed by circumstances we cannot control. Then we lie shattered and alone, a forsaken scrap of what we once were.

For Troy it was a motorcycle accident. For me, dreams were shattered when my husband was returned to me in a plastic bag of ashes. My bright sun slipped behind a veil of cloud. That's where I was, not knowing how to get up and go on living.

Just as Joe walked the beach searching for bits of tumbled glass, the eyes of God roam throughout the earth searching for the lost and broken. He picks us up and salvages every broken bit of our lives as the Psalmist declared. *"The Lord is close to the brokenhearted and saves those who are crushed in spirit... [He] heals the brokenhearted and binds their wounds."*[129]

The wisdom of the sea glass is a message of hope for all that is broken because our Redeemer lives! I can "hold *unswervingly* to the hope we profess *because* God is faithful."[130]

This is the "living hope" reserved in heaven, even though I may suffer grief for a season. Renewed passion and divine purpose emerge from ashes.

I once read that thirty-year-old eagles go through a reclusive transformation process called molting when they lose all their feathers and talons. Strength is depleted and glory stripped away. Obviously, eagles need their feathers and talons to live and it's a wonder they can survive the process.

It is a perfect illustration of what it feels like to lose your spouse after thirty years. You wonder if you will ever fly again or survive the loss, but the Lord promises to renew as the eagle.[131]

King David is a good example. That reflective soul put words to our passions and struggles, a man who grew in grace through failure and heartbreak. He roamed in the desert, lived in caves, and lost loved ones. David understood brokenness. He said, "I am poor and needy, and my heart is wounded within me." After mentioning life's challenges he added, "but I am a man of prayer."[132]

All his writings bring comfort to the grieving or broken, because he grappled so hard and well. He pressed in with God and experienced renewal as the eagle. David the shepherd-king molted with God.

---

[129] Psalm 147:3; 34:18
[130] Hebrews 10:23
[131] Isaiah 40:31; Psalm 103:5
[132] Psalm 109:4, 22

Looking back at a lifetime of experiences and battles, he wrote: *I praise the God who turns my darkness into light! As for my champion, this hero God of mine, His way is perfect!... Yes, it is the Lord my God who strengthens me and makes my way perfect!*[133]

This is the final sum of it all, and I echo David's praises. God is perfect and he makes my way perfect. I may not always understand, but that's okay. After all, He is the One who hung the earth upon nothing.[134]

He sees and cares for me, and He walks with me until the end of time just as He promised.

Have you talked to him yet?

---

[133] 2 Sam 22:29-51
[134] A favorite awe-inspiring verse of mine. Job 26:7

Glossary

Aumi (aow'-mee) - our home village on the May River.

Bilum (bee'-lum) — string net bag, usually colorful and carried on the head.

Expat - immigrant or non-citizen.

Haus sik — hospital or clinic.

Iwam (ee'-wahm) — name of our tribe in Papua New Guinea.

Kalabus (kahl'-ah-boos) - jail

Kiap (kee'-ap) — provincial police officer

Kina (kee'-nah) - PNG national currency or dollar.

Kowa ni Yenkam Purik (koh'-wa nee yehn'-kahm boo'-deek — God, the Highest Spirit

Lotu (loh'-too) — Bible teaching or worship meeting.

Mani (muh'-nee) - airstrip village and strategic tribal crossroads.

Mapu (hmuh'-poo) — snake.

Maski wari (mah'-skee wah'-dee) - no worries.

Masio (mah'-see-oh) - tribal leader who opposed our presence for years.

Masta — a European, mister.

MK — missionary kid

Mok (mohk)— large black hornbills resembling pterodactyls with wingspans up to 4'

Mozees (maw'-zees) — slang for mosquitos.

Puk-puk - crocodile

Sepik (see'-pik) - name of the 700-mile long river and province where we lived.

Sing sing - all night ceremonial dance to call blessing from ancestral spirits.

Sked — short for schedule, a slotted radio time.

Stori - to share or teach.

Tultul (tool' tool) - village chief.

The Chron (kron)- chronological Biblical teaching program.

Tok piksa — illustration.

Wantok (wun'-tawk) — friend, companion.

Wewak (wee'-wack) — coastal supply town on the Bismarck Sea.

Acknowledgements

Thank you to the staff at Ockenga Institute, Gordon-Conwell Seminary, and the members of my writers' groups, the FEW and the NIBS, whose encouragements from the earliest stages kept me plodding along.

Thanks to Ken Pedersen, formerly at Tyndale, whose praises meant the world to me, Betsy Newenheus at Moody, and Carol Traver at Tyndale, who threw down the gauntlet to get it down to less than 90,000 words.

Special appreciation to my brother Dan, who with MIT precision, painstakingly noted every questionable detail about tribal customs, names, and order of events while flying to Italy and back. To all my test readers and endorsers, a very special "thank you!"

I relied on the prayers of a host of friends who bathed my writing in love. Though I could never list all your names, I give my heartfelt thanks to Elizabeth, Diane, Doe, and Fran for constant encouragement. To the Divas of NEC, Crossroads and my PEGS group. To Fultons, Hanlons, Fozis who drove me to Wheaton, and Demeos who made me go!

For the staff at Paneras who let me stay past closing every night, and to everyone mentioned in these stories, thank you for sharing the journey.

My warmest thanks to Naomi, Jesse and Isaac, Nate, Jenn and Brianne for unfailing support, valuable brainstorming, for putting me up and putting up with me. I love you all so much!

To Frank, if you can hear this, my deepest thanks for all your love and smiles, for your hard work and faithfulness to the end. Your life was a gift to us all.

Lastly, to Jesus my Lord, no words are adequate to express my thanks for giving yourself that I might live. All praise and glory to your precious Name!

About the Author

Karen Low is a missionary, author and speaker. She and her late husband lived in Papua New Guinea for 16 years where they raised three children and worked as translators and teachers in a jungle tribe. Since then, she has continued working with prisoners, the suffering and broken. She recently served as street pastor to refugees in Europe, and now resides in eastern Massachusetts where she continues her journey with the God of crickets and thunder.

If you would like to view photos, contact the author, request a speaking engagement, or follow her blog, you can visit her online at:

http://cricketsandthunder.blogspot.com
or
http://faithwalkjourney.blogspot.com

You can also order Psalm 23 gemstone bracelets on her webpage for The Shepherd's Psalm at:

http://theshepherdspsalm.bbnow.org

Made in the USA
Lexington, KY
13 October 2012